"Garret Keizer's *A Dresser of Sycamore Trees* is the finest memoir I've read in years. Honest, moving, thoughtful, often very funny, and always entertaining, this story of a remarkably humane and observant man's lay ministry in one of contemporary America's last frontiers is a joy to read."—Howard Frank Mosher

"In *A Dresser of Sycamore Trees* Garret Keizer deftly plays the great organ of language and brings forth the thrumming music of life and the spirit. He has crafted a profoundly human book that catches and crystallizes the essence of being alive and joyfully riding our earthy planet in its journey through the heavens."—Richard Lederer

"Keizer exhibits a refreshing theological acumen and writes with verve and compassion. . . . His unusually compelling, sometimes humorous, and often moving nonfiction account deserves a wide readership."—*Library Journal*

"Keizer's story documents the doubts and joys of ministry, explores the reasons for serving others, and, finally, provides the reader with a role model and a guide."—*Booklist*

"At its heart, *A Dresser of Sycamore Trees* is a book about one Christian vocation. By sharing his own 'finding of a ministry,' Garret Keizer models the disarming candor and inclusive compassion which is a requisite of everyone's quest to serve God."—*The Witness*

A Dresser of
Sycamore Trees

A Dresser of Sycamore Trees

THE FINDING OF
A MINISTRY

Garret Keizer

HarperSanFrancisco
A Division of HarperCollins*Publishers*

Grateful acknowledgment is made for permission to reprint a
selection from *Zen Flesh, Zen Bones* by Paul Reps,
Charles E. Tuttle Co., Inc., Tokyo, Japan.

FIRST HARPERCOLLINS PAPERBACK EDITION PUBLISHED IN 1993
Library of Congress Cataloging-in-Publication Data
Keizer, Garret.
A dresser of sycamore trees : the finding of a ministry / Garret Keizer.
p. cm.
Originally published: New York : Viking, 1991.
ISBN 0–06–064357–9 (pbk : alk. paper)
1. Keizer, Garret. 2. Episcopalians—Vermont—Biography. I. Title.
BX5995.K38A3 1993   283'.092—dc20   [B] 92–56133

Display typography by Jessica Shatan

93 94 95 96 97 CWI 10 9 8 7 6 5 4 3 2 1

For the people of Christ Church, Island Pond,
Kathy and Sarah among them

ACKNOWLEDGMENTS

Thanks are due to Kristi Amadon Huling, for helping me prepare my manuscript; to James and Helen Hayford and Kathy Keizer, for reading the earliest drafts; to Don Congdon, my agent, for representing me well; to Chris Braithwaite, Father Robert Castle, Kharas, Ronald and Helen Langford, Dr. Thomas Moseley, William Weatherstone, and Lyle and Carol Willey, for granting interviews; to the staffs of *The Chronicle* of Orleans County and the Island Pond Public Library, for helping me to verify information; to the Right Reverend Daniel Swenson, Bishop of Vermont, for urging me not to distrust my writing or this opportunity to write; not least of all to Pamela Dorman, my editor, for supporting and guiding this book from the beginning.

A Dresser of Sycamore Trees grows out of my experience in the Church. While the Church deserves much credit for anything of value found herein, it deserves no blame for those faults it still labors to help me overcome.

CONTENTS

A Dresser of
Sycamore Trees

"By Setting
Me Free"

*I called to the Lord in my distress;
the Lord answered by setting me free.*
—PSALM 118:5

If I tend to my driving, and put off getting milk and gas until
tomorrow, I can be home before my wife goes to bed. She will
ask me how it went, and I will tell her I am happy with the visit.
I took Communion to one person, had supper with another, met
someone on the street who is "thinking about coming to church,"
and wound up the steeple clock enough to last until Sunday. Actually, I am intoxicated with the visit. The image of an old woman
taking the wafer reverently in arthritic hands overwhelms me as I
round a mountain and the full moon appears blessing the branches
of a great dead elm. The ionosphere has come down in the night,
like St. Peter's visionary sheetful of clean and unclean animals, and
my car radio is a feast of stations. A little more volume, a little
more speed—I give thanks for my family, my church, the Su-
premes. Next week, without fail, I will stop at the farm which it
is too late to visit now, but passing by I pray for the family who
live there. I pray for their cows and the land. And I tell myself by

way of exultation what I now tell my reader by way of warning: it won't get much better than this.

The story of how I came to be the lay minister of a small Episcopal parish in an old railroad junction town in the northeast corner of Vermont could begin in a number of places. It could begin in a city where I used to work, at a lunch-hour church service, after which a young priest approached me and asked, "Who are you, and how do you come to be here?" Or it could begin at the small Church of St. John in the Wilderness, built over a century ago by a wealthy woman in memory of her husband, who had died on their honeymoon. In spite of that ominous precedent, my wife and I were married there, because her Catholic parents and my Protestant ones could each claim their share of the Episcopal tradition, and because, quite frankly, we liked the way the building looked.

If I wanted more drama, more sense of destiny, I suppose I could begin with a great-grandfather, a Dutch Reformed minister, who according to the legend in my family had lost his wife and child— no one remembered how—and had cursed God, and left the ministry, and then returned later in life to serve until he died. More simply and to the point, I could begin with my baptism, the ordination rite of all Christian lay ministers.

But instead, I start out at an Anglican monastery, on the bank of a great American river, where I went eleven years ago, at the age of twenty-six, because I wasn't yet sure what I wanted to be when I grew up.

I was two months away from moving to Vermont's Northeast Kingdom and embarking on my first and present job as a high school English teacher. Signing the contract was probably what forced the issue. I was sure I didn't want to do *that* for very long. Believing that serious problems call for drastic remedies, I did the most sensibly drastic thing I could think of: I ran off to pray and fast in a monastery, just about vowing in imitation of the Buddha not to rise from my meditations until I was enlightened, but also asking that, if possible, enlightenment not take longer than several days. I was driving a rented car.

I had been thinking of returning to graduate school for a Ph.D. I had already taken my master's in English, writing my thesis on the poetry of George Herbert, the unofficial patron saint of Episcopal poets, priests, and graduate students. I would eventually make the pilgrimage to his church in Bemerton, England, and was just then beginning to correspond with his venerable biographer, Amy Charles, who had already cast her ballot in favor of my choosing an academic path.

But I was also thinking of the law. Law school occurs to most English majors as inevitably as suicide occurs to all of us. With most it's just a passing thought; a few try, and botch it up (one suspects that some of these are really crying out for help), and a few others actually carry it off. With a law degree, I reasoned, I could shore up the proletariat, defend the oppressed, put the fear of God into racists, expropriators, and polluters. And if I tired of all that, I could make enough money to *own* the car I was renting and to buy a new one like it every year.

Yes, I also wanted "to be a writer." I had wanted "to be a writer" since adolescence. I was just far enough beyond adolescence to begin asking exactly what I meant by the phrase. And of course I was thinking, like Mr. Herbert and my great-grandfather before me, of becoming an ordained minister. That was on my mind most of all. That was why I was going to a monastery to ask my question.

In my dilemma over vocations I was like so many others of my generation, with greater choices and higher expectations for a life's work, and therefore with greater anxiety about it, too. It's hard to imagine another society on earth for which this issue was or is so consuming. Was this the angst of my parents and their friends as they sat talking and listening to the radio before, during, or after the war? To have a job, yes, to have one that paid well, that had "some kind of future," that enabled you to "be your own boss"— all practical or even idealistic matters, but not quite *religious* ones. And for many of their children, I think, the issue is virtually religious. I think you can hear echoes of the question "What must I do to be saved?" whenever you listen to people of my approximate age talk about work. So I think there may be subtler explanations for my going to the monastery besides the facts of my religious affiliation and the ecclesiastical nature of one of my "career" choices.

Interestingly enough, very religious people do not always see the vocational quest as a monumentally sacred one—in spite of or perhaps because of the claim that all honest work can be holy. In a book about Lubavitcher Hasidim entitled *Holy Days*, Liz Harris tells how a convert named Moshe found his life's work. An obviously learned man, he thought of becoming a teacher. He sought the advice of his rebbe. Why not become a metal engraver? the rebbe suggested. No explanation on his part, no qualms on Moshe's. Apparently, the Hasidim feel that individuals are no more capable of finding happiness through their own vocational choices than they are at finding wedded bliss through courtship. So such things are largely arranged for them. I don't say now, nor did I say then, that vocations ought to be arranged. And yet I suppose my only real difference from Moshe was that I sought an unquestionably divine arrangement. I wanted God, no one less, to make the decision for me. Believing that vocations were made in heaven, I wanted the matchmaker to speak from that height. I came to the monastery hoping things might be quiet enough for me to hear my answer.

It was indeed a tranquil place. Its brick cloisters, guest house, chapel, and library sat on a gently sloping hill overlooking the river. One could easily walk to the shore through a small wood at the foot of the hill. Well-kept lawns and gardens made up the grounds. The monks were wise enough to know that visitors to such places have traditionally expected to revel in a little bogus asceticism, and so the rooms in the guest house were appropriately Spartan, though the refectory and reading rooms were as comfortable as those of any country inn.

The center of life there was, of course, the chapel, to which the monastic community came for matins at six, Eucharist at nine, diurnum at noon, vespers at five, and compline at seven. It was arranged in the monastic style, with opposing rows of choir stalls for the monks running from the altar to the rear of the church, where pews accommodated guests who wanted to attend services.

The bells at the altar, the red votive light, and the life-size, dusky wooden crucifix hanging on the stucco wall all exhaled "Cath-lick" in an incense-reeking breath that could make a man raised on Calvinism just about swoon. The sultry July weather added a disturbingly Mediterranean ambience to the whole effect. Like every other attempt to join eternity and time, this place was an enclosed garden, a fragment of Eden full of possibilities in which one vaguely heard a serpentine hissing. The impulse to fall to one's knees coexisted in a visitor like me with the impulse to head for the parking lot screaming.

Instead, I set about following the routine of the house, with details of my own regimen thrown in. I goofed almost from the start. Between wake-up and matins, the house was supposed to be in silence. I had no complaints about that. In fact there's a great liberty, especially in a dormitory-style bathroom like the one in the guest house, to be able to shave, shower, and pee without the need for any small talk—monastic small talk at that. But no sooner had I lathered my face when in walked a half-dressed middle-aged man with one of the worst cases of cerebral palsy I'd ever seen and something to tell me about his cigarette lighter.

After some difficulty, I understood that he wanted me to put in a new flint. I set to work, but, not being a smoker myself, I needed some instruction about the lighter. At this point the guestmaster stuck his head in the doorway and curtly reminded us that "the house is supposed to be in silence!" The other man grinned at me with an expression that seemed to say "We've been very naughty—and we'll probably be very naughty again" and headed back to his room with agonizing difficulty. I've been here for just a little while, I thought, and already I've violated the rule. I had been there just a little while, I see now, and how swiftly God had sent me an angel.

"We can talk now," he said to me when I met him after the service. He was a little easier to understand now that he wasn't trying to hide his voice from the guestmaster, though he continued to drool steadily. He was here after a brief stint in an Episcopal seminary. He had been visiting the monastery "since before you were born." His name was Jeffrey.

He asked a series of questions about my employment and education which inevitably revealed my reasons for being there. He even managed, without any hints from me as I recall, to guess some of the options I was considering. Of course, none of this was as strange as I probably took it to be. It would not surprise me to learn that I was one of dozens of young men who visited the monastery that summer, and other summers, with roughly the same questions on their minds. If Jeffrey had indeed been coming there for more than forty years, he could probably spot one of us a mile away—the sneakers, the notepad, the "man of the desert" beard, the constipated expression at prayer. Still, what is not unusual may nevertheless be uncanny. And there was something uncanny in the way he put his finger on so many of my concerns. It was like sitting down with a police artist who began sketching a true-to-life portrait of my assailant—without much help from me.

Nothing struck me so much as the fact that he was "back" from a place I might be heading to. "Seminary," he said, was not his "cup of tea." It was "overrated." Theology was "sanctified bullshit." It did not take an especially perceptive mind to realize that something very painful had happened to him there, something that nevertheless did not rule out his returning to the monastery or asserting, "I would die for this place . . . I would die for the Episcopal Church."

Near the end of the conversation, after he had been naming great writers with not-so-great educations, he asked me, "Who was the greatest failure that ever lived?"

"Jesus Christ," I answered.

"That's right," he said. "Yet he conquered the world."

Then he offered me a cigarette and, when I declined, asked me to light his. He said he was glad he'd met me.

No conversation could last too long if one expected to attend all the prayer services of the community—and especially if one also had things to write, read, see, and prayers to say on his own. I saw even then a real benefit in that forced halting of the day, throughout the day, to "do the work" which was the monks' main job. How many times are we in the secular world saved from some destructively stupid decision or impulse simply by having to break for lunch? "Saved by the bell," we say. Yet what a long and murderous fight it is when the bell rings but once or twice a working day, and that to eat, or drink coffee. What would it be like if we were all on monastery time? The disadvantages of such a stop-and-go sched-ule would have to be placed alongside gains such as a more humane pace, a more thoughtful production, a less ill-tempered work force, a less immodest consumption of the world's resources.

Services—and meals, too—provided one with occasions to see the community. Other times, many of the monks were in the cloistered areas. There was quite an array of men, from a princely African novice who served at the altar, to an ancient white-haired monk who filled the church with his consumption-like coughing. The abbot was a stern and virile-looking man; in the secular world he might have been a narcotics cop or a claims adjuster. He ran a tight ship, too; I heard some murmured complaints about his having changed the time of matins to an hour earlier, and once, after what was a less than flawless performance of the liturgy, he demanded "to see all of the brothers immediately after the service." Across from him sat a monk, one of the "culprits" in the incident above, with the unflappably beatific countenance one would expect to find in a monastery—or at some kind of group encounter weekend. There was also a slight, nervous man whom I liked almost on sight, an Alice-in-Wonderland sort of character who perpetually ap-peared to have lost something very important, unable to recall where he'd left it. Does it explain anything to add that he was the monastery librarian? Of every man there I wanted to ask the ques-tion put to me by that young priest when I'd shown up like a stray cat at an Episcopal cathedral: "Who are you, and how did you come to be here?"

However a monk had come to be there, his coming had meant a giving up of something—and that made all of the brothers fas-cinating and in some ways awesome. All of them had refused to believe that "you can have it all." In other words, all of them were challenging what has become the virtual battle cry of "yuppie" culture in the decade since I made my retreat. That battle cry is also the complete antithesis of any notion of social or ecological responsibility, even though people who claim "you can have it all" often affect to care about such things—why not, when you can "have it all"? Quietly the monks were saying, and have been saying for twenty centuries, "That won't work." If other persons, peoples, species, and generations are to have justice, no one can "have it all." There are choices to make and prices to pay for those choices.

If that had been their only message, their only reason for being, they would have been of supreme value to a young man who was wondering if he might not skirt the vocational question altogether by doing every worthy thing that occurred to him. Eleven years later, and quite settled into "my work," I still need a reminder of those monks and their sacrifices every single day. I am still tempted to believe that with good "time management" I can have all the pearls, including the Pearl of Great Price.

With so many men dedicated to prayer, it was natural that I ask one of them to pray for me in my dilemma. I chose Brother Philip, the old cougher, in part because his age might have meant a greater experience with prayer, and in part because I guessed his duties at the monastery were now quite limited, and so I might in a way be helping him by asking for his help. He accepted. "How old are you?" he asked. When he heard my age he said, somewhat wearily, "You still have plenty of time," and that was the end of our discussion. I did not tell him that I had stopped feeling as though I had plenty of time on my twenty-fifth birthday, and especially after taking that teaching job.

The next day, after Sunday Communion, Brother Philip rushed past me toward the refectory with a purposeful energy that, in him, seemed nearly supernatural. For an instant I think I may have wondered if he had some prophetic thing to shout into the abbot's face. He burst past several other monks and guests before stopping abruptly at the breakfast buffet, where he filled his plate with an almost obscene helping of bacon. Over the years I have grown increasingly fond of this image, the memory of this monk, and bacon. At the time I saw nothing but irony—that young man's sense of "Ah-ha, I see you!" For people such as I was, and have all I can do to resist being now, life is ablaze with epiphanies revealing the falseness all around us, when often nothing is revealed so much as our own immaturity. What we take for another eruption of the painful truth is just another pimple breaking out on our young soul's face. Perhaps Brother Philip was teaching me an important lesson, the corollary to renunciation, that when you have chosen asceticism for your life's work, and find yourself feeble and close to death, and the Lord deigns to provide you with some bacon, load up.

At that same meal I ended my own fasting. One of my most vivid memories of the monastery is the way my fast had renewed the taste of Cheerios, and how cool and sweet the milk was as the sun shone on my face through the refectory windows. Austerity will give you sensations like that, and I had come with a mind to be austere. My first night I planned to "keep watch" till dawn in the chapel. After an hour or so, I modified the plan to remaining in the chapel until dawn and sleeping on a bench if I could. Late in the night a monk came in and asked if I were all right. I said yes, and he left—perhaps, as I later realized, putting off his own reason for coming there in order to honor mine. Shortly thereafter, I went back to my room and slept. One of the psalms appointed for the next day contained the verse:

> It is in vain that you rise up early
>   and go late to rest . . .
> for he gives to his beloved sleep.

God also gave me an especially tight and fraternal embrace from that same brother when the kiss of peace was shared at Communion the next day. Though the monk and I hardly spoke to one another again, there was a definite sense of closeness, a shared understanding, whenever we took the Sacrament together.

Nevertheless, it was to Jeffrey that I grew closest. It was with him that I spent much of my time. I was quite conscious that he liked an audience, and a little suspicious that he liked to stretch a story somewhat. His contradictions were numerous. But in all he said was evidence of a genuine heart, and a profound hurt—the wounds of his handicap, and the wounds of his time in seminary.

"In my life," he told me, "I have learned to accept rejection. I have learned to do without all normal human desires, sex, friendship. . . . I have learned to love people without accepting love in return. The only regret I have is setting foot in seminary." It was hard for me to believe that was his only regret, though I didn't say so. He seemed to guess anyway. "What if 95 percent of the people in this world had cerebral palsy? To get a job or a girl you'd have to go like *this*"—but the cruel caricature of his own condition, all the more grotesque because he had to exaggerate an extreme disability, belied his point. Nevertheless, he did seem to have reconciled his fate with his faith. "If I were cured tomorrow at seven-fifteen, it would be the greatest tragedy of my life. Because knowing my weakness, I know I would forget about God by four."

What he certainly would *not* forget was what he regarded as the cruelty of certain officials at his former seminary. In his most bitter outburst, he exclaimed: "I have more respect for the Mafia than for the Episcopal Church. The Mafia is more honest about what it is doing." Apparently, the blow had come in the form of a controversy over a room. Jeffrey was told that if he came back for another semester, he would have to find his own apartment. I knew nothing of the details, of course, but Jeffrey was convinced that the crux of the whole matter was the unwillingness of the church to ordain someone in his condition. They were simply throwing up obstacles. "I'd have more respect if they'd said, 'Jeffrey, you're a paralytic, and you look like a monkey.'"

Eleven years later I can still hear him say "look like a monkey." In one of our talks, he abruptly asked me to write a letter as he dictated. The letter was to me.

Dear Gary,

It is about five months before Christmas. I like to think of Christmas in this way. I am very fond of dogs. I wonder how I would feel if God Almighty said to me: "I'm going to make you into a dog. And you're going to look like a dog, and eat like a dog, and sleep like a dog." You know, that is just what happened at the Incarnation when God Almighty became a man in Jesus Christ.

But I suppose one of the best ways to really get the significance and the joy of Christmas is to be heartbroken. Because when your heart is broken, then and only then can Christ come in. And a strange thing happens; our lust turns into love, our hatred turns into humility, our greed turns into gratitude, and suddenly we are surprised by joy.

Surprised by joy, okay—but what struck me most was the terrible juxtaposition of Christ as dog and Jeffrey as monkey. As with the Cross itself, there was an implied redemption in these images, but also the evidence of dreadful humiliation and heartbreak. I suppose that by now a reader may be asking, "This is all quite interesting, but what does it have to do with your going to the monastery to seek your vocation?" I ask myself that question again and again. Why, when I turned aside to consider the ordained ministry more seriously than at any time before or since, why was I confronted with this chain-smoking, drooling, hurting, pontificating, self-taught, iconoclastic, and perhaps heroic refugee from seminary? Was this a warning? A challenge? A reflection? An incarnation? A howling case of absurd irrelevancy to anything I can think of? I still don't know.

But I do know that I shall never forget him. And I also know from repeated experience that often when we pray for a "solution" to our dilemmas we receive instead an icon for our prayers.

At the end of Georges Bernanos's novel, *The Diary of a Country Priest*, the protagonist says, "[I]f pride could die in us, the supreme grace would be to love oneself in all simplicity—as one would love any one of those who themselves have suffered and loved in Christ."

As I reread the journal I kept in those days, I am sometimes moved by an impulse to love "in all simplicity" the man I was, if not the one I am. To be sure, I can get awfully annoyed with him, too. Should I phone my wife, he wondered, or endure the solitude for another day? "Call her, you jerk!" I shout across the decade. The angels turn to me with frowns of disapproval. "I don't care. He's an idiot. He never should have gone away in the first place."

Perhaps I was more fit to be a minister when I asked if I should be one than I am now.

But it is that "fitness"—rather, the burning desire to *be* fit—that I am able to love. I paid attention to everything, conversations, psalms, dreams, the flight of mating butterflies, believing it was necessary to note every detail and sift them all later in the hope of discovering a few nuggets of meaning. At times everything seemed meaningful, which of course everything is, but as Eliot noted, "Human kind cannot bear very much reality."

There were parables everywhere. Returning from a stay on the bank of the river, I happened on a cluster of black raspberry bushes. My first impulse was to strip them clean, hand to mouth. But the experiences of the past days made me want to share the berries with someone, even if there were only a few. I went back to the monastery kitchen for a colander. In the enthusiasm of my decision, however, I had forgotten to note where the bushes were. I searched for them in vain, until, frustrated and tired, I discovered another cluster of bushes, several times larger, and picked enough berries to share with the entire house. A pretty mundane incident perhaps, but in my state of mind at the time, it was as numinous and shining as the feeding of the five thousand.

A lot of my journal is simply the copying of certain passages from the Scriptures, which were read during the daily offices. When you come to the Bible in any state of agitation, its words seem to be activated—and I was coming to portions of the lectionary no fewer than five times a day. At its lowest level, this sense of activated Scripture is akin to augury; the Bible becomes a Ouija board over which the ego slides to its own conclusions while pretending that the power of God has moved its attention this way and that. Notwithstanding the temptation, I believe something supernatural *does* occur in any earnest encounter with Scripture. It is impossible not to find the marks of your life engraved among its details.

Of all the lessons, I found myself most drawn to the story of the Gerasene demoniac. He is the man possessed by a "Legion" of devils, crying and cutting himself among the tombs. Jesus exorcises the demons and sends them into a herd of swine. I had read the story many times, but this may have been the first time, speaking both literally and figuratively, that I actually heard it out loud. I immediately identified with the man tormented by a legion of voices. He broke the fetters brought to restrain him—he could damage the arguments of any professional guide or caregiver—but he could not silence the pandemonium within. I loved Jesus for rebuking the demons when they proclaimed him the Son of God: he cared more for health than praise; he preferred a man "clothed and in his right mind" to the accolades of a tormented religious neurotic. And his compassion extended to the demons themselves; he even answered their prayer not to return them to "the abyss"— "Send us to the swine, let us enter them." Wouldn't he answer mine?

Finally, I was impressed by Jesus' refusal to allow the cured man to follow him as a disciple.

And as he was getting into the boat, the man who had been possessed with demons begged him that he might be with him. But he refused, and said to him, "Go home to your friends, and tell them how much the Lord has done for you, and how he has had mercy on you."

Along with the call to go into all the world, was there also a call to go home? Maybe, I thought, that question could be put more simply: was there a call to stay out of seminary?

The theme that seemed to recur in the lessons, in my reading, in my conversations with Jeffrey, and thus throughout the journal I kept, was that God respected my freedom. "Only you can decide what will bring you fulfillment," Jeffrey said. "Love God, and do as you please," St. Augustine had written. "I called to the Lord in my distress," one of the psalms proclaimed; "the Lord answered by setting me free." That was beginning to sound like my answer, too, though it was not without a distress of its own.

At roughly the midpoint of my time at the monastery and of my journal, I attempted to clarify the situation this way:

I have come here to ask God what my vocation should be. And yet I almost think I hear him asking me what *I* want it to be. Do I know? If a voice thundered overhead, "Garret, choose your vocation, and whatever it is I will accept your choice, prosper it, sanctify it . . . ," could I answer? Do I really know what I in my heart of hearts want to do?

Is there some dishonesty in claiming to desire the will of God when one does not know his own will? Do I desire submission to God, or do I simply want to avoid the struggle and the risk involved in finding out what I want? Jesus asks that God's will, not his, be done—but only after he has made his own will perfectly clear: "Father, if it be possible, let this cup be passed from me."

So now I stand before God and say, "Should I be a priest?" Perhaps I should be saying "Father, I want to be a priest, yet thy will be done" or "Father, I dread that vocation, yet thy will be done."

I was not even sure which of those two petitions fit my case. But of the few things I did know with certainty, one in which my own desires and my sense of "God's will" seemed to converge was my talks with Jeffrey. Whatever I was meant to do after leaving the monastery, I was sure I was meant to talk with him as long as I stayed. During one of his diatribes against the seminary, when he said, "They ruined my goal of serving the Church," I interrupted to say that was impossible. He was indeed serving the Church, for he had helped at least one member of it—he had helped me. He seemed touched.

With Jeffrey's intercession I hoped to gain access to the monks' own library. This was not usually permitted, at least according to Jeffrey. He maintained that book stealing was a great occupational vice among priests, and that the monastery library had suffered accordingly. Even religious lay people were prone to the weakness. He told me he used to work in a library frequented by Pentecostals. They invited him to one of their prayer meetings, at which there was a display of glossolalia, speaking in tongues. "I wish the Holy Spirit would tell you to bring your books back!" he had spouted.

Anyway, permission was granted, and one of the last things we did together was to walk slowly—part of the way arm in arm—to the library within the cloisters.

Years afterward, when I read Umberto Eco's *The Name of the Rose* with its labyrinthine monastic library, I would recall the library at my retreat, not because it was so large or its denizens so sinister, but because it was a mildly forbidden place, and a forbidding and fascinating place, too, full of literature, theology, hagiography, ascetics, and the bowel-churning thrill that comes to me in any sizable collection of books. I suppose if I want to push the theme of providence to extremes, I could say that there was something providential in my making this little trip so close to the end of my visit. Jeffrey had taken me where *any* vocational choice I was likely to make would also take me—to a place where books were stored, and read, and sometimes written.

The last words my journal records Jeffrey's having said to me were "Pray for me, a sinner." I did not remember until later that these are also the last words an Episcopal priest says to a penitent after pronouncing him or her absolved.

My eagerness to go home—one of the most powerful recurring emotions of my adult life—was now even stronger than my wish that something would be "settled" by my prayers and meditations. I missed my wife terribly. One of the monks said that I should have taken her along, and certainly should do so in future, adding, "We'd even give you a room together, and, if you wanted, we'd give you a double bed, too." I was perhaps too distracted by the thought of putting a double bed to its best use smack in the middle of a monastery to grasp the import of what he was saying. Unless I could take my home to this spiritual place, or bring this spiritual place home, my "retreat" was just that—no more.

And maybe it *was* no more. I am at a distance where I can write about this; I am not yet where I can measure its value. It has occurred to me that I may have gone to that monastery with no more virtue than many a young man has taken to a whorehouse. At a very manageable cost, I was hoping to seize a significant experience that would confirm my "manhood," maybe change my life, at least make me feel better. Perhaps I am unkind to myself.

Certainly God was kinder. For I had called to the Lord in my distress, and the Lord answered by setting me free—rather, by letting me know, in what I now hear as a virtual choir of voices, that I was free; free to watch or sleep, to fast or eat bacon, to stay at the guest house alone or with my wife; free, if I could leaven freedom with faith, to accept my own handicapping limitations as part of "my way" rather than obstacles in my way; free, finally, to ignore a legion of the voices that said I was letting God down if I didn't become a priest, or letting myself down if I taught high school, or letting go too easily if I turned my back on both vocations to write down the story of my turning. This was God's answer. It was not the answer I had been looking for, but that was because God, also, was free. God was not subject to the terms of my question.

And as it turned out, the more specific and directive answer I had been seeking was on its way. I would very soon be presented with a ministry I could freely accept, or refuse. But first I would have to move to a wonderful place, and make the acquaintance of an extraordinary person.

The Monsignor of the Northeast Kingdom

When they had crossed, Elijah said to Elisha,
"Ask what I shall do for you, before I am taken from you."
And Elisha said, "I pray you, let me inherit a double
share of your spirit."
—2 KINGS 2:9

"Where's Father Castle?"

The child in the pew behind me sounded as if he really wanted to know. I was waiting for the service to begin in the little church of St. Mark in Newport, Vermont, on the south shore of Lake Memphremagog. It was the closest Episcopal church to my new home, and just as close to the Canadian border. I was a first-year high school English teacher in the rural "Northeast Kingdom." The monastery was several weeks and a million miles away. The cathedral in Burlington, where I had gone on my lunch hours to hear Bach practiced on a Baroque organ, and on Easter to hear the Resurrection proclaimed amid "smells and bells" by four priests, a full choir, and a brass ensemble, was just as recent and as far. "Where's Father Castle?" the child asked. And where, I wondered, am I?

The child's question is as clear in my mind as on the morning I heard it a decade ago. For one thing, I was struck that this squirmy-aged boy was so anxious to have the priest appear. And for another, his question was to become my own in friendship, anger, longing, and bewilderment ever thereafter. "Where's Father Castle?"—I haven't stopped asking. And where would I be if I hadn't met him?

I came to his church with other questions on my mind. The vocational question I had taken to the monastery was never completely absent in spite of my new sense of freedom. I was also playing with the issue of "engagement," i.e., what was the appropriate political response of a Christian to social and economic injustice? I had been dipping into liberation theology and finding it both bracing and scary. The priest who then served as my spiritual director, and who had recommended my visit to the monastery, encouraged me to strike up an acquaintance with Castle once I was settled in my new home. She had met him herself only recently and found him interesting. He had been "very active in the sixties"—a phrase which can introduce anyone from an avatar to an ass—and he seemed genuine to her. Certainly he could shed light on my own struggle with the idea of "revolutionary praxis."

I lost no time in letting Castle know what I'd been thinking, though I kept the matter of ordination to myself. It was he who would raise that one. I mentioned liberation theology—as I'm sure many in this country espouse it—more to establish my own credentials than to obtain a clearer vision of justice. I wanted him to know I was a guy whose brain, at least, was respectable. That's not to say I wasn't sincere in my uneasiness about "doing nothing" when so much needed to be done.

Castle's response was completely free of cant. It disarmed me. I was prepared for a position I could dismiss. Nostalgia for the sixties would get nothing but a loud raspberry from me. It was almost 1980. I was almost thirty! Anyone who said "movement" to me had better be talking about something that was still *moving*.

You could not just make a decision to commit yourself, Castle said gently, steadily. Nor was there any sense in berating yourself for "doing nothing." He had been involved in some "heavy stuff" in the sixties. But the involvement began because of what was happening to people he cared about. You cared about people. Then, as a consequence of that caring, you were pulled into their struggles.

Pulled in, all right. He had been arrested, jailed, gassed, and repeatedly threatened with violence. He had marched on Washington with Dr. King, participated in the first antiwar Mass at the Pentagon, and been arrested standing beside the Baby Jesus in the crèche at the National Cathedral. He had gathered garbage from the abandoned buildings in the inner city and dumped it by the truckload on the city hall lawn. He had organized for the United Farm Workers, removing parts of his dental work and dressing in dirty clothes in order to pass undetected into the camps. He had invited H. "Rap" Brown to Jersey City. He had worked with the Berrigans. He had cooked for the Black Panther breakfast program—and, rumor had it, cooked up some other things for them besides ham and eggs. Senator Eastland had it put in the *Congressional Record* that a northern Vermont farmhouse owned by Castle was being used by the Panthers for training in urban guerrilla warfare.

And it had all begun, apparently, because Castle had started playing basketball in the housing projects near his Jersey City church. The priest as athletic missionary—it was right out of *The Bells of St. Mary's* or Cronin's *The Keys of the Kingdom*, which turned out to be one of Castle's all-time favorite books. He had invited street gangs to use the parish gymnasium. He had staged a summit between two warring gangs, beginning with Holy Communion. Then two boys in his parish were forced to confess to crimes after being beaten in a police station. Castle was called to the station by a distraught mother. He took up their cause, and it led him to a larger cause. Eventually, the basketballs whizzing past his head turned into bullets.

After years of activism coupled with the most old-fashioned kind of pastoral care, having resigned his parish in the hope of being replaced by a black priest, and having seen a number of former comrades grow disenchanted or suicidal, he moved with his first wife and their four children to a ramshackle farmhouse in Vermont. The family opened a general store. "We ran it like a church," he once told me, "and I think it was a good church." When I met him he had been in the Northeast Kingdom for almost a decade. He had since sold the store. He had raised sheep. He had married hippies and baptized their children. He had buried his oldest son, accidentally drowned at nineteen. He was the rector of two parishes, St. Mark's in Newport and Christ Church in Island Pond, the football coach at the regional high school, and a night counselor at a halfway house for the mentally retarded. He was fifty years old.

When you first saw him, you might have found it hard to believe his past. He did not look as I had expected. How many people do? I had been looking for a scruffy, graying radical type, perhaps a beard, lots of touchy-feely mannerisms—some button pinned on a bogus blue-collar shirt to announce that his "progressive" pulse was still healthy and strong. In fact, I never saw him wear a button of any kind, though he always bought a poppy from the Veterans of Foreign Wars. He wore his hair combed over his balding pate, and in summer cut as short as a marine's. He was clean-shaven, with a clerical collar and glasses. His mouth brought to mind Hardy's description of the typical Anglo-Saxon face—"two halves of a muffin." My best summary description to date is that of the old comedian Phil Silvers, but with broader shoulders. A woman who would later become his second wife said that the movement of his head and mouth reminded her of "a Muppet."

Hearing him preach, though, one could believe almost anything about him, so long as it was good and brave. I do not mean that his sermons were daring or controversial; in fact, he seemed to avoid any divisive posturing or sloganizing—though he was not lacking in the nerve it took to invite a local serviceman dishonorably discharged for marching in a West German peace demonstration in *uniform* to "preach" from the pulpit. I mean you could believe anything about him because he seemed to believe so unreservedly in God. His God was the benign Father of the Gospels, and his Jesus was a stalwart "companion to the morning star." And all of us could be that, too. If this sounds like a theology with a few clichés, I suppose it was. Yet there was something gritty and rock-solid under his proclamation that Jesus had truly walked *on* the water, that unless a corn of wheat fell into the ground and died it abided alone—but if it were planted, oh, what one seed might do! And if I were to say in one sentence what Castle gave to me of more value than anything else, of more value even than the vocation that is this book's subject, I would say it was the sense of the Gospel as something real and important and liberating and full of high adventure. In the pews of his church, and in his company outside of church, I felt perhaps more than at any other time in my life how good the "good news" was, especially those springtime chapters after the Baptism and Temptation, when a voice called to you after a whole night of fruitless fishing on the lake and said "Try again," and you tried and enclosed more fish than your nets could hold, thinking to yourself "Here is luck and here is God and here is big trouble" as a man waved smiling at you from the shore.

Sundays after services, and weekdays after his shift at the group home or before afternoon football practice, Castle held court in the narrow kitchen of the parish house, at the head of a table almost as large as the room. We ate potato pancakes and drank coffee brewed on an old black stove, the burners of which we sometimes turned on for heat on winter mornings. For a while, we had a weekly Communion there at the table, passing the paten and chalice from person to person, but Castle soon found that "too easy" and moved us back to the chancel of the church next door.

"Us" refers to a small inner circle of which I soon found myself a part. My wife called us "the Gang of Four." Actually, it may have been closer to a gang of three, but since I'm the writer here, I will take the liberty of claiming full membership. One of the four, now dead, was a respected local dentist in his sixties named Ben. If ever I met a man I felt was beloved of God it was Ben. He was Simon Peter and Sancho Panza, too. His repeatedly stated goals in life were to reduce the size of his belly and to study his set of the *Great Books of the Western World* systematically. He was forever finding fault with himself for lack of dietary and scholastic discipline. Comparing himself with Father Castle, he felt like an indecisive coward, but I always believed, and Father Castle probably believed as well, that Ben was in some ways the bravest of us all. One of my last memories of him is that of "our local dentist" holding hands in a circle of Hiroshima Day demonstrators that included David Dellinger and Castle and a lot of sockless, braless, and perhaps a few witless people with whom he shared nothing but a planet, a biology, and a belief in the sanctity of both.

The other gang member, besides Castle and myself, was Anne, a middle-aged woman of incredible vitality and warmth. Her teenage children used to joke that nothing but her own relative poverty prevented her from paying for the groceries of everyone in any checkout line she happened to join. She would have been a bohemian in the Paleolithic Age, but she had been a bohemian in the sixties; I hesitate to use the word "hippie," though it was the word often applied to many of her friends—there was something too intellectual and sharp-eyed about her. Book for book, she could best some college professors for breadth of reading; it was almost an amusement to try to find a title she could not discuss. She was a talented artist, and in certain circles a legendary cook. She was full of stories and lore. Her grandmother, who lived by an Irish castle, once had her fortune told by a peddler. He said she would always be a Stafford and always live near a castle, seemingly a prediction of lifelong maidenhood. But she married a man named Stafford and went to live near his castle. It was just that sense of "maybe" and magic that she infused into our group.

In this company, of which Castle was always the center, I began to understand how water can be changed into wine. What a giddy sense of transformation there was in sitting with them on the shores of Lake Memphremagog—on the deck of the bar of The Landing restaurant, to be more exact—and realizing that the Sea of Galilee was only a bit larger than this body of water. They were both minor lakes, ringed by insignificant towns, disturbed only occasionally by fierce storms, yet charged with unlimited potential. Perhaps, just perhaps it was possible to board a small boat in the funky marina on the southern end and sail north to a Quebec town to cast out a devil or preach to the birds. It was just a thought—Father Castle himself refused to enter a boat on the lake. Ben had an old wooden inboard, hardly pretentious, especially for a dentist, but he claimed that Castle rejected all of his pleas to go for a ride. He'd drink on the deck of the restaurant, that he'd do, but the luxury of "boating" was apparently where he drew the line. Until everyone in that partially shabby town could come on board, the lake scene was not for him.

In spite of such refusals—and what kind of priest would he have been without them?—Castle abounded in humor: ironic humor, silly humor, often purposeful humor. There's a saying from the Desert Fathers, "If you see a young monk by his own will climbing up into heaven, take him by the foot and throw him to the ground, because what he is doing is not good for him." Had Father Castle written that, he would have recommended *tickling* the foot. When he saw someone too proud, too earnest, or too "holy"—in his catalogue of sins, the worst of all—he would often apply his feather to the toes. Even his own well-developed ego and occasional grandiosity were not exempt from a little gentle satire. When I first asked what form of address he preferred, he said "Monsignor"— though "His Holiness" would do. He once introduced me at a party as "director of the Lenin Institute in Brownington, Vermont." Was he mocking my very un-Bolshevist scruples, or jabbing at my occasional stridency? Was he doing both? Similarly, he cultivated a fiction in which my wife was a fiery Italian senora who might at any moment pull a stiletto from her purse and cut him to ribbons. By this they were able to burlesque a few stereotypes, but he was also able to say that he recognized she was not the fan her husband was, and that she was ready to do some of her own jabbing at whatever *she* deemed too holy, including the Monsignor.

It is a rare and enviable talent to make people laugh at themselves and enjoy doing so. At one particularly dreary vestry meeting, Castle suggested that we display the proceedings as a float in the Fourth of July parade. We were discussing at some length whether or not to cut down a tree that stood in front of the church. It was hiding the church and perhaps rotting some of the boards, but it was also a beautiful tree. Well, said Castle, we could have cardboard images of the tree and the church and all of us sitting there indecisively, rolling slowly down the main street of town. Once he and I were passing out leaflets describing the effects a nuclear war would have on Vermont. I was trying to show myself fit for the task by being a bit too aggressive, though friendly enough. Castle was more easygoing. He handed a leaflet to a middle-aged businessman who apparently knew him and liked him but confessed himself unsympathetic to the cause. "Ah," Castle said, "but do you know all the effects of a nuclear explosion?" Tapping the man at each point of his description, he went on: "Your hair begins to turn gray and fall out up here, you start to grow this big belly . . ." The man laughed and took a leaflet.

If you wanted to rub Castle with some of his own salve, the best place to apply it was his periodic enthusiasms, which took hold of him as of a young boy. For a time, probably under Anne's influence, he began to fancy himself "*un cook*." He made quiche and crepes, deliberately mispronouncing the latter as "craps." It was amusing to see him poring over a copy of *Gourmet* magazine, he who said his favorite eat-out meal was ground beefsteak with mashed potatoes, gravy, white bread, and creamed corn. He found a recipe for French bread in the *Boston Globe,* which naturally turned out to be the best French bread anyone had ever tasted. He never got tired of your telling him so. He began using the word "baguette" about as often as a soapbox preacher says "doom." The long brown loaves multiplied like rabbits on fertility pills.

It was this enthusiasm, not to mention the bread, that flavored the soup kitchens Castle and Anne began holding in the parish house. Privately, Castle expressed some ambivalence toward the whole "soup kitchen" concept. On the one hand, it struck him as a condescending acceptance of poverty, as a rescue effort gone awry and turned into an institution, with all the glib acquiescence to injustice that such a turn implies. On the other hand, "waiting for the revolution" struck him as just another version of pie in the sky. Who were we to say we had the food, but dared not share it because of serious ideological reservations? Still, he wasn't comfortable.

He may have worried too much. The soup kitchen at St. Mark's was a long way from Victorian "mercy." For one thing, the food was delicious. For another, everyone was invited, and nearly every kind of person came. Local professionals and shopkeepers broke bread—excuse me, baguette—with welfare mothers and street people. Guests donated what they could, if they could, and were enabled to do so discreetly. The question of "the truly needy" was *out* of the question. This was a parable as much as a project.

Ho, every one who thirsts
  come to the waters;
and he who has no money,
  come, buy and eat!
Come, buy wine and milk
  without money and without price.
Why do you spend your money for
  that which is not bread,
and your labor for that which
  does not satisfy?

With the kind of irony God seems to love, the heartiest, freshest, most gourmet food in town at that time may have been served at a church soup kitchen. And, as was the case in nearly all of Castle's undertakings, some of the served began to be servers. Customers became cooks and maître d's.

Watching Castle work with indigent people gave me an appreciation of the freedom that comes with commitment. I understood at least a part of what Jesus meant by saying "Take my yoke upon you . . . for my burden is light." When you are giving with abandon and acting with courage, as Castle did and had done for much of his life, you have won as your privilege an immunity from certain con games. Hustlers can smell a guilty social conscience a mile away. A religious guilty social conscience, so much the better. I'm not about to imply that Castle's social conscience was completely clean and completely his own possession, but, for the most part, the decision to be hustled or not to be hustled was his.

"And could you maybe give us a little cash?" the spokesman for a small group of vagabonds with remarkably good teeth asked him. Quite possibly he could—in exchange for painting the church steps. I shall never forget Castle expounding on "Take up thy bed and walk" as though the Lord's Aramaic had meant "Get off your ass and take some responsibility for your life." He did not say it so crudely as that, but however he said it, he had said it first to himself, and then, obliquely, to those who were ready to manipulate his heart. No one with a heart prone to hemophilia could help but be envious. Along with ordinary hustlers, there is a great

class of people one meets who have no intention of ever setting
foot in a church, but who can speak with enough certainty to shame
a pope about everything the church needs to be doing, especially
on their own behalf. Castle cut through that garbage with the
authority of a priest who'd been "there," in the struggle, longer
and harder and with greater risk than anyone who was likely to
challenge him.

Yet—and this I also find admirable—he showed little interest
in cutting through people themselves. One of the things we tend
to look for in a man or woman of wide experience and firm intellect
is the ability to penetrate human pretenses, to "recognize the rap,"
so to speak, and take it apart word by word. Castle often seemed
to recognize the rap and not care. It was as if he saw the posture
or affectation as a necessity, like clothing, because the poor human
ego cannot go naked on this earth. On more than one occasion I
waited in vain for him to pounce on something I regarded as pure
imbecility—some esoteric gobbledygook, or soft-brained cliché
masquerading as "free thought." If the speaker tried to justify or
belittle human suffering, he would pounce. Otherwise, he was more
likely to listen. By watching how Castle tempered insight with
tolerance, I began to believe that God's ability to see through the
superficial exterior of a man or woman is not necessarily the same
as God's disapproval of that exterior, however trite or quirky it
appears. Fortunately, I began to believe that at roughly the same
time as I began having an occasional painful brush with Castle's
complex exterior.

"The wind," Jesus tells Nicodemus, "blows where it wills, and
you hear the sound of it, but you do not know whence it comes
or whither it goes; so it is with every one who is born of the Spirit."
The saying came to mind more than once in my relationship with
Father Castle. I didn't always assume that he was "moved by the
Spirit," but if he was, I was apparently unsure of the movement.
I was licking my finger and holding it up in the breeze. I was being
telegraphed the latitude and longitude of a given position, but when
I rowed to those coordinates, all I found was the open sea. "Where's
Father Castle?"

We had begun holding a brief prayer meeting early Wednesday

mornings outside the Newport Federal Building. As originally discussed among the Gang of Four, this was to be the first part of an
action to protest the buildup of nuclear arms. It would eventually
lead to a "ghosting," which Castle said was a Quaker way of making
silent protest. Some of us might even be arrested.

The prayer meetings went on for several weeks. During my April
vacation from teaching, when Castle was away in New York pur-
suing job opportunities, I decided to "ghost" the Federal Building
on my own. I don't know exactly what pushed me to the decision.
I had just seen a film, *The Final Epidemic,* which was being circulated by the "freeze" movement, and it had left me shaken. I
was probably just as upset by the possibility that Castle might
leave Vermont for an urban parish. I felt he was growing impatient
with the small-town character of small-town activism. Well, he
would see that there were worthy battlegrounds—and worthy
comrades—right here at home.

Early on a Friday morning I awoke, prayed, and made the only
protest sign I have ever held in my hand out of cardboard, lath,
and Magic Marker. It was wordy enough.

I am here to bear silent witness against the senseless buildup
of nuclear arms, which puts the life of every creature on earth
in jeopardy. I am at odds with the policies of the government
represented by this building, not with the men and women
who work here.

Since I was still nursing my grudge against the Woodstock Nation,
I combed my hair and dressed in a sport coat and tie: protest
number two. I collected some leaflets and a prayer book; I kissed
my worried wife good-bye and drove to Newport.

I found a place to stand inside the door of the Federal Building.
Uncle Sam pointed disapprovingly from a recruiting poster. A dark,
ghostly image of me was mirrored in a display case; I used it to
check how straight I was holding my sign.

It occurred to me in a mixture of relief and disappointment that
no one might come, that nothing might happen for as long as I
stood there. A couple walked by without taking much notice. A

grizzled old farmer came through the door, paused, and said with a laugh, "I thought you was a statue." My reason for being there, why I was holding a sign and what the sign said, did not interest him in the least. He had thought I was a statue, and I wasn't a statue, and there's no end to the funny things you'll see in town if you can just find the time to get there. Five minutes later, his business concluded, he walked by and gave me the same glance and chuckle. "I thought you was a statue," he said, and went out the door.

A humorless army recruiter, whom I recognized from a brief verbal exchange between himself and Castle during one of our Wednesday morning prayer meetings, stopped in front of me and read the sign, standing stiffly "at ease." He then said, "You're entitled to your opinion," and left. Fair enough.

Almost immediately thereafter, a cigar-smoking janitor entered the lobby, noticed me, and let out the same sigh of mild distress he might have breathed had I been a leaky pipe or some dog's mess on the newly waxed floor. "I'm not sure you can be here with something like *that*," he said. "I'll go ask." And I began to ask myself, What shall I do? If he insists that I go, shouldn't I refuse?

He returned shortly and told me, politely, that I would have to leave. Otherwise, he would have to call the police. I could stand outside the building but not in it. It was nothing personal, he said. Nevertheless, he declared his position on the issue by noting that he had been in military service.

"I don't know if I can leave," I told him. "I would appreciate a few minutes to think about it." He said he would give me that long. Then he surprised me by adding, "And I hope you'll consider *my* feelings, too."

Hey, who was the practitioner of civil disobedience here, him or me? Consider his *feelings?* I was not sure what those feelings were, of course, but I was sure that he was asking me to value his dilemma and his conscience as much as my own. I had not prepared myself for that one.

Silently I said one of the Collects for Guidance from the Book of Common Prayer, which given my usual measure of decisiveness has proved as practical for me to memorize as my zip code. I

remember asking myself, What if a man had told Jesus to leave
the Temple courtyard on Palm Sunday? I decided to stand my
ground.

The janitor stayed away for a good five or ten minutes, long
enough for me to wonder if I hadn't called the bluff of some honcho
upstairs. Perhaps I'd heard the end of this. But I hadn't.

He returned, and again asked politely, "Will you leave?" I
reached out my hand, which he shook, and told him my name. I
told him he was very kind, but that I needed to stay where I was.
I asked him to try, as a former soldier, to understand how I felt:
to leave would be to desert my post. He said he could understand
that—but that if I stayed, he would have to call the police and call
his boss, and he didn't want to do either, and would I please go
outdoors. He said his name was Robert Reed.

That was it. I'd go—"for *you*," I said, but I might be back another
day. He began explaining his views on the issue, how we couldn't
"trust the Russians," etc., but I was scarcely listening. I felt completely outdone and undone by the man. What could the peace
movement not accomplish with a few dozen Robert Reeds in its
ranks? He thanked me for going and took a copy of *Nuclear War
in Vermont.*

I still don't know how much my surrender was a response to his
humanity and how much it stemmed from my fear of being
arrested—or, for that matter, how much my initial resistance had
stemmed from my fear of having to stand outside "in front of the
whole world." For I had resolved to ghost for an hour, and I had
about half of that to go.

I took up a new position at the top of the steps near the
door—as close to my indoor position as possible. By then I had
grown used to the heated lobby, and now I stood in the shade of
the building on a chilly spring day. I was cold, stiff, and embarrassed. The streets were full of shoppers and kids out of school.
Most showed only the slightest curiosity; I might as well have been
a statue. One woman stared at me from a phone booth. A couple
of men read my sign without comment. A usually affable member
of my school board strolled up the street, saw me, and crossed to
the other side.

The last thing I want to do is ascribe any pathos to what may well be one of the silliest things I ever did as an adult. It's just a simple statement of fact to note that this was also one of the loneliest moments of my life. And it is this moment that often comes to mind, however outrageous the association I am about to make, when we read the Passion Gospel where the crowd taunts Jesus to "come down from the cross" if he is really the Son of God. Certainly I was no Christ figure standing there with my cardboard sign and my conceit. But this experience is the closest my poor imagination can come to what it's like to be "nailed" to one spot, wishing you could be anywhere else, and wishing your friends were in sight. And I felt I could better understand, too, all the stories of the richly rewarded comforters on the Way of Tears, Veronica with her veil, and the thief promised paradise, and the Gypsies told they would "eat without working" because they alone had offered water to the Savior. When a woman walked up the stairs, read my sign, and warmly said that though she already had a copy of *Nuclear War in Vermont*, she'd take another copy for a friend, I wanted to be able to tell her that from henceforth all her lottery tickets would hit the jackpot.

Father Castle called me when he got back from New York. I told him what had happened. At first he sounded disappointed that I had not been arrested. "Oh, Gary," he said, as if I'd gone to Niagara but neglected to see the Falls. But then he said I had responded on an appropriately human level to that janitor. "You did right to leave, and you would have done right to be arrested," he said. "It's time we all went over there. You've upped the ante for us all."

I rather wished I had played a winning hand.

The next day my wife and I joined Castle, Ben, and their wives for breakfast. Things were not at their best in Castle's personal life, the New York trip had apparently renewed old doubts and longings, and he was not in a good mood. He brought up my ghosting of the week before. He said that being arrested at the Federal Building would be counterproductive. He said we'd be doing so "for its own sake." He spoke as though I'd come breathtakingly close to going over Niagara Falls in a barrel.

His mood and its causes aside, I cannot know the inner struggle out of which he spoke. Clearly, he strove to be both an example and a support to me. Perhaps he wondered if he hadn't misled his young friend. Perhaps he felt disappointed in himself for not having taken the first step—and a bit annoyed at me for jumping the gun in his absence. Perhaps the nature of my solitary escapade only served to convince him—to the point of depression—how paltry any activism was bound to be in Newport, Vermont.

None of this was important—for me. What was important was to ask myself how I would have felt *had* I been arrested, only to learn that in the final analysis Castle thought it "a bad move." If my aim was to play a minuscule role in saving the planet from nuclear holocaust, what did his praise or disapproval matter? But if my aim had been, even in part, to please Father Castle, I was on rough seas.

This may sound like a qualification to all the admiring things I have said so far about my priest. In fact, this episode, along with several others like it, may have been the most Christ-like gesture I received from a man so full of Jesus. "Call no man your father," it said, "for you have one Father, who is in heaven."

Call no man father. Easier said than done.

If I had to come up with an epithet for Castle, one to replace "Monsignor" and "His Holiness," I would call him "the Great Enabler." At the time of this writing, one of the buzzwords in America is "empowerment." Everyone seems to be "empowering" someone else, or seeking "empowerment" of some kind, and a lot of us are growing so downright empowered that I'm beginning to detect a powerful stink. But the word does describe what Castle could do: he empowered people with confidence in the strength of their talents and a sense of the importance of their choices. I know of chefs, priests, rock groups, entrepreneurs, and late-in-life, single-mother college students who got their idea, their first big push, or even starting money from Castle. Once he learned of my desire to write, and had read some of my pieces, he was constantly giving me encouragement. "He's so very talented" was as likely to be said as my last name in any introduction Castle gave to me, and he once brought me to the verge of tears by telling me over the phone that I should take my talent and just "throw it to the wind," use it with total abandon, and "get hurt," and he would be there for me.

Needless to say, he was a man of considerable talent himself—and not just as a preacher, pastor, and organizer. He had been an All-American quarterback in college. Though he had lost or given away a good part of his material resources over the years, I think he had a head for business. He had successfully run a machine shop in Jersey City, and I knew of no venture he ever suggested in the Northeast Kingdom that flopped. He had published a book of poems and prayers, not with a vanity press either. His rapport with people of every age group, class, and disposition was phenomenal. And he could make superior baguettes.

A key ingredient in the Castle ethos was the demand to use whatever talents one had to their fullest. "Stretching yourself" he called it. Most of us talk in terms of "spreading," usually followed by "too thin," but Castle's word was "stretching," usually followed by "not enough." For him Jesus had indeed come that men and women "might have life, and that they might have it more abundantly."

Castle's chief contribution to the abundance of my life began with a request that I help out an adult catechism class at the church. I had never been one to volunteer for any kind of auxiliary church activities. I was one of those who sat in the last pew at the earliest service, leaving at the earliest possible moment. But I agreed to his request. The season was Advent, my topic was the Incarnation, and I set about "stretching myself" to prepare the lesson along with all those other lessons I had to prepare as a full-time teacher.

You know you have been a success at presenting a theological dogma when your audience finds it so attractive and sensible as to wonder why they'd never formulated it themselves. I doubt I was that successful, but apparently I was close enough for Castle to ask if I wouldn't present my lesson in the form of a sermon for the whole congregation. This was a heady offer for me, since I don't think we had ever discussed my dilemma over seeking Holy Orders.

If I had felt driven to get up a good lesson, I was almost possessed by the urge to pen a great sermon. It might be the only one I would ever do. My recent study of George Herbert had immersed me in the sermons of his famous contemporaries, John Donne and Lancelot Andrewes, and though my own efforts were hardly baroque, they certainly made a "Batter my heart, three-personed God" kind of noise. Figures of speech abounded—the Second Coming was an elopement in which ladders would be thrown up against the world's windows, and the soul would thrill to the sound of the Lord's engines idling in the driveway. Gracious! But I was as elated to preach that sermon as a soul about to slip its feet through the window and get hitched to the Lamb. My love of words, and the Gospel, and God, and Father Castle—and let's not forget my own voice—came forth in one twenty-minute release that felt as good as anything I had ever done outside the intimacies of friendship or marriage. It was the beginning of something—and Castle knew that before I did.

He recommended a second sermon. And this time, why didn't I come with him after the service at St. Mark's and repeat my message at Christ Church in Island Pond? What is more—we were warmed up for some vigorous stretching here—if the parish were willing and I agreed and the bishop approved, why didn't I go several Sundays a month, to preach and read Morning Prayer? Castle could use the break and I would get a fee for going. Well . . . I wasn't sure. How did that collect for guidance go again?

I could not tell what kind of impression I made in Island Pond. Much of the tiny congregation seemed to be either overawed at what I had to say or at a great loss to figure out who in the heck I was supposed to be. Actually, a good number were simply hard of hearing. In any case, Father Castle did not say much about the Island Pond venture after that. I assumed I had probably blown it with the people there.

As at the monastery, I was keeping a journal in those days, and in an entry for March of that year, a few months after my second effort at preaching, I wrote in red ink the question Castle put to me: "So, are you ready for Island Pond?"

Thus began a very modest ministry which nevertheless has provided an answer to my vocational dilemma, a few warnings on the advisability of my ever seeking Holy Orders, and enough musings to fill up the rest of this book. The bishop's approval came, Castle gave me some rubrics, I was ready to go. Have prayer book, will travel.

Quite soon thereafter, at Castle's suggestion, I began to visit the people to whom I was preaching. My first visitation was as his partner, and I shall never forget it. Perhaps no one ever had a briefer apprenticeship in pastoral care; all told it could not have lasted longer than an hour. But I have yet to read a manual that taught me as much or as well.

We went to the home of a woman who had been sick. There was no stiffening when the door opened, no feigned surprise and pleasure, but genuine eye-lighting joy at welcoming someone who had come because he cared, and who would know when to leave. He sat on the couch and made conversation with the woman and her husband, easily, attentively, unhurriedly. When he was ready to go, he took the woman's hand and prayed for her. How carefully he gathered up the concerns of their talk, the dropped names, the lucky breaks, the implied fears, and made them the kindling for his prayer. When he was finished, we all rose and said good-bye; the prayer was still with us, like the warmth of a fire just extinguished. And just as fire is completely familiar and completely necessary—yet somehow never ordinary when it ignites—so was that prayer. Often we get up from a prayer as if we've just finished crossing the legs or zipping the fly that has let our underwear show. "Well, we'll all pretend we didn't see that." And of course there is also that priest who says "Amen" and leads his companions back to the profane world like a tango master escorting his partner to her seat with a flourish that says, "I've just about ravished you, haven't I?" This was different from either of those. This made you want to visit everyone you ever knew, and a number of people you didn't know, and say prayers with them all.

We visited one more person, then went for drinks to the Buck and Doe Restaurant, which turned out to be the second home for Christ Church's organist. So we visited her, too, though this time we didn't say a prayer. Late that night I drove home under a full moon past the misty hayfields and darkened houses of Charleston, Westmore, and Brownington, accelerating confidently into the turns, with Springsteen groaning "Born to Run," but my heart returning in counterpoint to his driving energy, born to start, born to stay, born for now and forever.

I was looking forward to years of shared ministry with Castle, quite content to be his straight man and second fiddle in Island Pond. But with his last child off to college, and a sense of his rural mission accomplished, his eyes were on an inner-city parish. He did not hang around for long. His first stop on the journey south was an Episcopal boys' home in the center of Vermont. He lost no time turning the place upside down. He changed the staff, cleared out the attic, and hoisted the Episcopal banner up the naked flagpole. He held services and athletic events that brought the community into the home, and took the boys for hikes in the mountains and to concerts at Dartmouth. He built coops for rabbits, chickens, and turkeys. He hustled Oriental rugs and antique furniture into the home. He nailed icons and art prints to the newly painted walls. He beat the scores of packages of frozen brussels sprouts back into a corner of the freezer and claimed the kitchen in the name of the baguette. Risking the very core of his image, he purchased a high-mileage but rather immaculate Mercedes-Benz sedan, and made a point of chauffeuring his charges to school, because "wayward boys" deserved to ride in style. Just last week as I write, several years after Castle left the home, I spoke with the chairwoman of the local P.T.A. I knew a little of her community, I told her, because a priest named Father Castle had run the boys' home there. "Oh," she said, "that man is still a legend in this town."

In any case, his legend there, like his legend in Island Pond, remained longer than he did. Castle finally made it to New York, to St. Mary's Episcopal Church, Manhattan, West Harlem.

So there I was—if not left holding the bag, at least wondering how I could carry what was now in my hands. With the help of the people of Christ Church, the diocese, and the one whom Castle preferred to call "the Lord," I have at least survived. And in some ways, Castle's absence has been an integral part of that survival.

Jesus said to his disciples, "It is to your advantage that I go away, for if I do not go away, the Counselor will not come to you." As long as Father Castle remained in the Northeast Kingdom, I would have remained his admirer, his limping follower—it does not seem truthful to say his disciple. I would have watched him, and in many ways tried to resist his influence on my life. But with him gone, I have had to assume a small portion of his spirit. I hesitate to give that statement its full Trinitarian weight, though if any ounce of that weight is there, I give thanks. What I rather mean, though, is that on the most ordinary level I have had to try to assume some of his moxie, his jovial evangelism, his blithe testing of every assumption and pretense, his daring of himself to go an extra mile—and then another—and in a very real sense, as with the Lord and his apostles, he is with me now more than when we sat over drinks at the Buck and Doe.

Shortly after he arrived in New York, I did something that seemed to indicate I had taken his mantle on my shoulders—or at the least was dragging it faithfully along the ground. I did not yet have his address and phone number. Then a wonderful way of finding them out presented itself. A friend of my wife told her the tribulations of a nine-year-old son, who had just started his own "detective agency." Customers were nil, and he had made the mistake of announcing the enterprise to some schoolmates who laughed mercilessly at his "stupid" idea until he came home in tears. This was all I needed. I would use the spirit of Father Castle to locate Father Castle; arrayed in his cape, I would come to the boy's rescue. I phoned the "agency," and with as much formality as I dared, I asked if a young detective might be willing to take on a missing-persons case which, for various reasons, I could not pursue myself. I knew that he could manage it, because Castle had relatives in the area who would certainly know the new address. The boy said yes, we agreed on a fee, and he went to work. My wife learned from his mother that our freckled Sam Spade was absolutely delighted. The new address and phone number came within days.

However pleased the boy had been with his first real job, he could not have been more pleased than I. It was such a trifling thing, and yet I felt somehow as though I'd really "gotten the knack" of ministering to others according to the Father Castle model. I smiled to myself about it for a long time. Weeks later I was daydreaming the details as I raked the lawn—and it hit me. I had never paid the detective. I had completely forgotten to send his fee. I rushed inside the house and phoned an apology. I mailed a check for a good deal more than I owed, and typed up a glowing letter of recommendation to go with it. I fell into a depression. My spirits were lifted somewhat, I'll admit, by learning from the boy's mother that only her intercessions on behalf of "a very busy man" had prevented her son from sending me a twenty-dollar "late charge"—through his *secretary!* The agency was expanding. The boy would do just fine.

But how was *I* doing? The lesson, for a lesson it was, taught me the dark side of the Castle commandment to stretch yourself, and spend yourself, and throw your talents "to the wind." It was very possible, and easier than I'd imagined, to extend yourself to a point where few of the seeds you planted ever got enough care to grow. I am not saying this was Castle's weakness; but it was, and to a great extent still is, the weakness of at least one young man who stood in his shadow. It is true that the Palestinian farmer in Jesus' parable of the sower casts his seed indiscriminately; some falls on the rocks, and some is eaten by birds or choked by thorns, and only a portion falls on good ground and bears good fruit. But I dare not fancy myself a sower, even though I share in the ministry of the Word. I am first, foremost, and forever a bit of dirt in which a seed has fallen, and without time and the ability to choose how I spend time, without nourishment and careful cultivation, I shall be at best a green shoot that withered and blew away. And most of my endeavors will share that same fate.

But I can talk myself only so far out of Father Castle's influence. As I said before, he is always with me. I get gas on the way to Island Pond, the cashier says, "Have a nice day," and I recall him saying: "There are no good days or bad days. They are all the Lord's days. 'This is the day that the Lord has made.'" "Don't worry, be happy," the car radio sings—and Castle replies: "We are not here to be happy. We are here to grow." But I am so tired tonight. I would just as soon turn around and go home to bed. "It is when you're ready to say 'I'm not going to do it, I've had it,' that the opportunity to do good is often most present. You have to die for people every day." Yes, but that's you—you're a priest, and you're Father Castle, and you're good at dying because you're so alive. I am in the wrong place and in the wrong line of work—I don't even belong in the church—and only a fool could believe anything different.

"Fools do go where angels fear to tread. But sometimes the angels go with the fools."

The angels, of course, can get to Island Pond any way they choose, but a fool has only a couple of routes if he wants to take a car. One of them goes past Lake Willoughby, Vermont's deepest lake and surely one of its most breathtaking landmarks. Glaciers cut its bed out of a mountain, and the sheared halves, which bear the biblical names of Pisgah and Hor, rise up haughtily on either side of the frigid depths. The place has its legends: an aquatic monster, and a story I've told probably as often as any local old-timer, about a man cutting ice off the lake, whose team of horses fell through and were found floating next spring in Crystal Lake, four miles away.

But these are not the legends I tell to myself when Willoughby suddenly appears on my way to Island Pond. That gap you see, that great chunk taken out of the horizon—that is the hole that was left in the Kingdom when Father Castle went away.

Island Pond

"Can anything good come out of Nazareth?"
—JOHN 1:46

When Father Castle asked me, "Are you ready for Island Pond?"
I am not sure he was referring only to a ministry there. I think he
also may have meant the place itself. Was I ready for that, too?

I suppose I was. But I have now spent quite awhile asking myself
if I am able to write the words that will "locate" Island Pond for
a reader. For it seems to me that Island Pond is like no other place
on earth. Island Pond confirms no one's belief in reincarnation: I
cannot imagine anyone standing for the first time at the intersection
of its main streets and thinking, "I've been here before."

When I close my eyes and try to imagine Island Pond—or Brighton, as it is properly called—I find that no single mental picture
can contain it. Instead, I see a kaleidoscopic view of discordant
images—from the Old West, from Appalachia, from the blue-collar
neighborhoods around Paterson, New Jersey, where I grew up,
yes, from Vermont, too, turning slowly in the pale light of a mid-
winter sun, and captioned with the original settlement's name of
Random. The same thing happens when I think in terms of time.

Island Pond is not Lake Wobegon, "the little town that time for-got," nor is it, as I once quipped, "the little town that time forsook," but a town in which time has come undone. At least that's how it seems, as one's eyes move from the classic brick railroad station, to the boom-box-toting kids leaning against the sheriff's car, to the gray-haired hippies leaving the new supermarket, to the World War II tank parked outside the American Legion Hall, to the kerchief-covered heads of the women of an ever-growing religious sect that has chosen Island Pond as a good place to wait for the Apocalypse. Of course, my inability to capture Island Pond in a single image or moment would not seem strange in a sprawling city, in any city—but it seems strange to me here, in a small town in northeastern Vermont.

The only way to take a comprehensive picture of Island Pond is to stand at a distance from it, and from there the picture is unequivocally beautiful. The town with its spires sits ringed by the wild, wooded hills of Essex County, the most untamed land in the most rural corner of the state. The author of a fulsome town history printed in 1900 begins, "Never in all her long centuries of won-derful picturing was Dame Nature in a gentler, more artistic mood than when with her giant brush and Divine inspiration, she fash-ioned the wonderful setting that was, thousands of years afterward, destined to be the resting place of the town of Brighton." The style may be exaggerated, but not the account of the view.

In town, however, the picture becomes kaleidoscopic once again. In one colorful facet I see the railroad station and maybe a small freight train, and on the hill behind, the steeples of the long-established churches, mine among them, and the Federal and Car-penter Gothic angles of houses built when Island Pond was a major railroad junction in the Northeast. There was certainly poverty in those days, but I suspect there is even more now, and that the decline of the railroad and the departure of the mills account for some other facets in the picture: dilapidated houses, sodden and lowly as toadstools in the little hollows at the bases of hills, and on dismal back streets.

In another view, I see Island Pond's main street, which makes me think of a frontier town, not only because of the square faces, false fronts, and railed upper porches of a few buildings, but also because of the packs of vacationers, snowmobilers, and motor-cyclists that usually fill its sidewalks and restaurants on the week-ends. Indeed, I was surprised to find in the 1900 history of Brighton a comparison to "a boomtown of the West," which foreshadows my own much later impression. That faint "Wild West" appearance plus the number of restaurants—four at present—plus the vast woods spreading to the north and east all give one a sense of Island Pond as a place where people provision themselves before entering the wilderness, or refresh themselves on the way out.

Hidden behind the main street, almost as if the town could not conduct its business without ignoring the distractions of its loveliest feature, is the lake called Island Pond. The pragmatic founders of New England towns seem to have understood "lake frontage" to about the same degree as they would have understood "life-style." A better view of the lake is from the hill that holds the churches; the best view I've had is from behind the clock faces in my church's steeple. Island Pond is a serene body of deep water, about three miles wide, fed by brooks and underground springs, and holding an uncannily round, wooded, twenty-two-acre mound of island in its center. I call Island Pond a lake out of deference to the turn-of-the-century historian, whom I quote one last time in a state of sublime indignation: "To Island Pond itself should the gods compel a never ending apology from the shade of the man who first called it a 'pond.' A more beautiful and beautifully surrounded sheet of water ne'er graced the poesy of Walter Scott, or stretched its placid depth over any portion of country." I would chuckle if I had never seen the pond—excuse me, the lake. The camps and suburban-style homes multiplying on its shores, the railroad track along its northern tip, the whining motorboats in summer and the motley village of ice-fishing shanties clustered on its surface throughout the long winter—nothing seems able to diminish the strength of its impression. In my sermons, it sometimes appears as an image for the Sea of Galilee, where Jesus called his first disciples.

One of them, the apostle Philip, went to his friend Nathaniel and announced, "We have found him of whom Moses in the law and also the prophets wrote, Jesus of Nazareth." Nathaniel's reply, this chapter's epigraph, reinforces my fancy of Island Pond as a town in the backcountry of Galilee. "Can anything good come out of Nazareth?" People have asked the same question about Island Pond.

Without a doubt, there is something depressed and depressing in this town, even for someone like me who has grown to love it. If a number of vacationers come here, so do a number of social workers. One magazine journalist called its main street "ugly," much to the resentment of many Island Ponders, but I've never heard anyone call its main street "picturesque." Actually, it's the lack of anything even remotely precious that forms some of my affection for the place. The first time my wife and I drove through town, however, it did not strike us as a place we'd want to come back to. It struck us both as strange and even a little sinister. A one-legged man in shabby clothes and a jalopy of a wheelchair sitting alone on the street corner seemed to sum up the condition of the town and its first impression upon us. Later on, I came to know the man. He boarded with two parishioners in an old house on the banks of the Clyde River, which runs out of the lake, and he considered the mallards that also lived in that spot his personal responsibility. He loved chocolate; I would take him some Hershey bars in the hospital a few days before he died. He continued to be a symbol of Island Pond—of how the town had revealed some of its humanity to me.

Nevertheless, it is often a hardened humanity one finds here. Island Pond has inhabitants as gracious as one could find anywhere; in the houses of my parishioners, and in grocery stores and repair garages, I have found a warmth no less than that reputedly found in the Old South or in the Old Quarter of Jerusalem. But I'll always think of Island Pond as a tough town, a stubble-chinned, large-caliber-bored, work-or-starve, fight-or-git kind of town.

Once I stopped my car on a rise just outside the village to help some lost French Canadians, a traditional Good Samaritan gesture in the Northeast Kingdom. I was parked off the road, mostly, but in a bad spot for any of my car to be hanging over the white line. As I was explaining the general direction of Burlington to a middle-aged man and his carload of neatly dressed, nodding fellow travelers, a woman came up over the rise, swerved around my car, and slowed down just long enough to deliver this tactful warning: "Move your car before some loggin' truck runs up your ass, ya goddamn fool!" I may not have the exact wording. I'm sure about the "goddamn fool" part, though. And I was sure, though this could have happened in any number of other places, that I was in Island Pond.

Not long ago in Island Pond a man followed his estranged wife and her male companion into a store lot and began blasting away at them with a double-barreled shotgun as they ran from their car. Somehow the companion managed to scramble to the counter and return, shooting the storekeeper's .44 magnum pistol. Though no one was killed, both of the ex-spouses were seriously injured. Some people in the surrounding area said that if such a thing were going to happen, it would happen in Island Pond. And it's true that in making my rounds through the neighborhood I've gingerly knocked at more than one door that bears a picture of a revolver and a caption such as "Never mind the dog. Beware the OWNER!" or my favorite: "If you are even thinking of breaking into this house be sure to notify your next of kin first so there can be a positive identification of the body." Of course, these kinds of signs exist all over the region. And Island Pond is not the only place where lovers and rivals attempt to kill each other. But it was not so much the violence, I think, as the degrees of broad daylight and firepower that made some outsiders say "Island Pond"—in that tone of voice that asks, "Can anything good come out of Nazareth?"

My own experience has been that it can and often does. My belief, influenced in large part by almost ten years of lay ministry here, is that there is no such thing as a "God-forsaken place." As Ronnie and Helen Langford have printed on the back covers of the menus at their legendary Buck and Doe Restaurant:

If you wonder what's to offer in this our little town,
Stop a while and look around.
P.S. We did.

Though not a native, Mr. Langford himself typifies some of Island Pond's toughness; outbursts of especially nasty weather have on occasion been attributed to the piquancy of his language. Through incredible stubbornness and hard work he and his wife have taken an enterprise that many said was doomed from the start, "a classy restaurant" in Island Pond, and achieved some national recognition for their pains. The Langfords are also examples of a great and varied tribe of immigrants who have come to the Northeast Kingdom and to Island Pond over the past several decades: New Age communalists, religious seekers, refugee executives, smugglers, outlaws, and people who simply seem to have "gotten lost." When Father Castle first introduced me to Ronnie, the feisty chef captioned the whole herd, himself, and Castle with typical peremptoriness:

"Anybody who wasn't born here, I don't give a damn who they are, they were running from something. You take a good look at them. I was running, and you were running, too. You can't tell me any different." Years later I quoted his pronouncement to him and asked what he'd been running from. "The city," he said, "and working for somebody else, and because if I went to a metropolitan area and opened a restaurant they wouldn't accept me because of my background as a Negro."

It has been more than twenty years since he came to Island Pond, with his Armenian wife, a hard-knocks education that began in Boston restaurants during the Depression, and a dream of opening his own place—and nearly ten since he told my priest and me that we were all running. At that time, and several times since, I've asked myself if I was indeed on the run, if I was in Island Pond as a matter of flight—from ordination, from the larger world, from God himself. Perhaps I am. But if I am running from anything that is really important, then it will be waiting for me wherever I go. "Lo, I am with you alway," Jesus says to his disciples, "even unto the end of the world."

When Father Castle brought me to Island Pond, seemingly to the "end of the world," to meet the owners of the Buck and Doe and to have me try on the vestments in the sacristy of Christ Church, he said, "There are very few people who attend here now. But then, there were not very many people at the Last Supper or in the stable at Bethlehem either." We were in the church at twilight, all by ourselves. We knelt in the large nave, built to seat almost fifty families, and he prayed with me, remembering people living and dead for whom that church had been important, and asking that my work there be blessed. It was a humbling moment. I was to know a few more like it.

The first time I went to Island Pond to preach, I went off the road. My text was from Micah: "What does the Lord require of you but to do justice, and to love kindness, and to walk humbly with your God?"—to which I gave a thorough, though perhaps less than humble exegesis. It had snowed on the way over, and in the sunshine after the service the roads were deceptively clear. There were borders of slush along the way, however, and it was one of these on a sharp downhill bend that sent me careening over the road, fighting to set my car straight again. I spun 180 degrees and crashed rear end first over an embankment, lodging in a trough of snow. A retirement-aged couple doing their dishes by a window facing the road saw the whole thing. The husband told me, when I climbed still shaken to his house to use the phone, "I says to my wife when I seen you coming through there, this fellow's going to go off the road."

It was not a good omen. Fortunately, I am less inclined to think in terms of omens than of parables. Island Pond would require a careful driver. There were tricky turns that awaited me, seemingly clear stretches of road that were not clear. But along with the good and merciful God (even my car escaped without major damage), there were good people watching me from the windows of their houses. They had seen others go off the road before me. I went to Island Pond not only, perhaps not even primarily to preach to them, but also to receive mercy and instruction at their hands. In the unsteady, embarrassed tramp to their doorways, and in the reassuring warmth of their kitchens, God would show the goodness of Nazareth to a goddamn fool.

A Dresser of
Sycamore Trees

*Then Amos answered Amaziah, "I am no prophet, nor a
prophet's son; but I am a herdsman, and a dresser of sycamore
trees, and the Lord took me . . ."*

—AMOS 7:14–15

I remember that my palms were sweaty, and my wife was pregnant,
and that at one point during the sermon the stained-glass windows
were suddenly flooded with sunlight. After two years of lay ministry
in Island Pond, the bishop had decided that he wanted to give
"formal recognition" to my work there. So he had come in mitre
and cope, with a silver crozier and a "Letter of Institution" affixed
with his red wax seal, to install me as Lay Vicar of Christ Episcopal
Church.

It was a glorious day, and because I did not have to preach or
lead any part of the service, I was relatively free to take it all in.
My parts in the liturgy were to receive the tokens of my office—
a prayer book, copies of the canons, a church key—from representatives of my parish, and to kneel once in the aisle, in the midst
of the congregation, and say this prayer:

O Lord my God, I am not worthy to have you come under
my roof; yet you have called your servant to stand in your
house. To you and to your service I devote myself, body, soul,

and spirit. Fill my memory with the record of your mighty works; enlighten my understanding with the light of your Holy Spirit; and may all the desires of my heart and will center in what you would have me do. Make me an instrument of your salvation for the people entrusted to my care, and grant that I may by my life and teaching set forth your true and living Word. Be always with me in carrying out the duties of my ministry. In prayer, quicken my devotion; in praises, heighten my love and gratitude; in preaching, give me readiness of thought and expression; and grant that, by the clearness and brightness of your holy Word, all the world may be drawn into your blessed kingdom. All this I ask for the sake of your Son our Savior Jesus Christ. Amen.

In my case the prayer had had to be modified slightly. I did not pray to "faithfully administer your holy Sacraments" because as a layperson I could not do so. Once a month a priest from a neighboring parish would come and celebrate Communion, consecrating enough bread and wine for me to take to the sick until she returned again.

That difference notwithstanding, I felt myself a very special person that day and thereafter. I was to my knowledge the only lay vicar in the state, and I know of none elsewhere. I thought of the prophet Amos, "a herdsman and dresser of sycamore trees," seized unaccountably by the call of the Lord and sent to prophesy to Israel. Like him, I had been raised to an important task. And like him, in spite of the ceremony and its insignia, I was completely without credentials. "I am no prophet, nor a prophet's son . . ." I had never been to seminary. I was trained to be a high school English teacher. I had been confirmed in the church only several years before. I felt exalted, yes, but also at sea.

Yet, as I look back on the service of my institution, as "special" as it seemed and truly was, it bears a striking resemblance to nearly every other service in the prayer book. It was like a wedding in which a couple vows to love and honor each other for a lifetime; like a baptism in which parents and godparents vow to raise another human being, as yet a stranger to them, in the image of Christ;

like a Eucharist in which we say "amen" to the announcement that
the flimsy wafer we are about to eat is the Body of Christ. In short,
it was like every other service in which we are sent out to sea in
a frail little craft with a few provisions and a few stars to guide us.

Irish monks in the Dark Ages would sometimes be set adrift,
literally, in just this way, hoping to land somewhere as missionaries,
but realizing they might just as likely drown. They were only a
little braver than the average bride and groom. Their mission was
only a little more desperate than that of a conscientious parent.
They looked only a little more precarious bobbing over the horizon
than I did rising from my solemn prayer that day. They required
only a little more faith.

So, when people have asked me what this book I am writing is
about, after I tell them it is about my ministry in Island Pond, and
after I tell them that the title comes from Amos, I say that the
book is about doing any work for which one has had very little
formal preparation. I tell them it is, essentially, a book about what
almost everybody I know is doing almost every day of his or her
life.

That sounds very universal, so I had better get busy with some
particulars. Authorities I trust, from Wendell Berry to Sri Rama-
krishna, all remind me that the particular is the only means we
have for touching the universal. We arrive at what is true for all
by committing ourselves to particular beliefs, tasks, persons, and
places that are true for us. One particular task I have to perform
in Island Pond is to preach. It is perhaps the *most* particular task,
the one in which I feel most "set apart" from other people. It may
also be the task in which I feel the most like Amos, a herdsman
and dresser of sycamore trees called from his regular labor to give
the Word.

You can get some idea of the difficulties a preacher faces by
considering the modern connotations of the verb "to preach," or
of the noun "sermon." The latter connotes a discourse as offensive
as it is dull. "Don't give us a sermon!" It's hard to believe that
sermons were once thought an art, even a form of sacred enter-
tainment. We find them quoted in Elizabethan commonplace books

side by side with bawdy jokes and accounts of high adventure. Needless to say, our ancestors did not use the word "preachy." Does any judgment damn a contemporary book more severely than to say it is "preachy"? I'll feel quite let down if no one has that to say about mine.

The idea of preaching is offensive to so many of us, I think, because we mistake the preacher for our would-be superior. (I am sure that a few preachers make the same mistake.) Instead of seeing him or her as an instrument, in fact a very lowly thing, like the other vessels used in worship, we see the preacher as attempting to mold us according to his or her own mind. This strikes us at the very least as undemocratic. Of course, it also taxes our meager supplies of humility. "What does he know that I don't know?"

My answer to that question is "nothing." Frequently, I have reminded my congregation and myself that for the most part I do *not* know anything more than they know. My lay status makes the job of convincing them a little easier. Yes, there are some facts about Scripture, liturgy, or church history that I may "have" and they as yet may not have. Encyclopedias have them, too. But as far as what is most important, I have nothing new to tell them. If they have read the Bible, if they know the Creeds, if they have been faithful in worship, they know everything I know. If they have lived with these longer or more intently than I, then they probably know more. All I can hope to do is to remind them of what they know, to enliven what they know—that is, to make it more accessible to their imaginations, and thus to their faith. I can help them see, even as I struggle to see for myself, the points of contact between our religion and the details of our lives.

In this sense, I see my work as not unlike that of a medieval painter. Like him I am hardly even an artist, at least not in the modern sense of a "creative" person. I am a craftsman. The subjects, the scale, even some of the colors and poses of my work have already been prescribed. It is my task to find the right face for the sin of envy, perhaps with the help of a mirror; it is my task to make the Virgin's robes such a blue that the sky will seem her mantle; it is my task, most of all, to dress the disciples and their

Master in the clothing of my own century, just as the medieval painter did, and to depict the Sea of Galilee with an island in its center and railroad tracks along its shore.

In attempting to "paint" in this way, I have two invaluable tools at my disposal. One is the example of Jesus himself, who took the stories of daily life and made them parables. "The kingdom of heaven is like a woman who took leaven and hid it in three measures of meal." I have tried to listen, as I believe Jesus did, for the stories that can become parables. So if an older man tells me what it was like, as a boy growing up in the Depression, to find a discarded baby carriage in the dump, and thus to have found a rare treasure, a set of four wheels, and how he and his companions ran home waving the wheels over their heads to build a wagon or racer— then I have a way of retelling the parable about finding a treasure in a field. I have a way of re-presenting the joy of discovering the Kingdom of God.

That brings me to my second tool, which, ironically, turns out to be my status as a part-time lay minister who makes his living in the "secular" world. As a schoolteacher I am a daily witness to countless little dramas of growth, judgment, healing, friendship, betrayal, sacrifice, suffering, reconciliation, miracles, rebirth—in short, of the central themes of the Gospel. So in one sense, at least, I have turned a disadvantage to my favor. I am not in church or in Island Pond as often as I would like to be, and there are definite losses to my parishioners because of that. But when I do come to them it is as one who lives very much where they do. My "vicarage" is a mortgaged home in my and my wife's name. The weekly meetings I attend are not opened with prayers. There is no clerical collar around my neck to remind me or others of what I am supposed to be.

Preparing a sermon is often a halting gesture of repentance on my part. I sit down to look at the lessons appointed for the up-coming Sunday—often a good deal closer to Sunday than I care to admit—and my sitting down with the Scriptures after a frantic week of cursing, complaining, and compromising is a moment of sobering recollection. Such moments have been too rare in the past week. And once again I've put off the sermon too long. The thought of getting up in front of my parish to preach the Gospel is mocked by all the ways in which I've failed to live up to it—in which I've failed even to remember it at all. Yet those shortcomings, illuminated by the Scriptures, can sometimes join with them as part of the "text."

Not long ago I preached on a passage from the Gospel of John: "I am the true vine, and my Father is the vinedresser. Every branch of mine that bears no fruit, he takes away, and every branch that does bear fruit he prunes, that it may bear more fruit." I started out by describing the remnants of an old apple orchard across the road from my house. For lack of care and pruning it bears little fruit, and I have often resolved—yet always neglected—to revive it. Here was an apt symbol of my own life. I talked about things that need to be pruned from our lives, and a few that needed pruning from my life especially. I suppose I was trying, once again, to get at the universal through my own particulars.

One of the things I needed to prune from my life, I said, was an obsession with justifying myself. There were simply too many judges in my head—too many suckers on the branch—and I was wasting too much of my moral sap in seeking approval. I shared a prayer that I had written, which is perhaps a bit much to quote here, but which may be the most concise way of making my point.

O God, who will judge me and all people on the last day, help me to free myself from the tyranny of appointing others as judges in your place. Help me to free myself from the need for their approval, from the urge to justify myself in their eyes; and forgive me, that I have strayed so far from the truth. Without judging others, and without contempt for their just criticisms of me, let me walk humbly before you, committing all my deeds and misdeeds into your hands, and on the day of your judgment, have mercy on me, a sinner. Amen.

I was "preaching to myself" again, but I was also inviting the congregation to put my preaching—and their minister—in perspective. If they read between the lines of my prayer, they heard me making a case for their liberation from any tyrannies growing out of my pulpit. Don't let my voice become yet another member of the unsparing tribunal in your head. Don't be needing to tell me why you weren't in church the past three Sundays. Get pruned.

Of course, like any rule of thumb, the notion of preaching to oneself has its limitations. It is not enough for me to examine my own life and to assume glibly that my particulars will automatically touch on the universal. I have to make an attempt to intuit the needs of those in the pews. But here too I am sometimes addressing problems close to my own heart, for I belong to their family. I am a part of the congregation.

All of us at Christ Church, Island Pond, are conscious of belonging to a small parish on the virtual edge of nowhere. Half of us are a good deal past what is commonly, if erroneously, referred to as "the prime of life." The resulting self-image is not enhanced by the memory that we were a thriving and "important" parish only a generation ago. Nor are we comforted by the prevailing notion of "parish growth" as an increase in parishioners. According to the same reasoning, we could say that a marriage "grows" when the spouses start putting on weight. But it is a hard notion to disavow, for the lay vicar no less than for anyone else.

In response to the tenuousness of our enterprise, I feel a need to preach "the wisdom of the desert," the beatitude of "the poor in spirit," the special affection God seems to have for "bruised reeds," "dimly-burning wicks," and for people who lack the prime or pride of life. Of course, in doing so I risk the danger of laying on the comfort to the thickness of complacency. We may get to liking ourselves too much. So I try to deliver the comfort in the form of a challenge. We *are* small, God *does* bless the seemingly insignificant—now what shall we *do* with that blessing?

What this all leads to is the old ideal of "the ministry of all believers." I hope that after the theme of "God so loved the world . . ." this is the most frequently recurring theme of my sermons. In terms of the discussion here, that means that the preached-to must become preachers. They must find the right words, the right parables, and the right opportunities for making the Gospel known in their lives. A necessary step toward their doing so is, once again, to put the kind of official preaching I do in its proper perspective.

Unfortunately, many people do not. I am sometimes amazed, even alarmed, at the extent to which people judge ministers by their preaching, and preaching by its rhetoric. To do so is to make the entirely spurious but nearly universal assumption that God is better served by a poet than by an accountant. It may be that the most eloquent sermons consist of the ways in which ordinary people bear pains in their hands and sides, their necks and backsides, in the daily crucifixion of being alive. I want my parish to see my Sunday preaching as little more than a classroom demonstration of this truth. I want them to understand that inasmuch as we are all carrying a cross, we are carrying a pulpit, too. The best pulpit.

In this aim I am helped somewhat by the structure of my church's liturgy. In the Episcopal Church, as in other "Catholic" branches of Christianity, the sermon is not the climax of the service. It is but a step, albeit an important one, to the altar. It always precedes, and never supercedes, the Eucharist, the sacrament of the Passion. I have a small role to play at the altar in dispensing the already consecrated wine. This has been an even more formidable task than preaching, because I am not the most coordinated or graceful of men. I am always fearful of upsetting the chalice, or spilling the wine onto a kneeling worshiper's head. I'm sure this is a concern of anyone who has served in any capacity at an altar. I remember Father Castle telling me of a seminary class in which the instructor told of a woman who, in a moment of fervent devotion, had seized the chalice he held to her lips and drenched herself in consecrated wine. "What did you do?" one of the seminarians asked. "We had to burn her," the instructor replied.

Recalling the humor of that story was of small comfort when the inevitable happened. I did not dump the chalice over, but I grazed it with my hand enough to spill some consecrated wine on the altar and on one of my sleeves. Episcopalians are not supposed to view such mishaps with as much horror as our Roman Catholic relatives are reputed to, but I viewed mine with horror enough. I was not at that time in the highest spirits to begin with, and the crimson stain on the altar cloth seemed to indict me. It said, in a voice I have heard several times since, that my ministry was a failure and my "vicarhood" a joke.

It took a little time for me to comprehend what had really happened, and what had not happened. It took a little time, in this and in so much of my ministry, to see the universal and the particular intersecting in a cross, plain and simple. Why was I suddenly so worried about the wine? I had been spilling it every day of my life. Two thousand years ago, the blood of Christ was poured out over the rocks and dirt for my sins. In other words, even in my peculiar accident, occurring in the midst of my peculiar work, I was just like everybody else.

Another part of my work as lay vicar is visiting the members of my parish. I call it "the other foot." "How beautiful upon the mountains are the feet of them who bring good tidings," says the Book of Isaiah. Preaching is the one foot; visiting is the other. If my feet are somewhat less than "beautiful upon the mountains," I hope they will at least be sturdy and reliable.

Some of those I visit are people too old or sick to attend church. I am permitted to take Communion to them in their homes or nursing homes, or in the hospital. I carry it in a silver Communion set presented by the people of Christ Church to Father Louis A. Arthur in July 1881. So I'm carrying a sacred mystery, and a little history, too—all of it enclosed in a broken wooden box, held together with a thick rubber band. I like the symbolic unfolding of it all: the band snapping off; the box, which someone long ago attempted to dress up with a covering of wood-grained Contac paper, coming apart as it opens; the purple-velvet lining and the antique silver vessels like pearl and mother of pearl within an outwardly drab shell; and within those, the "food of salvation."

I love the service itself, which is a radically abbreviated version of the rite for Communion said in church. The brevity is a gesture of mercy toward the ailing communicant, for whom the mere act of swallowing is sometimes a struggle. The "table" is whatever lies at hand, sometimes a kitchen table, an end table beside a bed, a folding snack tray, the seat of a chair. In the midst of crumbs,

Kleenex, unanswered mail, pill bottles, remote-control channel changers, and catheterization tubes, Jesus lays out his meal. I am often reminded of the mystic Julian of Norwich and her visions—experienced while she lay sick in bed—of the "homeliness of God," and of the whole of the universe perceived as "a little thing, the size of a hazelnut." Perhaps someone had brought hazelnuts to her room, and one of them lay on a table next to her bed, near a comb, a candle, or some other "homely" thing, when a priest came and placed Communion bread beside it.

I am often touched by the way people will prepare a place for the Communion. Patients in neighboring beds will sometimes turn off their televisions, or lower their voices to a whisper. Whatever they do, we always pray for them during the service. One elderly woman keeps a clean linen cloth on hand to place over a folding metal snack tray; she hobbles to her closet to take it out whenever I come. Perhaps the most memorable of these preparations occurred in a slowly collapsing house which I was visiting for the first time. I asked the woman if she and her husband, who was then suffering from dementia, would like to have Communion. She said she thought that would be nice, especially for her husband, who was not able to get to church. Then, without a word of explanation, she walked out the front door.

After several moments she still had not returned. It suddenly occurred to me that she had taken my offer as an opportunity to step out for a while, perhaps to run some errands. Her husband seemed to get the same idea and was growing visibly agitated. What is more, I was supposed to be leaving for a long trip within the hour, and I could hardly leave the man alone. Why do I always get myself into these messes? I thought. To the best of my ability I assured the man that I was "coming right back" and went to the door to see if I could sprint up the street and catch his wife.

But she had not gone. There she was, bending over in a weed-ridden vacant lot across the street. Was she sick? What on earth was she doing? Back she turned, grinning at me, with a bouquet of wild flowers in her fist. "For the Communion," she said.

On every level, Communion and the visits of which Communion is a part "come from" the church. I try to emphasize that to myself by making the church building my first stop. That sometimes takes a little resolution, because I'm often coming to Island Pond after a day of work, and with only a few precious hours to spend on "making the rounds." But of course this is one of the most important things I have to do as a minister: to quiet myself, and to make intercession, by myself, in silence. It took awhile for me to recognize how important a job that is. I think an ordained person would have realized its importance sooner. It is typical of an amateur to be dazzled by the extraordinary aspects of a given work. The pre-med student dreams of using a stethoscope or scalpel; a good doctor is probably more absorbed in listening carefully to what a patient has to say.

When I first came to Christ Church as a preacher, an elderly woman shaking my hand after the service said to me, "This is a beautiful old church. Sometimes if you're not feeling good, and you come and sit here for a while, you'll feel better." She was right. It is usually quiet there. Sometimes the clock in the tower rings, or I hear the pigeons cooing on the roof. Once I heard through the floorboards, like an antiphon with my prayers, the Girl Scouts who meet in the basement reciting the Girl Scout Promise: "On my honor, I will try: to serve God and my country, to help people at all times, and to live by the Girl Scout Law." Sometimes I walk to the front of the nave to see the waning sun brighten the faces of the two little angels in the window, memorials to the daughters of Edward Payson Lee, a Civil War captain who became the church's first rector. Both girls died of smallpox. On the way out, I will glance up at the marble plaque for Doctor Linehan, who died at the age of thirty-five—from contracting the same disease while treating Lee's daughters, I am told. In a strange way, I feel they are all there with me. Father Castle smiles at me from the pulpit, and so does the ghost of Father Clark. "Dad Clark," they called him, who drove his Model T Ford over the backroads to baptize children on remote farms, and through Island Pond late on Friday nights, picking up passed-out railroad men and lumberjacks from the gutters and taking them home. Is he the ghost or am I?—with such an example to live up to, I scarcely feel substantial. But I do "feel better." It is then time to wind the clock in the steeple, make a few phone calls around town, and set to work.

I enjoy my visits. And I think most of the people are glad to see me. "Gary!" a man calls out, as I pull into his drive at the dead end of a dirt road. "Come in and have a beer." "Gary" sounds almost more refreshing than the beer—it reminds me that I have known these people from before I decided to go by my full first name. My family calls me Gary, too. Inside his house, a widower's camp in the woods, we sit on the couch with our beers, his old dog across from us in his bed. "They say every man is entitled to one good woman and one good dog," the man tells me, "and that's been true for me." He has been a widower for a long time. His wife died when their daughter was still a girl, and he raised her by himself, moving away from Island Pond for the sake of a job, then moving back when the girl had grown. "So, what's up?" He's been tearing up the inside of his place and redoing it. He's teaching the hunter safety course again. His star pupil is a girl, and he seems proud of her and of that fact. He's been reading, too—*The Clan of the Cave Bear* and Paul Johnson's *History of the Jews.* In this room, not long ago, he told me what it had been like to walk next to the American tank that knocked down the gates of Dachau. He did not tell me a single grisly detail. All I saw was his face when he said, "I've been to hell."

I have no idea who benefits more from these visits, the people or me. I know I am supposed to be "the minister." I pray that I will bring God's peace when I enter someone's house. Yet it often seems that I am conscious of bearing God's peace only after leaving. Perhaps it was I who needed it, and the host who gave. In any case, I give what I can, and gratefully acknowledge what I take. I am grateful for the practice that has enabled me to overcome a little of my awkwardness in social settings. I'm grateful for the piece of blueberry pie baked from wild berries picked along the railroad tracks. I'm grateful for the jar of blueberry jelly I take when I say good-bye, and for the care in the warning to "drive carefully" and "watch out for the moose."

Lately, I have started doing a few of my visits in the form of taking someone for a ride. As with my quiet times in the empty church, I am surprised at how long it took me to think of this. I have always found it easier to pray walking than kneeling. In a moving car I may be a better visitor also. Awhile ago I took a drive with a woman almost ninety years old up through the still-wild country east of the little town of Newark where she had grown up on a farm. Having grown up not far from Newark, New Jersey, I always get a kick out of the sign announcing entrance into Newark, Vermont. But she took me on winding roads even more desolate than those I knew. She showed me the farm where she had been born, and told me how in winter the crews would come with a massive horse-drawn cylinder to "roll the snow." She showed me the one-room schoolhouse where she had taught for a year before marriage, and another house where she had boarded and had had to pay for damages when the horse who pulled her wagon to school had chewed up the landlord's stall. Passing an embankment studded with boulders, she chuckled, recalling a recent bus trip to Plymouth Rock with the Island Pond Seniors. "I thought to myself, we've got bigger rocks than that to home." With Martha Washington somewhere in the branches of her family tree, and the memory of all those glacial deposits "to home," she was probably a good deal less impressed by her trip to Plymouth Rock than I was by our drive through Newark. Anyway, we came home with plenty of forage for our prayer.

I try always to end a visit with a prayer. I follow what I took to be Father Castle's practice of incorporating the concerns of the preceding conversation. Issues, worries, ailments, plans, the names of loved ones—all of these enter the prayer as essential ingredients. If, as has happened on several occasions, my visit interrupts a game of rummy or Scrabble, then my prayer gives thanks for games, and asks that God will be present during them. I hope this practice reinforces one of the stated goals of my preaching, that is, to make the Gospel and its parables come alive in the day-to-day doings of my parish. At the very least, it helps keep my prayers concrete. I said one of my parting prayers in a basement where a young logger had taken me in order to show me his new chainsaw. Ministers and priests have blessed everything from bombers in wartime to puppies on St. Francis Day, but I may be one of a very few who ever said what amounted to a blessing of a Husqvarna 266.

Trying to pray in this way requires one to listen carefully. I have come to believe—again so embarrassingly late—that this is one of the most important things I have to do in Island Pond. "Of course, of course," we're inclined to say, "listening is very, very important." But when we say so, we are almost never listening. We're thinking about what we're going to say next. We're trying to formulate the "answer" that we imagine is required of us, when often all that is really required is that we pay attention.

That may sound like just another notion cribbed from the social sciences, but for me it is a theological one. More and more I see God as the Almighty Listener. More and more I see how preoccupied we are with the "answers" to our prayers, never acknowledging the utterly omnipotent and compassionate act of God's hearing them. In contrast with the half-open ears of even our dearest friends, we have a listening as large as the universe, a listening so profound we can almost hear it—and it unsettles us, like the breathless silence of someone on the phone who does not even mutter an "uh-huh" to our confessions until we feel compelled to ask, "Are you still there?"

Jesus, too, was a listener. In his parables of lost coins and disappointed fathers, of fruit trees needing manure and cultivation, of labor pains suffered and later forgotten, I hear the traces of conversations in which it was always his honored part to listen. When the Samaritan woman at the well says, "He told me all that I ever did," I wonder if that is because she, without realizing it, told him all first, and he listened. By that I do not mean to question Christ's prescience, but only to acknowledge his full possession of a gift that I have increasingly come to regard as divine.

Ironically, I have sometimes been granted a share of that divine gift through being so mortal. In some conversations on some evenings I am simply too exhausted, flabbergasted, unqualified, or inexperienced to do much *besides* listen. When a woman relates some of what it had been like to live with a pathologically abusive husband, when a hospitalized Vietnam veteran tells of the terror of smelling the Southeast Asian jungles in the earth of his own cellar, when another woman tells me of waking from a nap to hear the voice of her dead husband speaking from a misty human shape beside her bed, what is there to do but listen, to say as little as possible, and to say that in the form of a prayer?

Visiting my parishioners, and listening to them, makes me a witness to their loves. You cannot minister to people effectively without that knowledge. You cannot lead them to a greater love of God without knowing about the other things they love, which I believe God has given them as steps to the vision of Love Itself.

In a parish made up largely of older people, this means learning or attempting to learn the litanies of their grandchildren and great-grandchildren. I have even started a small file of family trees for some of my older people, adding a name here and there when I hear it dropped in conversation. This is not a matter of mere data gathering. You cannot pray for someone at the deepest levels of intercession without including the pictures on the piano and on top of the television set.

When I go visiting, I am often given a glimpse of the affection people feel for their loved ones. A wife lays her hand on her husband's shoulder; a father tousles his son's hair. Of course, we all see those things when we go visiting. But on a pastoral as opposed to a purely social visit, those glimpses take on an extra significance. Just as the minister comes to bear witness for God, to show people, by "showing up" at their doors, that God cares about them, so he or she also bears witness for the people, acknowledging their affections—and their anxieties for those they love—before God. I suppose one could say, "Doesn't God see that affection without your help?" I am sure God does. But one of the mysteries of prayer, indeed of all our relationships, is that of telling the other what the other already knows. What "does not need to be said" is frequently and paradoxically what most needs saying. I love you.

Along with witnessing the affections between people, a minister "making the rounds" is also able at times to witness their other "loves," their enthusiasms and diversions: a quilt in progress, a snowmobile engine torn down to the block, a prom dress, a remodeled kitchen, a watercolor, a garden. These projects are as much differentiae in the definition of humanness as speech, cognition, and an opposable thumb. What was Eden, after all, but the best of backyards to muck around in? I imagine heaven itself as a place for tinkering and making. Somewhere in the "many mansions" of the Father's house there must be the equivalent of a sewing room or a power shop.

I stop at a farmhouse and the man who lives there asks, "Would you like to see what I've been doing?" I know the question. It is one I have grown to love. It leaves someone's mouth furtively and lights on your head like a crown. I will show you a place in my house, and in my heart. I will let you see what I've been doing, deliberately and freely.

I wish I had Homer to help me describe the farmer's special room, to tell how a man wakes up one Saturday morning and sets to work after milking his cows to strip an old farmhouse door down to the wood, of how he lays wooden panels parallel and interlocking along all four walls of the room—or even how, after years of living in northern rural towns and eating in luncheonettes, you can look intently at wood paneling and smell coffee, eggs and bacon, diesel fumes, cedar smoke, and autumn rain in your mind—of how the man built gun holders all along one paneled wall and hung deer trophies on the other three. I wish I remembered the models, dates, and calibers of all his guns, laid side by side in the racks, muzzles aimed at the ceiling, from a worn but durable 12-gauge to a recent indulgence almost too fine to fire. Each had its story: with one he had shot his first deer; an old man had found another abandoned in the woods on top of a mountain. The farmer took down gun after gun, allowing me to take them in turn, and hold each to my shoulder to feel its weight and balance, then wiped their barrels with a red flannel rag before returning them to the rack.

This room was a sacred space, a place that he had chosen to make especially his own, a place redeemed from mere "use" in which he would make a conscious attempt to be at rest and to put a part of his life in order. In short, this room was the evidence that the man was able to pray. And if I can find a way to tell the man, if he even needs to be told, that his special room prefigures prayer and might itself become a prayer, then perhaps I have done my work. But the work on that day was to acknowledge his kindness in showing me the room and trusting me to appreciate what it meant to him—never mind my suggesting what it might mean. "Thank you for showing me this," I said to the farmer, and later to God.

Of course the various "loves" of my parish are not the only things I see when I go visiting. I also see my friends' struggles. The same farmer who showed me his gun room has told me some of the harsh economic realities of farming within a system where milk sells cheaper than soda, where farmers "sell everything wholesale and buy everything retail," and where everyone associated with dairy agriculture seems to be making money hand over fist except the people who milk the cows.

I also remember visiting his farm when he and his wife were engaged in a local political struggle to have frayable asbestos tiles removed from their children's elementary school. Unfortunately, the issue was polarized between "local" people who tended to see the asbestos fears as grossly exaggerated, and environmentally conscious émigrés who saw asbestos as an intolerable threat to children's health. The battle lines were not softened any when police discovered marijuana plants and even a few opium poppies growing on some of the more prominent antiasbestos people's property. Some of their opponents went so far as to have bumper stickers printed with the facetious imperative: "Don't breathe asbestos. Smoke pot instead!" I'm sure I had no more than a glimpse of the difficulties faced by this couple, a man from one of the valley's oldest and largest farm families married to an outspoken downcountry woman "with ideas," and of the courage it took to fight their fight—and to try to do so with charity toward all their neighbors.

It is here that we arrive at the limits of what I've been saying about listening and its importance. Listening *is* important, but it is not always enough. Neither is talking. Yet talking, in prayer and from the pulpit, is all I have really done to address the economic and environmental issues represented above. In many instances, the pastoral rightfully becomes the political. Yet, as I look over the struggles I have seen as a part-time pastor, I also see how consistently I have failed to take the next logical step. In some cases I have lacked the time; I am simply too involved in my own struggles. In other cases, I have lacked a sense of direction, the reassurance that the church at large would be standing with me and guiding me. Sometimes I have lacked the right sense of relationship with those in the struggle; we have not known each other well enough or long enough for me to feel I have a right to "join" them. Yet, in all cases, what I think I have lacked most of all is the guts. And in spite of all my talk about love, perhaps I've lacked that, too. Anyway, it is all too easy when you are "not a prophet or a prophet's son, but a herdsman and a dresser of sycamore trees," to excuse yourself from going to "prophesy to Israel," though that is the very thing you are called to do.

Lately, perhaps in answer to my prayers that I be a better minister, I have begun to "butt in" once in a while. No, I'm not yet engaged in anything like a political struggle, but I'm at least taking a few gingerly steps off the platform of "godly" neutrality. I have begun, for instance, to tell the relatives of a few of my elderly parishioners that they need to respect their parents' and grandparents' desires for independence and self-determination. Laugh, if you wish, at the modesty of the undertaking. It is at least a step, and a step in keeping with the profile of my parish.

The beginning of the end for an old person living in his or her own home is when he or she begins to fall down. If you have any dealings with old people "on the loose," you know that there comes a time when they quite simply begin toppling over. The falls are nasty in a lot of ways. We all know about brittle bones that break easily and take a long time to heal. But there are also bruises that seem to happen as easily and last as long. A little wrinkled arm bruised from the wrist to the shoulder, or an old face with a black-and-blue cheek, looks like the result of a major beating. And it also looks, to younger family members, like a bitter accusation. Look what's happened to Grandma! Look what's come of your unwillingness to face facts!

But broken bones and ugly bruises are only the periphery of a family's worst fear. The truly dreadful thing to contemplate is that Grandma will fall down with no one nearby to pick her up. But perhaps the family dreads this more than Grandma does. One elderly woman in my parish, who's taken some seriously bruising falls, got into her bathtub one day and discovered she couldn't get out. So, quite in character, she pulled down a towel from the rack, wrapped herself in it, and took a nap until some relatives found her, nearly dehydrated but calm. "Oh, Nanna," one of her great-granddaughters exclaimed after the doctor had come and gone, "it must have been so awful!" Nanna replied coolly from her bed, "You mean to tell me you spent four years away at college and never slept in a bathtub?"

Of course this was no joking matter. Yet wouldn't it be fortunate if the worst fall you could take was down a flight of stairs or even out of a window—instead of out of your home, out of your neighborhood, out of the familiar surroundings that keep many of us from going out of our minds? Wouldn't it be a relief if the worst thing your family could do to you, at seventy-five or eighty-five or ninety-five, was to let you die in your bathtub?

In this regard I think that my religious tradition has something important to say. The second thing about God and humanity which the Bible teaches after the fact that God made us is that God loved us enough to let us fall. None of the disastrous consequences of our disobedience outweighed the value of our freedom in the mind of God. Now I realize that such a value cannot be applied indiscriminately. So I am gentle and tentative when I remind people that the elderly have the same right as other adults to decide which risks to their *own* well-being they are willing to take. They are entitled, warn them as we might, to their share of the Forbidden Fruit.

The rejoinder to this bit of theologizing is the Great American Dogma of Senility. When an old person cannot remember what day of the week it is, it follows that he or she has no sense of personal destiny either. I thank God that my relative youth prevents such a rule of thumb from being applied to me! Setting aside the more extreme cases, I wonder if "senility" might be viewed more accurately, and more religiously, as old age's version of the basic unconsciousness that afflicts all human beings. Children are naïve, teenagers are careless, adults are busily oblivious—and older adults are, well, forgetful. Of course this means that each group needs to be warned, advised, protected, and in special circumstances even restrained. And I am not questioning the necessity of some hierarchy in determining how the generations care for one another. But I am saying that to eliminate all choices for one group on the grounds of *its* peculiar version of unconsciousness is to make our own version all the more glaring and intolerable.

As for those people who do seem to have "lost it," or lost most of it, I find myself asking questions about what they have indeed lost—and what, as a result, they may have found. If we believed more in eternal life, I think we would believe less in inevitable deterioration.

I will never forget one old woman who would haunt me whenever I came to visit one of my parishioners in a nursing home. She would wander into the bedroom during our visit, or follow me out to the front door. She wore a seraphic countenance which may have been fed by the blithe conviction that her son, whom I suspect she never saw, was "the second most powerful person in the country." The joke would have been on me, wouldn't it, if one day a limousine had pulled up to the home, and out had stepped the Reagans' astrologer.

Anyway, she was a great pest. And on one visit in particular I was in no mood for her. I had had a hard day at work, and I could tell that my parishioner, patient as she was, also wished that Maggie would go away. What is more, at that time my mind was over-wrought with the fear that something had gone wrong with my wife's pregnancy. I could scarcely keep my attention on the visit, and Maggie's interruptions and non sequiturs didn't help.

Finally, she left us alone and sat down in the TV room. I walked past her on the way out, feeling a little guilty that I wasn't saying good-bye, but excusing myself on the grounds that I needed to get home on time. When my hand was on the doorknob she called out to me, out of the blue, out of my innermost heart.

"Do you have any children?"

"No," I said. "But my wife and I are expecting one."

"God bless you!" she cried, adding nothing more to detain me.

One of the nursing homes I used to visit was run by French-speaking Roman Catholic nuns, and presided over by an elderly sister of unquenchable cheerfulness. I don't think she was senile. She had spent much of her life in the African missions, and I suspect she never quite got over the pleasant surprise of ending up in Vermont. On one of my visits she was entertaining a superior in the order, and when she saw me pass the office, she called me in to be introduced. "Now this is Mr. Reverend Keezer, he's a"— I'm always curious to see what people say next—"Lay Apostolate with the High Church of England." Wow! And there I stood, looking like a lay apostolate if ever there was one, with horizontal stripes from the chalk tray at school running across my groin and backside, a rummage-sale-condition prayer book, and, as it so happened, a rather hefty bunch of bananas. If only I'd had the wit to reply that all my friends just call me "Apostle."

That's a good story to use in opening a talk or meeting, something with which to break the ice when a new acquaintance asks, "Now what is it you do with the Church?" I often wonder, though, how much less silly it is to say I am the Lay Vicar of Island Pond than to say I am a Lay Apostolate with the High Church of England. I often wonder, "What am I doing here? Who am I kidding?"

One of my favorite anecdotes has to do with a man known as the Curé d'Ars, eventually St. John Vianney. At one point in the career of this uneducated and irritatingly zealous rural priest, a number of his flock circulated a petition declaring him "unfit" to hold his post. When at last the Curé was able to get his hands on the petition, he signed it. I think I know exactly how he felt.

Often my sense of my own ministry is nothing more than an awareness of missed opportunities, of gains that might have been won but for my being too blind, timid, forgetful, or otherwise employed to seize the moment. In spite of all the friends I've made here, I often wish that I had never come to Island Pond. The thought that I shall one day be called to account for what I have done in this place often seizes me like the realization that I've failed to turn off an iron or stove, and that it was hours and miles ago. I can smell the smoke.

Yet there is a way through these doubts, and it leads to the recognition with which I opened this chapter: I am much like everybody else. Granted that a layman's preaching and then writing about it are a little outrageous, can't the same thing be said for every human being's praying, joking, hoping, lovemaking, child rearing—inhaling and exhaling? It is outrageous just to be alive. All of us are like passengers strapped into the wildest ride at the amusement park, who suddenly recognize as the gears begin to whine and the faces of the other riders blur that only a few screws and bearings stand between themselves and death, that people can die, do die, on rides just like this one, and you can't get off simply by wishing you hadn't gotten on. The only decision one really has then is to believe or not to believe that the apparatus and its operator are trustworthy. The best that most of us manage is a lopsided vacillation in favor of belief—but oh, in those moments of belief, one knows what it is to fly, to positively scream for joy in the ecstasy of "the Love that moves the sun and other stars."

So there are highs and lows, moments of exultation and moments of near despair, and thankfully more than a few moments of sobriety to ask the question I posed above: what am I doing here? Is there any special contribution one makes as a "lay vicar," as a lay anything?

I think there is at least one. By being a lay minister, I can remind my parishioners that the practice of our religion will take place, for the most part, outside the church building. This is an obvious truth—Sunday services end with the dismissal "Let us go forth . . ."—but it is a truth that can be obscured by clerical professionalism. Full-time ordained clergy often tend to remake parishioners in their own image. Their particular work takes place in and around the church premises, and the assumption follows that the Christian work of the laity will take place there, too. In many cases, church-centered projects constitute a parish's whole definition of "lay ministry." That notion, it seems to me, ignores the vital work people do in their own homes, communities, and places of employment. It also ignores the need for scale in people's often over-crowded lives.

That need is especially apparent in Island Pond, where community involvement is a long-standing tradition—and sometimes a mania. Samuel Johnson spoke of the ungregarious as "unclubable": a few of my parishioners are nearly clubbed to death. If church is just another way to "club" them by giving them just another office or duty, how has it helped them grow?

Women are often those clubbed the hardest. If you hang around a church for any length of time, you will probably see something like this: A solitary woman comes to church. As it turns out, her husband or ex-husband has agreed to keep the kids for the morning. She works outside the home for five days a week, and inside of it for seven. She is not looking for a job. She's looking for sanctuary. She's looking for the strength to do the jobs she already has. Unfortunately, what the church often seeks to give her is yet another job, often adding, ironically, some babble about "making time for yourself." The woman knows all about making time for herself. It has just recently dawned on her, however, that to do that in any profound way she must first make time for God. That time might be more meaningful if we let her have it without trying to find her a new chore.

Admittedly, there are chores that need to be done. And there are vital, important missions a church ought to undertake, which my church often doesn't undertake because of the limitations of its part-time, unordained leader. But in preaching to my parishioners and in visiting them as one who always has to "go to work" the next day, I may serve to remind them where the greatest part of their mission lies. When the last dish of the church supper has been washed, when the last chorus of "We Shall Overcome" has been sung and the last singer bailed out of jail, we go home. If we expect to live very long at home, we eventually go to work. And if we fail to live the Gospel in those two places, it is highly unlikely that we shall have succeeded any place else.

I will only add, before turning to my next point, that I myself have been especially slow to grasp what I have proclaimed above. It took awhile for me to recognize that I did more of my ministry in front of a blackboard than I did behind a pulpit, and that the most important "parish visit" I often made was when I dropped my car keys and prayer book on my own kitchen table.

I suppose the other contribution I can make as a "lay vicar" is to show my parish a model for doing work without credentials. I can emphasize for them the importance of prayer, of seeking consensus, and of seeking advice of those who *have* the credentials. I have a bishop, a sacramentalist, and a spiritual director—and from time to time I let my parish know how lost I would be without any one of these. I quote St. Bernard: "If anyone makes himself his own master in the spiritual life, he makes himself scholar to a fool."

Perhaps I am making an important statement in this time of rebellion against expertise, of home schooling, home birth, and a locust plague of dubiously trained "counselors." The rebellion has its own rationale and right to exist. In many ways I think it needs to go even further. But seeking a new independence from the experts ought not be the same thing as seeking their abolition. It was a *young* Luther who said "Every man a priest." It is necessary to have experts to locate new trails for us to follow. If the experts understood that more fully, and defined their role more creatively, they might be less threatened by the laity's demands to walk well-beaten paths on its own two feet.

I am fortunate to have had for my sacramentalist at Christ Church a priest with a very developed sense of the laity's importance. Unlike many priests, who went off to seminary as young men and came out shellacked in the same gloss as other "professionals," she was not ordained until after becoming a grandmother. When she first came to Island Pond to do our once-a-month Eucharist, I was a bit skeptical. As neat and proper as a hat on a schoolmarm's head, extremely methodical, Jeannette McKnight made quite a contrast with Father Castle's rough-and-tumble style. Was she going to sit me down, make me take my medicine, and send me off to bed with a good scrub behind the ears? Far from it. In fact it was she, perhaps more than the Father, who "made a man out of me," ecclesiastically speaking, and then led me to question phrases like "made a man out of me." A committed but extremely unaffected feminist, she refuses to call any priest "Father," after Jesus' injunction, or to let anyone call her "Mother." Yet she wears a dress whenever she wears her clerical collar to avoid "threatening" those as yet unadjusted to a woman in a traditional man's role. Her local reputation for quiet courage is perhaps the best-kept secret in our diocese. She offers sanctuary to battered women, disarms their pistol-toting husbands, presents seminars on gay awareness—in Lyndonville, Vermont—then walks briskly home to make lunch for herself and her husband or to catch up on her sewing. She kills me. Her parish recently sent her on a trip to Portugal, where she presented the Anglicans there with a priest's stole she had sewn for them to have on hand when they finally got around to ordaining their first woman. Perhaps she more than anyone else has brought the issue of gender-biased language home to me—not so much through anything she has said as through some things she's compelled me to say. More than once I've caught myself exclaiming, in ill-phrased admiration, "That five-foot grandmother has got more balls than half the . . ."

The Reverend McKnight immediately recognized my ministry as legitimate, and treated me as a peer. In her, I saw some glimpses of what "authority" in the church might look like. It is a thing worth looking for—especially when one is trying to define one's role as a "lay vicar." Clearly Jesus had intended for there to be authority, but of a radically different kind:

> The kings of the Gentiles exercise lordship over them; and those in authority over them are called benefactors. But not so with you; rather let the greatest among you become as the youngest, and the leader as one who serves. For which is greater, one who sits at table, or one who serves? Is it not the one who sits at table? But I am among you as one who serves.

If his intention had been to abolish hierarchy entirely, he simply would have said, "No one should be first," not, "The one who is first needs to behave in this way." Jeannette McKnight struck me by the way she was able to offer direction without "lording" it over anybody. She seems to think that women are more inclined to exercise authority in this way, and what I see so far of our new sacramentalist, also a woman, leads me to suspect she may be right.

In any case, the question of my own authority in Island Pond remains a murky one for me. That doesn't mean that my parish is forever questioning my authority—far from it. I rather mean that I need to decide how much of the authority they are all too willing to grant me comes from God, and how much is a delusion that belongs to the ways of "the Gentiles." I need to be sure I'm behaving like a lay vicar and not like a Lay Apostolate with the High Church of England.

In this regard, consider the question of "taste"—that is, of "good taste" in the house of worship. All parish leaders probably find themselves at one time or another in the awkward position of arbiters of taste. It may be that Episcopal ministers find themselves in that position more than most. Taste would seem to be very important to us. Less prone to quibble over doctrine than some other denominations, ours will sometimes choose a matter of "good taste" to wrangle over instead.

Artificial flowers are a good example. A number of my parishioners are fond of artificial flowers, and have on occasion donated arrangements to the church. An Episcopal priest from another diocese who has worshiped with us on several occasions has more than once taken me aside and said, after some compliments on the sermon and the seeming health of the parish, "You've really got to do something about those artificial flowers on the altar." The first time he said so, I thought to myself, "Well, yes, I do." But the next time I wasn't so sure. "Maybe God likes the artificial flowers," I retorted.

"I don't think so," he said undaunted. "God doesn't like phony. And artificial flowers are phony flowers."

Perhaps he has something. But I don't believe he has everything. Granted that God dislikes the phony, are these flowers phony merely by virtue of their being imitations? We worship God in Island Pond, not on Martha's Vineyard. Perhaps fresh boughs of apple blossoms in artsy ceramic vases would be more artificial in this factory town than artificial flowers. If people in Island Pond love cloth and plastic flowers and put those flowers on their dining room tables and beside their marriage beds, shouldn't they be on the altar, too?

Now, the light-up 3-D picture of Jesus in the Garden of Gethsemane is something a bit larger to swallow. I found it packed away in a storage room behind the oil furnace one Saturday morning when we met to clean up the church basement. It had probably lain there for thirty years. I suspect that a past rector had attempted to contribute to "the beauty of holiness" by moving it one step closer to the trash. "Oh, boy," I thought, "if they ever get their hands on this . . ." Naughtily, stealthily, I slid the thing into a box destined for the dump. But a woman with her mind on rummage sales decided that all dump-bound boxes had best be edited first, and so the picture was discovered a second time.

I do not think that some of my fellow laborers would have been more impressed by a piece of the True Cross. They wiped the glass carefully. An anxious hand took up the plug. Would it work? It did. I'm a little ashamed to admit that I more or less hoped it would explode. I was also a little ashamed to speak up when they began to wonder aloud how such a thing could ever have wound up in the garbage. But my confession emboldened me, as they went on to discuss the proper place for such an object, to mutter "*Not* upstairs!"

Yet here, as often in the past, they knew something I didn't know. The picture was indeed venerable, and numinous—like those Russian icons reputed to weep inexplicably. It seemed to endow all those who stood nearby with some of its electric radiance. It may even have spoken to me. "Don't you realize," it seemed to say, "that these people have been pulling me out of the garbage for generations? They have doggedly rescued me from the dumps where your kind has always wanted to throw me, because I am a little embarrassing, a little too accessible, a little too much. I tell you, if it were necessary to suffer and die for them a second time, as utterly 'tasteless' as that might be, I would."

Tonight is the Great Vigil of Easter. It is also the first time in memory that Christ Church has observed the Saturday evening before Easter as anything special. In the Early Church this was the time when catecumens, who had spent at least a year in preparation, were finally baptized. It was a night of expectation and mystery. It has taken me almost nine years of ministry in this place to realize that tonight may be the most important day of the calendar for us; for we, too, are keeping watch on the verge of Easter. We, too, have heard the Great Proclamation, but in darkness, longing to hear it in the light of day.

There are two people, a husband and wife, in the church when I arrive at 7:30 P.M. It was they who hosted the breakfast that morning, when some of us met to "break fast" from Good Friday. They are "new folks" in the parish. I explain that we'll begin by lighting the Paschal Candle, with some prayers. We extinguish the lights in the church, except for one small lamp on the organ by which to read our prayer books.

Dear friends in Christ: On this most holy night, in which our Lord Jesus passed over from death to life, the Church invites her members, dispersed throughout the world, to gather in vigil and prayer . . .

O God, through your Son you have bestowed upon your people the brightness of your light: Sanctify this new fire, and grant that in this Paschal feast we may so burn with heavenly desires, that with pure minds we may attain to the festival of everlasting light; through Jesus Christ our Lord. Amen.

The candle sputters in the half darkness, like a voice too embarrassed or overwhelmed to proclaim the news: "Christ is risen." But it catches fire, and there we are, three people and a flickering light—in an old church, on a Saturday evening in spring, with the noise of the cars and their winter-rusted mufflers outside. The moment is filled with the ambiguities of all such quiet observances among few people, in the midst of an oblivious population in a radically secular age. The act is so ambiguous because its terms are so extreme: the Lord is with us, or we are pathetic fools. I like it that way. I believe God likes it that way. My worry is always that others will be discouraged rather than exalted by the omnipresence of the two possibilities.

We light a profusion of candles from this one source and place them around the church. Appropriately or inappropriately, the candles are that short, white drippy kind sold in supermarkets to have on hand during power failures. They fill the church with a soft light, and, in the movement of their flames, with a sense of the place as alive and stirring.

By rights, this should be the beginning of a great and lengthy liturgy of lessons and prayers. But I don't want to overfeed people who are already full of Holy Week liturgies. In a place where a faithful few attend every service, and where many of those are elderly, a minister has some obligation to see that he is feeding, not stuffing, the sheep. So I have simply invited people to come and go throughout the night, from the lighting of the candle until dawn.

Others arrive and sit quietly in the pews. We have never "done a vigil" before, and I have done a less than adequate job of preparing people for the observance. I fear that some of them, after a few minutes of prayer or contemplation, are frustrated by a restless sense of "Now what?" There's to be a film downstairs, but that's an hour away.

One woman goes to the little Hammond that serves as "backup" for the intimidatingly capricious pipe organ and begins to play. She is not the church organist, ever, but I know she comes here sometimes by herself and plays the organ—as release, as worship, I would never presume to ask. I only know that she has an organ at home, probably a better one than this, yet it is this one she comes to play in her most private moments. So I am gratified to know that in spite of my shoddy direction at least one person knows that a vigil is for prayer, and that prayer is however we lay ourselves open to God.

She begins to sing, softly. I love her voice. Only a few voices in the world are dearer to me than hers. Her "official" role in the parish, besides her unofficial one as its mother and "first woman," is that of lay reader, and in the gentle but insistent tones of her voice I have so often heard the Bible become the Word of God. When the prophets speak comfort to Israel, in her mouth the words are truly the Balm of Gilead. When they warn or chastise, I detect in her voice a hint of sadness intermingled with her own faithful assent to the proclamation—like a mother saying "Your father's right" to her child, but wishing at the same time that her husband could be calmer in his discipline. I wouldn't take all the voices in a Cambridge choir for the sound of her singing tonight.

Two voices join hers. Then another woman mounts the pipe organ and they try to play together, though they have some difficulty finding the right key. The attempt to do so is a bit raucous; wrong keys ricochet around the church—there is laughter. Well, now, the High Church, spiritually sophisticated voices whisper in my head, this will never do. Better for us all to sit in reverent silence, some of us practicing some quasi-Christian form of meditation, some of us simply holy, and a few of us a little horny. That's fine, I answer, yes fine, but not better. We are waiting for the Lord, and it behooves us to sing a little, even to clown a little until he comes.

The film I've chosen is *The Mission,* which tells the story of the creation and destruction of a Jesuit mission in South America in the eighteenth century. I've chosen this one because it avoids the glib pieties of the usual Easter movies, because it touches on some current issues, and because I can rent it locally. The man at the TV repair store in town, whose wife I buried a year ago, lends us the television. Someone has brought her brand-new popcorn maker and we read the directions. Once we figure out how to use it the machine quickly pops and butters enough popcorn for all of us. Plus we have other snacks, sandwiches, coffee, and soda that the vigil-keepers have brought. There are two families, several faithful women—as at the first Easter—and me. We watch the film in an all-but-empty room. The Head Start preschool that used to meet here has recently left in favor of another site. We are all that is cozy about the place.

I've seen the film several times before, so I take charge of making sure there's food and drink all around. From time to time I go back upstairs and replace burned-out candles and briefly pray. I wonder if it qualifies as a vigil if the nave is left empty at any time. Our own modest premise was that the church building would be occupied the entire night with at least one soul awake at any given hour. There was a time I would have worried more about "qual-ifying"; I wonder if I have matured or simply gotten sloppy.

The film ends almost too late for any discussion. People seem to have liked it—at least to have been moved by it. I wonder, though, if it was the right film to show. Perhaps its Calvary was too devastating and its Resurrection too understated. Perhaps the image of a hard-won mission put to the torch and sent over the falls was the wrong one to present to those whose own mission must at times strike them as tentative and possibly even doomed. But once again, I trust that God blesses the ambiguity. Were the film a "triumph," I'd have doubted no less. Anyway, I ask God silently to cancel any ill effects, and whatever was ill-advised in my choices, and I try to let go.

The last part of the "program" consists of keeping watch for the remainder of the night and making hot cross buns for the service tomorrow. I had originally conceived of the whole "vigil" idea, with its suggestion of a party and a sleepover, as something for young people. But we have few young people to begin with, one is away on vacation, and only one of those here tonight plans to stay. The poor kid is tired, I know; she fell asleep through the last part of the picture, but she is determined to "go the distance." Mature, intelligent, and personable, she will be good company. My only worry is that I will fail to be as good.

Neither of us has ever made hot cross buns before. I have brought a recipe and ingredients, but the kitchen proves to be much less well-equipped than we thought. Apparently a number of the utensils belonged to Head Start and left when it did. We have trouble finding a proper-sized saucepan for scalding the milk; on the other hand, we have a potato masher that could be used for the arming of heavy infantry. We have to boil the potatoes in a pot intended to cook spaghetti for half a town. Who ever suspected that hot cross buns contained potatoes anyway?

Amid all the things I remembered to bring—raisins, a kneading board, a VCR, candles, and even the potatoes—I have forgotten to bring the flour. There is no flour in the kitchen. All the stores in town are closed. The girl suggests calling her mother, who I'm sure has just managed to fall asleep and is now dreaming fitfully about Amazonia, but under the circumstances I can raise only the most fainthearted objection. And if her mother would happen to have a medium-sized saucepan, and some . . .

We drive to her family's cabin in the pouring rain. Miraculously, neither of us has run out of conversation or good humor. When I first met this girl, she was about seven years old; now she is in high school. I prepared her for confirmation, and taught her how to serve as an acolyte. I wrote her a letter once during a hard time in her life. I am happy for all this, but regretful I have provided so little else. Somehow I fear that in her life, too, I have neglected to bring some essential ingredient. Yet I trust she will rise quite well without me.

With the right utensils and all the ingredients we feel a sense of second wind. We make the sponge. So far so good. But the number of risings required seems intended to take the strength from a cook's knees. Christ may have risen all at once, the gospel according to Betty Crocker seems to say, but flour and yeast and people made of dust require successive chances to reach their stature. And those who would attend such mysteries require patience.

We decide to do the risings in shifts, with one of us minding the kitchen and the clock (our "timer" is nothing less than the old steeple clock, which we must step out in the rain to read) while the other gets some sleep upstairs. My companion decides to lay her sleeping bag on the raised floor of the chancel, just in front of the Communion rail. We say a brief prayer, and I return to the kitchen. I find myself thinking of the story of the boy Samuel, who slept in the Temple and heard the Lord calling, and thought at first it was his mentor—and I hope this young woman, too, will hear God's voice in the holy place where she sleeps.

When I wake from my own turn upstairs on the floor, the last rising is complete. We ice the buns in the half-light of a gray Easter morning. I take the young woman home, where she will get ready for a family trip to spend Easter with relatives. She will not be able to hear the compliments of those who taste our work after the service. But she has taken a hot cross bun home for her younger sister.

The Vigil is accomplished. Easter morning is here. It is raining again. I return home for a shower and for my wife and daughter, and come back—fifty miles and a couple of hours later—to preach with the help of God's good grace and good adrenaline. God only knows if what we did last night was pleasing to him or meaningful to those who participated. God only knows the same for this whole enterprise. Christ is risen—and I'm ready for bed. The church is filling up with that deceptive Easter fullness. I have not seen some of these people ever before, nor will I see some ever again. I know that at the end of the service someone will say, "If only the church could be full like this all the time." I will reply, "Yes, that would be so good. And perhaps someday it will be."

But what I will really mean to say, to that person and to myself, I say now in an inaudible whisper as I walk into the church and the congregation rises to begin the liturgy. It is something Jesus said to his friends thousands of years ago, and I have whispered at the beginning of services here for all the years of my very modest "vicarhood." It is my prayer, my motto, and my excuse for everything I have said, done, and written as a dresser of sycamore trees.

"Fear not, little flock, for it is your Father's good pleasure to give you the kingdom."

I Am the
Clock-Winder

And God will wipe away every tear from their eyes.
—REVELATION 7:17

I am the town clock-winder for Island Pond, Vermont. I have been so almost as long as I have been the lay vicar of its Episcopal Church. Twice a week, on Thursday and Sunday, I climb through the vertical tunnel inside the Carpenter Gothic spire of my church up to the little wooden house that holds the clockworks. With a key like an antique car crank, I wind two drums of steel cable, one for the time on the four clock faces and one for the great bell that rings the hours. I also make adjustments, minor repairs, and lubricate the bearings with a special oil made for the few mechanical clocks still keeping time in our towns.

Along with my ministry this minor job has given me a focus for thinking about work, faith, and time, and about the particular places in which individuals come to reckon with those things. From a vantage point much higher than a pulpit, I have looked out from behind the clock faces at the railroad tracks far below, and wondered about my own coming and going, and about the town's history and future.

Island Pond was made and almost unmade by the railroad. It

stood as the chief junction between Montreal and Portland, Maine—I like to say, between Canada and the sea. The railroad yard in town was once thick with tracks, as if a giant had pulled a broad rake over the valley and each tooth had left rails and ties in its wake. There were fifty locomotives stabled here, sometimes so many cars that whole trains of them had to be moved down the line for storage. A legion of local men worked for the Grand Trunk in those days: brakemen, bridge builders, section men, ticket takers, freight conductors, engineers, machinists, stokers, boiler welders, inspectors—all shifts, all year, every hour the trains came and went packed with wheat, lumber, bauxite, machines, and passengers. And on a hill over this railroad town, above the train yard in work time and strike time, over the black locomotives huddled thick like pollywogs in the spring, above the steam of engines, the mist off the pond, and the breaths of men working in the subzero cold, was the clock. A former railroad man tells me he could hear and see it clearly from the yard, always running, always right.

The town prospered with the railroad, which means, of course, that it contained some prosperous citizens, and the rest had work. There were no fewer than five hotels in operation at any one time. Choice cuts of lumber came on the train to build the church that would hold the clock. Then, having built it, the workers along with their bosses filled the pews. The pipe organ also came, piece by piece over the rails—followed by the clock, up from the E. Howard Company in Boston. The organ pipes played like melodious train whistles, thanks to the boys who pumped the bellows and left their initials in the little curtained closet behind the instrument. And at the first moment of the liturgy, the clock rang, wound twice each week by one of those same boys, dreaming in his tower of the day he'd exchange his meager clock-winder's wage for that of a full-fledged railroad man.

Island Pond began to decline at roughly the same time as railroading did, more specifically when diesel replaced steam, and when the Canadian National bought out the Grank Trunk. The descent was gradual; a generation grew old as the railroad went down, many retiring in what for them was the very nick of time. As the tracks began to be pulled up, families came up with them, like wheat with tares, and Island Pond joined the list of those places where an industry has enjoyed a good time, and is happy to help tidy up a little on the way out, and will be pleased to see its hosts if they ever happen to be in South Carolina or Singapore.

After the railroad, Island Pond's dubious fame rests with a controversial religious sect that moved here more than a decade ago, and with the fact that Rudy Vallee was born here. His house still stands. Old-timers tell me that the man with the megaphone never took any pains to announce the place of his origin. But now his music is as quaint as a steam locomotive; his name is almost as obscure as the town's. The bell that tolled for Island Pond tolled for thee, Rudy.

Then the bell was still. For years, ever since the railroad declined, and long before "the church people" arrived, the clock in Christ Church tower was broken. The motionless hands on each of its four faces pointed to different numbers, and no sound came from its belfry but the cooing of pigeons. One day, for a reason they might not know themselves, the people in the church under the clock, who number fifteen on a good Sunday, maybe thirty-five on an Easter, elected to repair its faces, the steeple above, and the machine behind. They found a clock repairer and a clock-winder. The town graciously supplied them with funds to pay both. Somewhat fitfully, like a steam locomotive starting from a long standstill, the clock began to run.

I first met Bob Ross, the clock repairer, at the top of the tower in the clock house that lies squarely under the cone of the copper-shingled steeple. It was only my second or third climb up, and I still clung very deliberately to each of the iron rungs, which appear to have come from the side of a boxcar.

The first part of the ascent is on a short ladder outside the church sacristy. One goes straight up about a dozen feet to a wooden trap door; on that day in July it was already pushed up and open. Once through the hole, the climber is standing on the roof of the sacristy, looking up at least twenty feet to the ceiling, or belfry floor. This first high-ceilinged room, dimly lit by one bulb, is cobwebby and barnlike, its floor littered with old rope, straw, clock weights, a piece of log. At diagonal corners, one by the first ladder, are upright wooden tracks in which the clock weights rise and descend on cables. The entire steeple is built with the same sturdiness and doubtless some of the same materials and know-how once found in wooden railroad trestles. Single timbers, one piece each, run straight up the corners. What trees they must have been hewn from!

The second ladder, this one at a slant, takes me as high as the belfry. The few remaining rungs are bolted to the steeple side and lead to the last floor, on which the clock house sits. The belfry is a squat room, lit during the day by slatted windows in the steeple and at night by nothing but the moon. The bell is about one third the size of the Liberty Bell, uncracked, and hangs in a carriage of gray wooden studding. Raised letters around the waist of the bell read: "Cast by Henry N. Hooper & Co. Boston 1862," indicating that the bell is about fifteen years older than the church. It is rung by a sledgehammer set on a spring by its side and connected to the clock house above by a metal rod, and to the sacristy below by a new bell rope. In the past, there was no way to ring the bell from downstairs. One of the parishioners told me that on Easters some years ago he would put coveralls over his Sunday clothes and climb to the belfry with a croquet mallet to ring in the holiday. "I don't think I could go up there now," he added with a look of sincere worry that someone might ask him, at eighty-four, to perform the feat again.

I found Bob Ross under the light bulb in the clock house, wiping a clock part with a rag. He and his assistant, a fellow industrial arts teacher from New Hampshire, had spent a good part of that morning cleaning the clock, the clock house, and the area around it, some of which had been cleaned earlier by the crew that repaired the steeple. But there was still some more cleaning to do, even when I arrived, and, as I was to learn, cleanliness is essential to the smooth running of a mechanical clock. Outside the clock house were several grocery bags full of pigeon skeletons, egg shells, and droppings; apparently the former condition of the steeple had afforded good housing to several generations of pigeons. Inside, the partially disassembled clock, its heavy pendulum asleep on the

floor, was being wiped and rewiped, and, where appropriate, lu-
bricated with light machine oil. Boards in the clock faces had been
removed, providing extra light, a breeze, a glimpse at the back
sides of several clock hands—so much larger when closer—and
four commanding views of the town.

I introduced myself to Bob Ross as the man who would be
winding and looking after the clock; he greeted me warmly and
immediately began to tell me everything he knew about that clock,
working as he went. Listening to him I had the impression of
standing before a benevolent but zealous archivist with a greasy
rag. His language was as exact as the toothiest gear of the clock—
no thingamajigs, but no impatience either when I asked for repeated or simpler explanations.

Under his tutelage the clock became intelligible. It was the same
as a grandfather's clock or cuckoo clock, he said; the three of us
had stepped into the works of a giant's timepiece. In between two
cast-iron arches bolted to the floor are the gears of two separate
but cooperative mechanisms, one for the clock and one for the
bell. Each is driven by the pull of weights lowered when the pendulum swings and the bell rings, respectively. The pendulum, kept
ticking by this pull, regulates a succession of gears that move the
clock hands; it "feeds into" (Ross said this better) the clock by
means of an escapement, an object like a curved pair of open
calipers that swings with the pendulum, its points rocking in and
out between the teeth of a rotating wheel. When the pendulum is
lengthened—that is, lowered—the clock runs more slowly since
the pendulum moves in a greater arc. A vertical shaft rising out of
the timing mechanism turns the gears of four horizontal rods, which
form a cross over the clock and extend through four holes in the
clock house to each of the faces. Ross had tied red rags on these
rods to prevent our bumping our heads on them—I felt dizzy
enough following his tour at the same time as I tried to stay out
of the way.

Mostly I was interested in the maintenance of the clock, though
I have since found myself grateful for Ross's "theoretical" information, without which I would have been unable to improvise the
few repairs I have had to make. Ross showed me how to set the

clock by pulling a pin to disengage the faces from the mechanism and moving a dial marked for sixty minutes. He also instructed me to lubricate bearings, pulley sheaves, and the universal joints behind each face. I have since learned from a helpful man at the E. Howard Company that the exposed works of the clock itself, which suffer no friction, should receive no lubricant whatsoever. They should be kept as clean as possible. But Bob anticipated even this; he concluded his directions by saying that if I studied the clock, I would soon know things about it that he could never have told me.

By early evening the clock was reassembled. We wanted an hour or so in which to check its accuracy, and eat our supper. After washing up we headed down the street to a restaurant. On the way, we met Bob's sister Andrea, who was responsible for bringing him to the clock, and who was just then coming home from work. She said that if a simple meal of chicken, potatoes, and salad was to our liking, the three of us were welcome for supper. She and her husband would stop at the store for some things; we knew the way over.

Andrea and Larry Roth live with their three daughters in a new log cabin at the foot of a mountain in East Brighton, just outside of Island Pond. One crosses a railroad track at his "own risk" and enters a dense woods on a bumpy driveway that climbs to the cabin. It is an impressive dwelling, with five or six different pitches to the roof, completely surrounded by forest. They have seen a bear, a moose, and a bald eagle, literally in their backyard; their daughter, Aggie, fishes for trout in the brook behind the garage, and rabbits tear back and forth across the clearing chased by the family hound. The Roths will be as good a choice as any if ever an American family goes into outer space as emissaries or pioneers. They are all hearty, hospitable, and handsome. They built their cabin from the ground up, Ross working alongside his brother-in-law on those tricky roofs. They make their own soap, grow their own vegetables, slaughter and dress their own chickens. Larry, a local boy who journeyed to Los Angeles via the navy and stayed for the car craze, who has a hot-rodder's lean and intrepidly optimistic look, took the risk of opening an auto parts business in

Island Pond, which has proven a smart venture in a town twenty miles from the nearest spare parts, a town that runs on cars—hopped-up cars, wood haulers, collections of junk cars one tries at inspection time like a ring of skeleton keys. At supper we asked about the auto parts trade, and the Roths talked about the clock trade, and then we got down to business and talked about Indians.

The ones in the woodland were as fierce as any, Larry says, and I agree, having read the public library out of Indian books as a kid, and Ross, behold, an American history buff who casts and fires replica Civil War cannons, begins the round of stories—how one chief mustered ten thousand braves from as far away as Michigan and Kentucky, and not a white person in the East had wind of their movements until the first tomahawk struck; how the Sauk and Fox and Ojibwa played lacrosse outside the stockade of an army fort, passed the rawhide ball through the gates, and ran screaming past the blue-clad spectators only to run out again with everyone's scalp—we stopped with a "shhh." It was eight, and Ross wanted to listen for the clock ringing far away. All quiet, we looked out the cabin windows into the shadowy woods in the direction of town. I really don't remember whether we heard the bell or not; it was faint at any rate, perhaps too faint to count.

We returned to the clock after nightfall and made a few minor adjustments. It appeared to be keeping good time; the metal slide that regulates the number of chimes, to which Ross had welded three new teeth to replace broken ones, was in its correct post–eight o'clock position. After a few final squirts of lubricant, a few parting wipes of the rag, Ross and his friend wrote their names and the date on the inside walls of the clock house, urging me to do the same. I felt I had not earned a place there, but Ross said I had, probably meaning that in time I would have. We picked up the tools, lowered them down the ladders with a rope, closed the trap door, shut out the lights, locked the church. I was left to learn the secret idiosyncrasies that were lost years ago when the clock and its most intimate tenders had stopped ticking.

When you acquire the use of a new word, you suddenly begin to see it everywhere. I began to see clocks, clocks, clocks. Like a hungry traveler, antique postcard collector, gravestone rubber, or boozer, I'd drive into an unfamiliar town with hunting eyes and one question behind them: "They got a public clock in this place or what?" I had seldom worn a watch before; now I often carried two, one with the exact time as told by radio station or phone operator or, in the case of divergent readings, as figured from an average of the two; the other set by the clock in Island Pond the last time I had driven to check it, which was usually no later than yesterday, sometimes no later than that morning—and I live more than twenty miles out of town. Against these two I was likely to check any other timepiece I saw.

I began noticing the number of clocks on town halls and churches that do not run or run wrong. Island Pond had not been so unusual in this respect after all. I also realized that the public keeping of time has passed from the church and possibly the municipal building to the branch bank. In most towns of any size, that is the place to look for a digital display of the right time. The location of the public clock has something to say, I think, about the way a culture gives meaning to time. It was logical for a church to tell people the time when one of the things they needed to know time for was when to pray, and when church feasts and holy days colored the calendar. Equally logical is it that the bank should tell the hours to a populace for whom time is not liturgical but financial, who inhabit a fiscal year broken into quarters and the maturation periods of certificates of deposit.

Island Pond also has a bank clock, albeit a modest one with hands, inside the bank window, but I do not check that clock against the steeple, though one can check both standing in the same place. The latter clock has been running erratically, I suspect not merely slow or fast, but slow *and* fast, and correctly some short times in between. I prefer to have a more comprehensive report comparing real time and Island Pond time over a twelve-hour period, so I stop first at one of the service stations in town, not only because the elders leaning back on chairs inside the office will have such a report, but because I want an excuse to lean back in one of those chairs myself. I love a garage, a store, a barber shop with a circle of regulars—each one a third part customer, a fifth part helper, and the remaining part permanent fixture. I find this one of the things most wanting in my work as a teacher: we are a sadly croniless profession. Oh, for some wizened old geezer with a reserved seat under the bulletin board and his own dog-eared copy of *The Great Gatsby* lying next to a spare cane on the radiator cover to totter in of an afternoon and say, "How they doin' with their compositions? I just been down the hall. You ought to see old Harding givin' 'em hell on the Punic Wars. Think it'll rain?"

The men on chairs give me a list of scattered data with commentary. "It was five minutes fast at six 'clock this morning." "What's an ol' fella like you doing up at six o'clock? You was probably still half asleep. It was running fine when I seen it—that was at ten o'clock. Just taken my wife for her beauty appointment. I stood right outside and listened to the bell—was ten on the nose." "You should've gone in with her, Frank." "I just been over for a paper, and I think it's a minute or two *slow*. What time you got now?" Everyone looks down at his watch; no one has the same time. "Well how's the bell?" I ask. "Is it ringing the right number of times?" "Yup. Least it did at three."

I get my tank filled and go over to the church. The clock is three minutes slow, not a considerable discrepancy in itself, but I set it correctly and made an adjustment the day before, when it was two minutes fast from the day previous. I have apparently overcorrected. My goal is to have it lose or gain no time in four days; accuracy beyond that is immaterial since I wind it every four days anyway and the clock can be reset then. For some reason I am unable to calibrate what fraction of a turn on the adjusting wheel will quicken the clock by a minute in twenty-four hours. I have kept logs, made charts—all useless. The adjusting wheel is unmarked except for a dot of paint on the circumference and a curved, two-pointed arrow marked "S" and "F" for "slow" and "fast," which Bob Ross scratched into the metal. I am to turn the wheel in the "F" direction to make the clock run faster—or am I? I begin to wonder if I may have misunderstood his instructions, if the "F" direction is for when the clock is *running fast,* not for making it run faster.

Framed on the clock-house wall are the antique "Instructions for a Tower Clock," which I had not bothered to read before, thinking I had all the information I needed by word of mouth, thinking also that my source had himself read the plaque. According to *that,* one turns the wheel left to make the clock run faster—the opposite of what Ross said, or at least of what I remember him saying.

So, I change the meanings of "S" and "F" and adjust accordingly for a week. If anything, the clock runs worse. But I have forgotten those "theoretical" principles that Ross took such pains to teach me; in my independent study I have grown careless of what I learned in the required courses. The pertinent question is not "What did Ross really say about turning the wheel?" but "Which direction on the adjusting wheel makes the pendulum shorter?" That a shorter pendulum makes a faster clock is beyond dispute.

With a little measuring, I find out that Ross was right if he said what I remember him saying; turning the wheel in the "F" direction shortens the pendulum and thus makes the clock run faster. The original instructions hanging on the wall were undoubtedly right, too, when the clock had all of its original parts and threadings. Nevertheless, having finally established how to raise and lower the pendulum, and thus how to make the clock run faster or slower, I am still unable to make it run as accurately as I wish, as accurately as the old people in town remember it. For that part, I can tell myself that the memory of the aged always makes the past more perfect than it was, and that in the days before the quartz crystal and television, people were less likely to notice or be disturbed by a slightly quick or sluggish clock. But I cannot even make the clock consistently quick or sluggish; it seems to run at will, a propensity made all the more maddening by brief periods when the clock keeps literally perfect time. I feel like those physicists who abandoned the clock model of creation, who watched as Newtonian law gave way to relativity and relativity to uncertainty, their quarks like my clock's quirks—nothing but vapors and winds to stand on.

And how much more troubling is the clock's misbehavior in an age of microseconds, when precision is as sought after as youth. A man can scarcely enjoy listening to recorded music because his space-age sound system picks up the tiniest motes and scratches like a radio telescope catching nebulae light-years away; he chases hysterically after his wife accusing her of the infidelity of his record—perhaps she has been lending it to his best friend on the sly, a dissolute man with a cheap turntable. I struggle with my erratic clock as computers are fed the archprogram: "Be ye perfect, even as your father at the drawing board is not perfect."

I discovered the secret of my clock's imperfection in the autumn, which comes to Vermont like a painted Indian brave with cold flint arrows that never miss. During the first frigid spell, the clock began accumulating twenty to thirty extra minutes in a three-day period. The clock is affected by the weather. Cold temperatures make it run faster, presumably because the moving parts contract somewhat and work with less resistance. By turning the adjusting wheel and by varying the number of weights on the cables—another determiner, discovered at the suggestion of Larry Roth—I can make my clock keep very good time providing that the temperature is roughly constant. But I can as easily make a perfectly precise adjustment as I can predict the weather—the Vermont weather no less. With the whole world waiting for its machines to start acting human, there I was, waiting for my poor, fallible clock to act like a machine.

• • •

THE CLOCK-WINDER

It is dark as a cave,
Or a vault in the nave
When the iron door
Is closed, and the floor
Of the church relaid
With trowel and spade.

But the parish-clerk
Cares not for the dark
As he winds in the tower
At a regular hour

The rheumatic clock
Whose dilatory knock
You can hear when praying
At the day's decaying,
Or at any lone while
From a pew in the aisle.

Up, up from the ground,
Around and around
In the turret stair
He clambers, to where
The wheelwork is,
With its tick, click, whizz,
Reposefully measuring
Each day to its end
That mortal men spend
In sorrowing and pleasuring.
Nightly thus does he climb
To the trackway of Time.

Him I followed one night
To this place without light,
And, ere I spoke, heard
Him say, word by word,
At the end of his winding,
The darkness unminding:

"So I wipe out one more,
My Dear, of the sore
Sad days that still be,
Like a drying Dead Sea,
Between you and me!"

Who she was no man knew:
He had long borne him blind

To all womankind;
And was ever one who
Kept his past out of view.

When Thomas Hardy published this poem in 1917, my clock was also punctuating the prayers of a decaying day, though inaudibly; one does not hear its "dilatory knock" until halfway up the steeple. Unlike Hardy's winder, I have a wife, a past cheerfully open to view, the desire to live long, and plenty of fragile reasons to believe that I shall. Perhaps because of this contrast, I am not without some care of the darkness, which Hardy's bereaved parish clerk had climbed through and beyond.

I drive over to Island Pond on a Thursday night after a well-cooked meal and a teacher's day of youthful enthusiasms and impertinence, a myriad of death-defying distractions; after winding the clock, I return to a place where even the refrigerator has a cozy light within, and four hands pull the covers up when darkness has at last settled throughout the house. So in the tower, even in the darkened Gothic church below, I am in an unfamiliar place, with a somewhat unfamiliar me, and sometimes I am afraid.

I twist the old-fashioned turn switch at the foot of the ladder, and a light visible through a crack in the trap door tells whatever may be up there that I am coming. The black hatch thuds away from the hole; my head emerges facing the corner of the first room. I turn around almost immediately, and complete my entrance looking behind. The light of the one bulb here is quite diffuse in the high room, but I have enough to see all the rungs of the next ladder, which makes a dull knocking against the steeple side as I climb it. Nevertheless, the ladder is steady, its iron rungs firm underfoot and to the grasp—but so chilling on winter nights that I wear gloves. The belfry is pitch-dark, except when a little moonlight slips in. It is here, and above, that I often hear a pattering around the outsides of the steeple—and perhaps up in the rafters under the apex—what, I do not know. I have looked with a flashlight for bats and seen none. I have grown somewhat used to the pattering now, but I confess that the first few times I heard it were unnerving. Once, as I climbed with a sideways glance at the dark hulk of the bell, dreadfully silent in the moonlit midst of that pattering, my heart jumped at the sound of a loud slam, followed by an awful hiss. Several seconds passed before I came to the logical explanation: two freight cars coupling outside on the tracks below the church.

One thinks of the damnedest things clambering up a steeple on a howling winter night. A picture comes to mind: bright in my head, an icon in the Orthodox monastery of St. Catherine in the Sinai desert—terror with a footnote—shows gray-bearded ascetics climbing a ladder to heaven, a ladder that, as I remember or contrive, looks exactly like this one, while demons cast lassos and grappling hooks to yank the unwary down to perdition. And thinking of pictures, I go on to remember learning in an anthropology class about some tribe or tribes that cannot discern the images of a photograph; the point of the example was that the ability to read three dimensions in two is acquired, not innate, something we learn in our parents' laps with storybooks held open before us. So it occurs to me: what if we *un*learn the reading of other images, if we are as blind as pictureless aborigines to the demons leering from the closet because we were repeatedly told as children that there was nothing in there but clothes and shoes? If I lost some of my childhood vision, if some inner eye was closed by an adult's conditioning, I'd prefer not to have it opened now as I climb to the clock.

On the uppermost level, with the bright light shining through the clock house's lone and dirty window, I complete my ascent from superstition to a sublimer awe. Inside are the ticking and the light, no longer vague as at the ladder's lower rungs, but distinct and canny as my breath and heartbeat. Here in the night, floating almost among the clouds, yet anchored by long, arboreal bones to the earth, unseen, unthought of, discreet and patiently relentless, the clock marks time, turns its moon-colored arms each minute of the sixty in the twenty-fourth part of the earth's rotation in a darker, infinitely vaster steeple. I am the mystic now, at the top of his tower, flinging open the door to behold the vision of the clockworks and the light—as inviting as a snack bar on a dark wooded road in summer—homely, as more than one of the adepts have described it.

The pendulum is the most mysterious of all, the tool of hypnotists, and dowsers, too, I learned. One morning I ate breakfast with a couple of dowsers, and tried to augur their gentle, Quakerish faces. They showed my companions and me their pocket-sized pendulums, like little tops swung from strings. It is a common misconception that dowsers use only forked sticks and dowse only for water. Dowsing is an ancient art, and the most advanced dowsers practice device-less dowsing. Jesus was one of these, according to the couple; he dowsed for "the great draught of fishes" and knew right where to tell Peter to cast his net. There are stories of dowsers being sent the floor plan of a house hundreds of miles away, and by swinging a pendulum over it, they can "find" a lost object that has eluded the house's own occupants for months. The woman said she used her pendulum to make almost every decision; she even took it with her to the supermarket. Dowsing works, I was told, by utilizing the entire nervous system of the dowser's body as an antenna to pick up the invisible energies and emanations of the cosmos. The human body has hundreds of miles of these nerves, as compared with (though no one at breakfast said so) a mere two or three pounds of brains. I smile at my pendulum and see the dowsers swinging their smaller ones over packages of sandwich meat, dowsing to decide the best brand of baloney. How quickly I have climbed from savage to seer to skeptical rationalist—all in a few tick-tocks. I think I like myself better shuddering on the lower rungs of the belfry.

What if the dowsers have something, if those two faces were not only kinder but wiser than mine? Then what of this mighty pendulum at my side—what arcane knowledge might I apprehend by shedding my sneer and hooking my central nervous system to its swing with a downturned palm on the adjusting wheel? It is true, a dowser's pendulum must be free to move with his hand, but perhaps along with deviceless dowsing there is a "way of the fixed pendulum" known only to a few initiates, masters of both dowsing

and clocks. With access to that, I could become an oracle in Island
Pond, a bigger business than the railroad, with five hotels of pil-
grims waiting their turn to try the perilous climb to my sanctuary.
And there, stiff and half blind, like a man-pigeon, an oracular bat,
I would give the people knowledge, dowse the very depths of the
earth, answer every question put to me—every one, that is, but
"What time is it?"

To answer that question, I would need to climb down from my
tall steeple, walk out of the church, and stand on the street.

Just outside the center of Island Pond is a little yellow house close
to the side of a dirt lane. I go there sometimes after I've wound
the clock. Behind the house are railroad tracks, and beyond these,
overlooking the pond, is a steep bluff topped by tall cedars. "When
I first came here," the old woman in the house tells me, "I hated
to look at those trees going back and forth in the wind. They
looked like crazy old women waving their arms." She says she got
used to them and came to love them along with the passing train
that rattles the kitchen but lets her know that "all is well." So she
has her "clock" out here where the ringing of the one I wind is
very faint. There used to be an old garage next to the house, when
the cedars were still crazy, and on its weathered boards, which had
once fenced the tracks, she read the messages and marks the hoboes
had left each other about handouts and dry places to sleep. She
never understood how the authorities could lock a man up for
being poor and taking his food and lodging as he found them. A
former governor made her angry with his condescending talk about
the disadvantaged—"as if it's really their fault." She has been poor.

Her house is the best it has ever looked, very neat inside and
out, with clean paper, paint, and panels—no one can picture its
former condition who did not see it, she tells me. I know several
houses like this one, each with a railroad man's widow within,
bought of necessity in a hard time and restored as slowly as nature
restores an abused landscape, now as polished and significant and
lovingly worn as a wedding ring. And I've seen several other Bibles
of the kind she shows me with pride, gifts of the railroad workers'

brotherhood, bound in white leather in a fragrant cedar box with the dead man's name and a colored picture on the inside of the lid showing Jesus feeding his sheep.

A year has passed, summer to summer, since the clock was repaired. Miriam takes me outside to show me her flowers and vegetable garden. She has chrysanthemums, gladiolus, lilacs, fuchsia, pansies, bee balm—and down below, on the level of the tracks, peas, corn, carrots, beans, beets, squash, lettuce, broccoli, cucumbers, tomatoes, all from seed she or a grandson planted in the ground, and which needed her as much but no more than my clock needs me. We have had to tend to both, but their changes happened without our watching, like changes in the weather, like the changes that made Miriam old. Standing in her yard, she is a strange and beautiful vision; she can barely stoop to touch the plants, she cannot chase after the birds, and because of this she seems to stand more intimate with every bird and plant than anyone younger can. They seem to reach for her, to enfold her. Naked children romping in the grass may be an image of paradise, and the man and woman lying beneath the tree, but no less is Miriam in her garden an image of paradise.

I have other stops to make going to and from the clock, other stories to hear. I see Rebecca, with her immaculate house by the river, once a dump—"That's all you could call it"—and her white Bible in its cedar box. I went to see her just after she had qualified for the Bible. She was animated by a sight in her backyard: Years ago she and Owen had torn up a patch of Indian poppies to plant their vegetable garden. No poppies had grown there since, none were there on the day the ambulance came, but that first morning of widowhood, when she looked out the kitchen . . . it must have come up in a night. And there it was, absurdly large and orange, bobbing in the rain like a sprung jack-in-the-box.

He had come into her life long ago, when her father hired three men on a street corner in Island Pond to help him cut hay. Owen was the only one who showed up that afternoon. He was already a railroad man. He had gone to the station asking for a job when he was only seventeen. "How old are you?" the man there had asked—then told him to come back when he was twenty-one. He showed up three days later to have the same man ask the same question. "Twenty-one," he answered, and was hired on the spot.

Rebecca's brothers were determined to show this railroad man what "real work" was. They fired him volleys of heavy bales, never letting up. He worked without a complaint. That evening, when the train stopped at the farm to pick up the cans of fresh milk, Owen showed his tormentors a trick he knew of mounting and dismounting a slowly moving train. At the right moment, a moment he knew quite well, he jumped off and waved at Rebecca's brothers as they rode helpless down the tracks. They trudged back from Island Pond and made peace with their future brother-in-law.

How is the clock running? Rebecca asks me. Do I mind the climb? Years ago she and Owen took a summer job at a forest station; they lived in the observation tower. One day when her husband was gone, she heard her two boys holler from the woods below, "Bears! Mommy, there are bears!" Down the rungs she flew, a miracle that she reached the ground with an unbroken neck, only to see a standoff between two little boys and two groundhogs. I should let someone know whenever I intend to wind the clock, she says. It is not good that I should be alone—up in that steeple. Have I climbed it yet this morning? Have I seen Mart and Bea?

I am going there next. Mart is the man who hit the bell with a croquet mallet on those Easters long ago, and he also held a fire hose to the roof of Christ Church the whole night that the great Stewart House hotel next door burned down. He loves that church, and he loved the railroad, and he loves his beautiful Bea, his wife of sixty-five years. She nods and smiles as he plays his tape recordings of locomotive engines and whistles; they defer back and forth to each other with the telling of every story—the very curtains and cushions redolent with their mutual courtesy like a church that has burned incense for so many centuries that standing there one thinks that even if the whole place were demolished, the odor would remain. Mart worked welding and inspecting the insides of locomotive boilers, hot even after they had cooled. Bea says he would come home with spark holes all across his shirt front, and many a night he sat up in bed worrying that something was not right in the train yard; he'd dress and go down, always to find it right as he had left it, but then he could sleep.

These people are all reasons why the clock must run, and run as well as I can make it, not because it ran when they were young and their lives require that consolation, not for nostalgia or as a souvenir, but for the sake of faithfulness, which in its every nuance has been the stuff of their living.

Sometimes, it is true, I think about the good and ill uses of my clock. It tells the unemployed when they would have finished work, the disabled when their favorite game shows are on, the philandering when the third parties are due back, the child abusers how long a time their victims yet have in the closet. The bell awakens a pleasant memory, and awakens as well a person who desperately craves sleep. But I need to ponder this no more than rain and sun need to be pondered—they fall with the time on the just and the unjust, the happy and the many, the young, for whom sun and rain and time are endless, and the old, for whom the first two are ever immoderate, and the last is ever more swift.

The clock will die a second death, I am sure. Its parts cannot last indefinitely, no one manufactures mechanical tower clocks any longer, and the whole idea of a clock, how it should look and where it should be, has changed along with our theories of time itself.

Not long ago we reconciled science and what remained of religion in the "clock model of creation," which saw God as the maker and onetime winder of the cosmos. We have since outgrown that model—or at least most of us have. I confess that I find myself rather fond of it lately. But in my version, the winder is not an eighteenth-century Intelligence snoozing in a stuffed chair someplace inside the chambers of a divine Royal Society as the cosmos efficiently ticks on the mantelpiece. He puts on greasy coveralls and climbs a tower through the void, past the bones of prehistoric animals, fallen angels, and the turds of ancient bats, as the Big Bang echoes in his ears like railroad cars coupling. Rung by rung he rises through the terrible darkness. At the top of his ascent, he

winds up the sun and other stars with a cranklike key, adjusts for
the weathers of unknowable dimensions, and lubricates each equi-
nox and comet. Then, stooping to a tiny gear amid the wheelwork,
he wipes away the surface dirt of railroads and religious strife and,
with a fresh rag, every human tear. And I am one of his ministers;
I tend one of his metaphors. I am the clock-winder of Island Pond.

Conscience and
Common Sense

You will know them by their fruits.
—MATTHEW 7:16

I may be the clock-winder of Island Pond, and I may be the lay vicar of its Episcopal parish, but when people learn about the work I do "over there" the question they are most likely to ask me is "What can you tell me about the church people?" They don't mean my church.

They mean the members of the Community Church in Island Pond, a utopian commune of biblical literalists who have lived there since the late 1970s. People in and around Island Pond also call them "the Moonies," though they have no affiliation with Sun Myung Moon; "the Cult"; or, more colorfully, "the Hanky Heads." Women of the sect wear kerchiefs on their heads as a sign of submission to male authority. Men wear beards, headbands, and short ponytails. Members claim to own all of their possessions in common. They do not vote. Except for odd jobs, they do not work for employers outside of the commune. The message of the New Testament, according to one of their publications, "condemns forever the notion that a 'good Christian' can be a witness for God while working for IBM." The community sustains itself through carpentry, a print shop, a restaurant, and by making soaps, candles, and other crafts. Children are not sent to school and, with very few exceptions, not vaccinated. Members refer to Jesus by his Hebrew name, Yahshua. They see themselves as the demonstration of a way of life taught by Yahshua, but not lived with any effectiveness since the earliest centuries of the Christian faith.

How these people came to Island Pond is one of those stories of migration, idealism, and irony with which the Northeast Kingdom abounds. The popular account is that they moved here with their founder, a man named Elbert Eugene Spriggs, from Chattanooga, Tennessee—another tribe of "downcountry" invaders—but that account is incomplete. Prior to their arrival, a small nucleus of French-surnamed, charismatic Roman Catholics had begun to worship together in Island Pond. They were all local people, most of them farmers. One of their number met Spriggs's people at a wedding in Chattanooga, and acknowledged them as kindred spirits. So, the Chattanooga people were *invited.* Of course, the same can be said for the Crusaders who eventually sacked Constantinople, but in view of the tendency of some Vermonters to be more than a little xenophobic, I think it important to clarify the point. It is also fair to add at the outset that my own experiences with the sect, not all of which have been pleasant, took place on "their turf." They never came to the steps of my church to shout their gospel. Any harangue or sales pitch came at my own prompting. I had in a sense "asked for it."

In any case, the arrival of the Community Church in Island Pond was a turning point in its history, perhaps no less significant than the coming of the railroad. It occurs to me that the book I am now writing may be read mainly for its curious chapter on a group that now has sister communities in several New England states, in Canada, France, New Zealand, and Brazil. And, giving all due credit to Chattanooga, this expansion began in Island Pond, where the group now comprises about a fifth of the population, and owns some of the town's largest and oldest houses and buildings.

It is not easy to define this group, or any group of human beings, however simple their life or homogeneous their worldview. The best I can do is to say that they are a strange mix of southern fundamentalism and New Age utopianism. Actually, that is not such a strange mix. At least I don't see it as one. The hippie culture of the sixties and the "old-time religion" bear several key resemblances: apocalypticism, antiintellectualism, a reductive view of history, an unsparing view of "the others." But this observation, in the present context, is quite inadequate. The members of the Community Church are also in rebellion against their roots, that is, in rebellion against the "white bread Jesus"—to use their phrase—of their parents' churches, and the druggy hedonism that characterized the youths of some of them.

Nevertheless, the roots are still the roots. For example, two important targets for the group's evangelism have been Billy Graham crusades and Grateful Dead concerts. A publication they prepared for the former, entitled *When You Wish Upon a Star,* asserts that when Graham allowed his name to be engraved on a star in the sidewalk of Hollywood Boulevard, he betrayed a "fundamental flaw" not only in himself but in "the whole of Christianity." Another publication, this one addressed *To the Deadheads,* says, "We're interested in bringing to you the essence of what you longed for in following the Grateful Dead but now realize has not really come about in a real and lasting way." You can read both papers together and see them as a laughable contradiction, or, more cynically, as an unscrupulous way of cutting different bait for different audiences. I tend to see instead a real genius for recognizing common ground.

Virtually all of the group's publications include directions to one of its communities, and an invitation to come and "see the life." I must say that most of my own glimpses of "the life" have been stolen over the shoulders of "witnesses" who attach themselves to me as soon as I enter the community's domains. The "way in" is through the front door of the Common Sense Restaurant, which serves as the center of the Community Church. Though the restaurant stops serving customers after sundown on Friday, for Sabbath, its doors are always open. It is a dark, cozy, spicy-smelling place, just recently renovated, with barnboard booths, varnished tables, a fireplace, and macramé hangings. The religious purpose is understated, almost esoteric: overturned half-bushel baskets

serve as lampshades, a reference to Matthew 5:15 where Jesus tells
his disciples not to hide their "lights" under bushels. The menu
makes mention of a man who found a great treasure in a field and
sold all he had to obtain it, but no mention is made of Jesus, or
Yahshua, whose parable this is. The menu does what a menu
should: it arouses your interest. It whets your appetite. You can
order a pizza, or a Reuben sandwich, or a sprout salad, or you can
ask to hear about the treasure in the field.

You may get to hear about the treasure in the field whether you
ask to or not. As I hinted above, a member of the community will
often approach you with a few friendly questions—"Where are
you from?" and such—and if not shooed away, he will attach himself to you. You will then hear his story, his variation on the group's
core evangelical theme: he had some experience of Christianity, it
stank, he was lost, he heard about this community, he was skeptical,
he came here anyway, what he found was something he had been
unable to find anyplace else, the Gospel as a living reality.

On Friday evenings the hardwood floor above the Common
Sense Restaurant literally undulates from the dancing feet of a
multitude of men, women, and children, whirling and stomping
and clapping their hands as they sing. A visitor who has never
listened patiently to the testimonies served up downstairs cannot
guess what this part of Sabbath celebration must mean to many of
these people. A number came from a southern fundamentalist
tradition that regards dancing as a snare of the devil. Perhaps theirs
is not so harsh a bargain after all: to relinquish one's possessions
and adopt a rigidly prescribed way of life in exchange for being
able to take one's neighbors by the hand once a week and dance
with them in a ring.

Nevertheless, having said that, I cannot imagine for very long
the retired railroad men of my parish dancing in circles with tam-
bourines and ponytails—nor do I want to. The Island Pond sect,
it seems to me, has fallen into the same trap that inevitably catches
all attempts to "purify" Christianity of its "extraneous" historical
and cultural accretions: they simply create another culture, nar-
rower and more restrictive than the first. The Word must have
flesh. True, when the Word goes abroad in the society or in the

world, it ought to take on the cultural flesh of the people it meets. But among the eaters of Wonder Bread, we quickly discover that in rejecting the "white bread Jesus" we can end up baking some whole-grain version so nutty that only a few nuts will be able to eat it.

The music at Sabbath celebrations comes from a live band of men and women, playing piano, bass fiddle, violin, clarinet, tambourine, and guitar. Both the music and the dancing have a Judaic flavor; some of the songs contain Hebrew phrases. Most are the compositions of church members. Many of those assembled are men and women between twenty and forty, the bearded men in jeans, corduroys, and plain, casual shirts; the women in jumpers and peasant dresses, and spangled or tie-dyed babushkas. There are children everywhere, dressed like smaller versions of their parents. There are always a few pregnant women. Around the edges one sees some demographic variations: a pair of women who must be in their sixties at least, a black couple, a deaf man standing face-to-face with a woman who signs the words of "the prophets."

Part of the celebration consists of spontaneous testimonies by men, and sometimes women, at least a few of whom are regarded as "prophets" by the group. Most of these testimonies consist of commentaries on Scripture, or accounts of experiences during the week. Sometimes a letter is read aloud. The testimonies rarely call forth a full hush from those assembled; people generally pay attention, but those conversing quietly on the benches or children meandering across the dance floor do not appear to be breaking any taboos. Sometimes a speaker has appeared to me a little embarrassed, and sometimes the listeners appear a little bored. Perhaps I am merely projecting two emotions that I feel quite often on these occasions. It seems that the church praises itself almost as often as it praises Yahshua, and with a good deal of redundancy. Yet I have also been touched by some of these testimonies, usually those of people who I guess are neither "prophets" nor leaders here: a young man tearfully telling how he has enjoyed doing carpentry with his "brothers," a father groping for the words to tell how parenthood has helped him to see his sins and inadequacies and to appreciate God's fatherly anxieties over him. The dismissal of the assembly seems to be as spontaneous as the prophecies: someone rises and says something like "We should go home now and enjoy our sabbath meal." The people call out their assent, and slowly disperse, chattering and embracing one another warmly as they go.

In the pattern of their worship, in their various affected Hebraisms, the Community Church is making a concentrated effort to duplicate the Church of the first century, as they understand it. I do not know if I believe that goal is either possible or laudable in the twentieth. Admittedly, I have sensed some of the pungent evangelical flavor of the Pauline Epistles in these gatherings. I must also say, however—and it is a measure of the affection I hold for at least a few of these people, that the next words come hard—if this is a reflection of first-century Christianity, then I feel some sympathy for the Romans.

These people can irritate me. They see themselves as the only legitimate church on earth. They are willing to grant that there may be others, unknown to them, in the same way a paleontologist may grant the negligible possibility of a Loch Ness Monster. According to them, the Holy Spirit abandoned the church, perhaps as early as the church's decision to make Sunday its Sabbath, but at least by the time of Constantine's conversion. In other words, Antony of Egypt, Gregory of Nyssa, Julian of Norwich, Teresa of Avila, George Herbert, John Wesley, William Wilberforce, George MacDonald, Florence Nightingale, Martin Luther King, Janani Luwum, Dorothy Day, Oscar Romero, and Mother Teresa are all more or less sincere people who did their work without God's Spirit and who represent curious anomalies within an otherwise defunct Christianity. To put the matter another way, Jesus or Yahshua discovered his bride to be a shameless whore, and instead of going like the prophet Hosea to rescue her, he has spent almost two thousand years cruising the schoolyards of history for a virgin. The church that runs the Island Pond delicatessen is she.

Of course, theirs is not the first religion to make exclusive claims for itself. Elements within Christianity, and until very recently Christianity as a whole, have made claims no less outrageous. At least the sect in Island Pond is not ready to consign Buddha or the Baal Shem Tov to everlasting fire. They believe in three places of final reward: the Lake of Fire; the Nations, reserved for sincere people from all traditions who acted according to their conscience; and the Holy City, reserved for the true church of Christ, i.e., themselves and their Galilean peers. That's the *good* news. The bad news is, if you have met the Community Church in Island Pond and felt your conscience pricked by it—and few denominational Christians with any conscience left would not feel their conscience pricked by it—then you are running the risk of ignoring your conscience and willfully clinging to a corrupt culture and condemning yourself to the Lake of Fire.

It is in their constant appeal to "conscience" that I find these people most astute, in spite of whatever else may appear naïve or anachronistic about them. They have chosen a virtually unmissable target. The average American of my generation has a knowledge of history, an awareness of global suffering, and a karmic sense of interconnectedness unequaled in any group of people who ever lived. We know about the rape of Africa, the Inquisition, the defoliation of the rain forests, the bombing of Cambodia, and what happened eighteen hours ago to a child living at the end of a hallway on the twenty-seventh floor of a building in a city we have never seen. We also know something of the economic and political threads that connect our every privilege to another's woe. We suffer from what might be termed "moral obesity." Instead of taking in as much sense of social evil as we can exercise off through responsible social *action,* we sit at the table gorging ourselves, too polite or weak-willed to refuse yet another helping, until we are so full we cannot even stand up, let alone move in a constructive direction. Then a lean man who looks just like Jesus begins to talk to us about our conscience. He is nimble and obliging; he can bring us as many helpings as our poor bulging hearts can hold, all the time telling us how very fat we are.

A good example both of the sect's exclusivity and of its effect on a Christian conscience was an "ecumenical" meeting held in Island Pond several years ago. One of the clergymen in town felt the churches should all get together, and he took the bold step of including representatives from the Community Church in his invitation. They came. Our discussion, however, was very soon hamstrung by the rhetorical questions arising from our visitors' "hearts" and "consciences." Many people, some of whom probably resented the "Moonie" presence to begin with, were visibly annoyed.

So was I. Look, I told them, let's for the sake of argument grant all your points. Some of us are the church of Jesus Christ and some of us are the church of Judas Iscariot. Okay? Jesus could still sit down to supper with the man who would betray him. So can we find some concrete thing, however small, that we can do together—even if it is only sweeping a step or brewing a pot of coffee? If we can, let's do it. If we can't, let's go home.

At this point, the Roman Catholic priest, who said the least and probably made the most sense of anyone present, reminded us of the Ethiopian famine. This was exactly what we needed. Let's have a dinner and raise money for the people of Ethiopia, I said. It would be a paltry crumb for them and the most negligible gesture of unity for us, but it would be something, perhaps even a mustard seed to plant God's kingdom.

As it turned out, the Community Church could not join with us on behalf of Ethiopia. For all their readiness to identify the established churches with the Pharisees of Jesus' day, they showed themselves quite "Pharisaical" in their scrupulous refusal to be defiled by us.

But that is not the end of the story. The ecumenical dinner that we agreed to hold without them never came about. The clergyman who had first called the ecumenical meeting, and whom we had elected to call the next, became ill. The Catholic priest was also ill. Remote places like Island Pond are not always sent ministers in the prime of their lives. I was "busy," as usual, and almost relieved by the delay. Within a year I saw posters around town for the usual church suppers, and our parish was planning its own summer picnic. Somewhere in Ethiopia a child who might have been granted a precious space of time, the time from one cup of milk to the next, was dead.

There in stark terms is the best statement I have on the fundamental difference between "them" and "us." They saw no need to work with us, and as I was to learn later, see no need whatsoever for the church to engage in such acts of charity as we had proposed. We saw both needs, but failed in any major way to fulfill either. If you believe in some concept of "Final Judgment," and I admit that I do, then you have to ask which of us would look worse in regard to the respective charges brought against us. I have a feeling we would, especially if that Ethiopian child gets a chance to testify.

So I do listen when someone in the Common Sense Restaurant talks to me about the lack of zeal in Christianity. But I try to listen carefully, with my common sense as well as my conscience. "There were two groups of Jews after the Exile in Babylon," one man told me in the restaurant. "One group was content to remain in Babylon, while the other returned to rebuild Jerusalem. We see that as a reflection of the situation today. There needs to be a people who have it in their hearts to go out from Babylon and build a community obedient to God. We need people like Nehemiah."

After reminding him that the people who stayed behind in Babylon were those who gave us the first written form of the Torah, I said, "Let's hope that God will send us some people a little more gentle than Nehemiah." He gave me an uncomprehending look. "Nehemiah dissolved all marriages with Gentile women. He took Jewish husbands unwilling to comply and beat them up, and pulled their hair out by the roots . . ."

"But God honored Nehemiah," he said, with a hurt in his voice that made me ashamed. I realized I was being "cute," and I checked myself.

"Don't misunderstand me," I hastened to add. "What Nehemiah did and the way he did it were probably necessities within his historical situation. I'm just saying that he seems a long way from Jesus Christ."

"I don't think Jesus would have taken exception to Nehemiah," he said.

Not long after the Chattanooga people appeared in Island Pond, serious questions began to arise regarding the care and punishment of their children.

Accounts from visitors to the sect, eventual defectors from the sect, and even responsible spokespersons of the sect all joined in painting a disturbing picture of children trained by the rod. The degree of severity was, and in some circles still is, a matter of dispute, but a few facts emerged as virtually incontestable. Children were routinely "disciplined" by their parents, and sometimes by other adult members of the church. Disciplining involved striking a child repeatedly on his or her naked buttocks with a thin, dowell-like "balloon stick" until the child "received" the lesson. Disciplining began at the age of six months, though at that age children were reported to be struck lightly on the hand instead of on their backsides. Disciplining was administered routinely for offenses such as lying, refusing to respond immediately to a parent's command, or for "idolatrous" play. Children were forbidden to fantasize; their parents wanted their attentions focused on "reality."

These facts were given complexity by a few others. Corporal punishment is not illegal in Vermont. Corporal punishment becomes illegal abuse only when it leaves marks. Abuse is difficult to prove in many cases. Abuse is especially difficult to prove when child welfare laws designed to deal with individual (and usually low-income) households are applied to a communal situation in which people are relatively educated, in which many people have been renamed, some more than once, and in which children suspected to be "at risk" sometimes go for extended visits out of the country.

The sect's own position was that it disciplined its children not out of anger, but out of loving self-control. This all sounded pretty self-righteous, of course, but so did some of the indignation that came from the outside community. I remember when the controversy was hottest, sitting in what was then my apartment and overhearing a "normal" nine- or ten-year-old neighbor out on the sidewalk shouting to a girl that he was going to cut off her nipples. And I remember thinking sardonically to myself, "At least some religious fanatic hasn't crippled *his* capacity for imaginative play."

We in the northern counties of Vermont lived then and live now in a sink of child abuse and neglect: kids leashed to woodstoves like dogs while their urine-soaked clothes cook dry over the stovepipe; toddlers locked in apartments with nothing in their reach but a pot to excrete in while their mothers go out on a twenty-four-hour drunk; little girls crying out in their preschools that they are "tired of playing married" with their stepfathers; boys tied to trees with tractor chains during lightning storms to teach them a little respect for their parents. After a while, the atrocities begin to be trivialized as mere local color. In the jargon of the "dysfunctional family," which nearly every dysfunctional family seems to have learned like a second language, a kid driven to suicide is discussed like a problem of faulty wheel alignment. But in the case of "the Island Pond Cult," whose children were all clean, clothed, and given plenty of those hugs the bumper stickers tell us "kids need . . . everyday," some of us were ready to rise up and execute the wrath of God. The words reeked of hypocrisy as soon as they entered the air. We knew it. And the sect knew it. They knew about our conscience.

But they seemed to have no appreciation for the other side of our conscience: the remembrance of all those people—the "damned" of our secular religion—who "stood by and did nothing," the neighbors of Kitty Genovese and Auschwitz. Instead, the sect reminded us of the witch hunts and Joe McCarthy. There were ugly historical precedents for everything we might do, even for doing nothing at all. I shall always wonder if our sense of history was a help or a hindrance in the mess that followed.

Perhaps the most troubling and widely publicized incident of church discipline had to do with the caning of a thirteen-year-old girl. The details remain somewhat clouded due to conflicting testimonies and retracted testimonies. All parties seem to agree that the girl was brought to her parents to be disciplined for having been "deceitful," and that her father asked for the help of a church elder—not because he felt himself too squeamish for the task, but because he feared he would overreact. She was disciplined, questioned, and instructed by at least one church elder, in the presence of her parents, in a session that lasted for seven hours. For part or all of that time she was stripped to her underpants. Accounts differ as to how much time was spent striking the girl and how much time was spent otherwise. A doctor at the emergency room of the North Country Hospital examined the girl after the incident and sketched a drawing of welts on her back, bottom, and legs, which the hospital retains in its records. The girl was taken to the hospital because her father decided to leave the Community Church. He also decided to file assault charges against the elder who had struck the girl.

Eventually the girl's father would drop the charges, claiming he had been pressured into making them. He would rejoin the church and issue a statement of "repentance." For its part, the church would apologize to the father—not for the practice of discipline, but for taking over what the father should have done for himself. The official church position at present seems to be that they made a serious mistake, but that the incident was distorted and exploited by malicious individuals in the larger community.

It is fair to say that the larger community was in something of a turmoil. People seemed unsure of what to believe, and baffled by the seeming inability of their society to "straighten things out." Needless to say, many were forced to examine their own standards of acceptable behavior in the treatment of children. What Yeats said in "The Second Coming," that "The best lack all conviction, while the worst/Are full of passionate intensity," was probably true to some extent here. Shots were fired through the windows of the sect's restaurant and rocks thrown through the windows of its homes. Apparently some people were so concerned with the welfare of the Island Pond children that they were willing to risk killing a few to make their point.

Before dawn on June 22, 1984, ninety Vermont state troopers drove into Island Pond with search warrants and drove away with 112 church children and their parents. What has come to be known as "the Raid" was authorized by the State's Attorney's Office. The plan was to have the children examined and photographed by physicians for signs of abuse. If evidence of abuse was found, children deemed at risk would be taken into state custody.

On the afternoon of that same day, before any children had been examined, a district court judge named Frank Mahady declared the raid unconstitutional. He ordered that all persons be returned to their homes along with all property seized. Lawyers, police officers, doctors, and journalists involved in the raid concur that the conduct of the church people was calm, cooperative, and dignified. Where opinions differ is in whether that conduct, under the circumstances, showed remarkable faith or a nearly inhuman detachment. The judge's ruling was never challenged by the state of Vermont.

Purely by coincidence, I drove into Island Pond that afternoon, perhaps at the very hour that the judge was making his ruling. I saw one of my parishioners, a mother with young children, standing at the edge of her driveway, and I stopped to chat. "Did you hear what happened?" she said. I thought by the tone of her voice that she was going to tell me one of her family had been taken to the hospital or died. "A bunch of state troopers came into town— Gary, there must have been a hundred of them—and they went into the church people's houses and took away the children. They loaded them into buses . . . and they just drove away with all the children." She was in tears.

If this were a different kind of book, or I were a different kind of author, there is much that could be written about the Raid and its place in legal or regional history. But I think it is that woman's tears that are closer to my subject. They speak more eloquently than any words, of course. And though there was no single emotion that they expressed, it may be that a single word can cover all of her feelings: helplessness.

Well, my religion teaches that we are all helpless without God, helpless in the gravity of our sins. But what impresses me about the whole affair, and what may be the great common denominator between the Community Church and the rest of us poor whores of Babylon, is the way our minds work to deny the helplessness. There is so much, it seems to me, that both of us refuse to admit or recognize.

I wonder, for example, if the Community Church has asked itself the hard questions called for by its own theology. How can one enter the Kingdom of God as a little child—as Jesus said we must—if one strikes his own children for some of the very qualities that make them childlike? Or how can the Community Church see itself as a collective Christ figure in view of the events described above? That is how they wished us to see them. One of their publications at the time of the controversy contains an "Open Letter to the Attorney General of Vermont" and a picture of Jesus standing before Pontius Pilate. Yet, if this was Calvary, who was crucified? Nearly every official who had anything to do with the ill-fated Raid has suffered some loss of fortune or standing. After a number of cases involving allegations of child abuse, neglect, unregistered deaths, and truancy, the only offense for which a member of the Community Church has been successfully prosecuted is the unauthorized practice of medicine in the removal of a wart. A wart. If this is the Good Friday mockery, who, may I ask, is wearing the crown of thorns? If we in the world are the rabble of Jerusalem, we have certainly been an innocuous rabble. Though there may have been scattered cries of "Crucify them, crucify them!" it seems that the cry which has prevailed is "Live and let live."

I believe in the essential goodness of that cry, as do many of the people in my community, but I also believe we have been slow to think on what it means. We are as deafened by our own cant as the church people seem deafened by theirs. Both of us have unrealistic ideas of community. *We* think we can choose whether to live in community or to be the self-sufficient individuals who live in our myths; *they* think they can create their own community apart from us. The fact is, however, that all of us are living "in community," the same community, whether we choose to or not.

This idea was brought home to me in an interview with Dr. Moseley, a local pediatrician to whom I had come for a medical view of the Island Pond question. One of his concerns is the Community Church's stated position on immunization. Supposedly, the church's elders view this as a personal matter left to the conscience of individual parents. Nevertheless, most of the church children are not immunized, despite an exceptional offer by the Vermont Health Department to immunize them *without asking for their names*. "My concern about a closed community," Dr. Moseley told me, "is that they are a menace to people around them. . . . A lot of our protection from infectious diseases comes from the fact that 90 percent of the people are immunized against them. The remaining 10 percent are protected by what's called 'herd immunity': if the disease is not around to catch, the fact you're unimmunized does not present a danger to you. . . . By refusing in large numbers to take part, they [the sect] minimize the effectiveness of immunization practices."

In other words, without meaning to, the Community Church has threatened the health of Island Pond. (This is not purely hypothetical; in 1989, the church suffered an outbreak of whooping cough.) Furthermore, the larger community, also without meaning to, may have "blessed" the church with some of its own immunities. It seems to me that the indisputable fact of our biological community challenges both the church's practice in the area of immunization, and the Vermont state laws that permit parents to forgo the immunization of their children as a matter of religious faith.

In some ways I think that the "Island Pond issue" is merely one form of a question that lies at the bottom of many social, medical, and cultural controversies of our day. Is there a point, I wonder, at which a liberal, humanistic culture needs to "draw a line" in order to remain liberal, human, or even a culture? I worry a lot about this question, because I see it being debated, in numerous arenas, by right-wing demagogues who want to draw the lines all over everyone's back, and by liberals who are loath to admit that a single line needs to be drawn. The Island Pond controversy strikes me as the perfect paradigm of both. The response of a Republican administration in Vermont was the infamous Raid, what might be called "the Grenada approach" to the problem. Send in the marines. Kick some ass. The policy of the liberal Democratic administration that followed was to distance itself in every observable way from the issue, or from any admission that an issue even exists.

And yet past a certain point such ideological distinctions may scarcely matter. In the Island Pond controversy, and in a number of issues related to it, we see the authority or the beliefs or the "life-style" of adults almost always upheld in spite of, or even at the expense of, their children. This is the bed in which the New Right and the New Age inevitably lie down together. This is one

reason why I said earlier that in targeting Billy Graham crusades
and Grateful Dead concerts, the church people show a real genius
for recognizing common ground.

In the end, the Community Church may have challenged our
social and political faith even more than it challenges post-
Constantinian Christianity, or contradicts itself. For whether or
wherever we go to church, or however we identify ourselves politically, most of us believe in two gods called Truth and Justice.
Yet in the case of the Island Pond tragedy, we have failed to
establish *either* truth *or* justice to any reasonable degree of community satisfaction. For this reason, if for no other, the Community
Church in Island Pond is holy. I mean "holy" in the sense of
illuminating a crucial human situation, and inspiring an almost inhuman dread.

The reader is mistaken who thinks that the Community Church is
in this book merely because the book is set in Island Pond and
the church people live there. The Community Church has a place
in this book because, like other persons and experiences mentioned
therein, it has influenced my faith and touched my parish. The
discussion has simply needed to be far-reaching because the Community Church's influence has been far-reaching, too.

In regard to the "church people," the members of my parish
probably typify the mix of views found in Island Pond. The oldest
parishioners tend to be the most tolerant, perhaps because the
"church people" are always available to do the kinds of odd jobs
and small repairs that elderly people living on their own are often
unable to do for themselves. They work carefully and steadily;
among all the charges and slanders ever leveled against them, I've
never heard them called cheaters or goof-offs. I know a man who
hired them to haul a lot of refuse to the dump. In one of the loads
a church person found a piece of jewelry. I think some workers
would have called that "a tip," but he dutifully returned the piece
to its owner, who had never meant to throw it away. In acts such
as these, and in the members' simplicity and courtesy, I think many
older people see an image of earlier, happier days in their own
lives. They probably see the "spanking business" as just a modest

form of progress; many of them doubtless got much worse in the woodshed, or even in the schoolhouse, half a century ago.

Finally, I think that the older people take less heat in the form of proselytizing. I'm not sure the sect is overeager to embrace the Kingdom of God in its geriatric incarnation. Well, neither are we. I also don't think that the terms of their particular evangelism are very accessible to people over sixty-five. The elderly are struggling with failed bodies more than with failed idealism. For them the Grateful Dead are people who never went to a nursing home.

On the other hand, those of us younger can take more heat. I'm back to the theme of conscience, and of the ability these people have for afflicting it. My discussion here is about "taking the heat," both the sparks scattered carelessly on your shirt and the unquenchable fire aimed at your heart.

A person who undertakes to go among these people for a while had better know what he or she believes. I have even thought of requiring a trip to the Common Sense as part of my course for adults seeking confirmation. There's a man there, a former seminarian, who never meets me without a little verbal thrust. "So what's this stuff I've been reading about the Episcopal Church ordaining homosexuals? Maybe it's a few churches—no, I guess it's just the Episcopal Church. Are people blowing it up out of proportion, or is this some kind of cutting edge, or what?"

"Well . . . I guess it's a little of both." Impeccably liberal answer. "What's being discussed about ordaining gay people *is* something new, although the church has been ordaining gay people for centuries." He laughs heartily, though I did not intend the statement to be funny. "But there are, yes, people who fixate on this controversy and exaggerate it as a way of distracting attention from deeper issues."

"So what are the deeper issues?" It's here where you hold your nose, close your eyes, and jump.

"The issue," I say, "is whether the God we worship is a good Creator who makes people a certain way with a certain purpose in mind, or whether he likes to play practical jokes. Another issue is how seriously we intend to take the example of Jesus in calling a society's outcasts into Christian community. And another issue has to do with defining sexual responsibility and confronting our own smugness about that whole question. For instance, am I a sexually responsible person just because I'm heterosexual and monogamous?"

"We'd have to ask your wife on that one." These people, at least some of them, are not without a sense of humor.

And others of them are not without charm. One man in particular comes to mind. Like nearly every other person I've met at Common Sense, he gave me his testimony—the disappointing journey through denominational Christianity, the haven of grace found here—adding the unusual twist that he had been raised a Jew.

Then he turned to me and asked, "How do you see us?" I had at that time been reading some of the sect's more vitriolic indictments of Christianity, and I let him know exactly how I saw his church. Along with the words "sincere" and "committed" I'm sure I used at least one of these: "smug," "arrogant," "self-righteous," "uncharitable." He looked defensive. "Come on, come on," I challenged. "I've read some of your stuff. White bread Jesus, the whole bit. We're all harlots. That's your line, isn't it?"

"We've repented of that," he said. I've since come to doubt that there was ever any such "repentance" in the group as a whole, but I believe he was telling the truth for himself. "In fact, for whatever part I may have had in whatever offended you, I offer my apology. I'd like to learn more about what you believe and about your church. Can you help me do that?"

I was so disarmed—perhaps even threatened—by this that I responded less than politely. "If you really want to find out, if this isn't just part of the rap, I can bring you a book." He said he did. So a few days later I stopped at Common Sense and left a copy of *What Is Anglicanism?*, by Urban T. Holmes III.

Unfortunately, we didn't get to discuss the book. I was told some months after our meeting that he had left the church and gone "back to his mother's, back to Judaism, back to New York"— perhaps, I thought, where Yahshua had meant for him to be all along.

Where a visitor to Common Sense can feel most vulnerable is on the subject of property. Jesus' words to the Rich Young ruler—"Sell all you have, give to the poor, and come follow me"—are an undeniable part of the record, though everyone seems to ignore the fact that Jesus had been willing to let the young man go with advice to "keep the commandments." When pressed for something more challenging, he obliged. Nevertheless, one feels at a moral disadvantage sitting, quite literally on his wallet, across the table from someone who claims to have "left everything."

The experience is not unlike that of being fourteen years old, fresh from your first date and your first tentative kiss, and being confronted by an eighteen-year-old who's "gone all the way." They say he notches his steering wheel every time he gets a girl in the backseat. He used to drive to school with a brassiere hanging from his rearview mirror until the principal made him take it off. He could have fought that one in court, you know. "So I hear you've been on a date. I used to 'go on dates,' too. All little boys 'go on dates.' So, does she do it? 'None of my business,' okay. You probably haven't even felt her up yet. Do you want to know where anything is? I could draw you a picture if you need one. You want to know where *I* was this Saturday? You want to hear *my* testimony?"

The implication is very clear. You're supposed to be a man, or at least a boy. But are you really? You look like a boy, that's true. You take gym with the boys. You go to church with all the other so-called Christians. But is that what you are? Maybe what you are is a little flaming faggot. Maybe you're going to the Lake of Flaming Faggot Fire where all the little flaming faggots go.

As with the young man in my analogy, I suspect that some of the church people's confident exteriors mask the faces of "little boys" who are very much afraid of life. Their need to make us insecure about our orientation suggests a basic insecurity about their own. I also suspect that many of these poor, good folk did not have that much to leave.

A friend told me of a church member who assured him that prior to entering the church he'd had a manuscript of poetry under consideration by half a dozen major publishers. I couldn't help but wonder: Had he waited for all six rejection slips to arrive before going away? Or had he left sooner than that, guaranteeing himself the illusion that he had sacrificed a dream, not failed at it? I knew of another young man who joined the sect after a very brief bit of celebrity in the nuclear freeze movement. With a note of romantic devotion in her voice, his wife stood beside him and told me, "He gave up peace." Did he? Or did he give up his chance to read the telegram that comes to every would-be hero sooner or later: YOU'RE AN UNEXCEPTIONAL THIRTY-SEVEN-YEAR-OLD ASSHOLE, AND YOUR VISA BILL'S OVERDUE. It is the person who opens the telegram, reads it through once, and uses it for a bookmark in his or her Bible who is *my* hero.

This is not to say, however, that everyone on "my side" is heroic. Many responses to the Community Church, including some from priests in my own diocese, are discouraging to say the least. In response to cant, they offer cant. They suggest that we are elect members of a vast cult of fierce free-thinkers. People who "defect" to outfits like the Community Church are simply those too weak or lazy to think for themselves. Am I supposed to believe such drivel? Is there any surer indication of lazy thinking than a cliché, and is there any cliché more beaten to death than that people join "cults" or turn to orthodoxies because they are simply too lazy to think? Most of us wouldn't even take a stand on an issue without first checking out its media certification as "liberal," "conservative," "progressive"—whatever camp we ourselves wish to be certified as belonging to. I would dare some Christians I know to walk into the Common Sense, seek out a person in their own mental "weight class," and walk away an hour later claiming that their own beliefs are more thoughtfully held than those of the "robot" they talked to.

I suppose that in some ways I gave myself the dare. I cannot deny that some of my visits to the Common Sense have come in the form of daring myself, or of answering the dare I heard coming from its doors. Ultimately, I would realize that the challenge was not to a mental contest. It was a challenge to a spiritual struggle— something very different. No one wins such a struggle all by him or herself. At least that is my conclusion to the story I am about to tell.

Before I had ever met the church people or contemplated this book, I wrote an essay entitled "I Am the Clock-Winder," which in its revised form appears as the chapter before this one. An earlier version was published in *New England Monthly,* and later condensed for *Reader's Digest.* It referred to the Community Church as a "cult" that had received national attention for its "harsh" child-rearing practices.

Almost immediately after the article appeared, I received a letter from a man in the sect. He had been one of my first contacts there, and remained one of my favorites, a gentle and seemingly guileless person. He wrote that he and another member wanted to talk with me about my article. It is an indication of my naïveté that I suspected the two were going to tell me how my clock-winder metaphor was somehow fulfilled in their community. Or perhaps they would simply urge me to clarify and expand my references to their group in the future.

Of course, I was wrong. When I met with the writer of the letter, I found him angry and hurt. My use of the word "harsh" to describe the group's child-rearing was irresponsible; it risked reviving all of the ugliness that had finally died down.

I was also "not stating the truth" when I said that those "harsh" practices had brought their church national attention. The Raid— "when they came and took away our children!"—had brought the attention. It was a nice distinction, but he was right.

He went on to say that those in the community who knew me and who had read the article felt betrayed. The evening before my first appearance among them, he now told me, they had prayed that God would send them Nicodemus. He is the Pharisee in the Gospel of John who comes to Jesus by night to hear the words about being "born again." They had thought I was he. I did not ask him how they could be so sure I was Nicodemus. Instead, I asked myself how he could have known that Nicodemus is one of the characters in the Gospels with whom I most poignantly identify.

He was also incensed by the word "cult." The connotations were admittedly grave. And, I asked myself, hadn't I been lazy in failing to revise a phrase that predated my actual encounters with these people? Hadn't I assumed they would never read the essay, and thus minimized my sense of responsibility to them? I was not helped any by a second man, not a member of the church, who sat beside the first. He was a writer then working on a book about the church and the Raid; he had written another, critically acclaimed book about New Age communes in the United States. He was more scathing than the elder was. As far as he was concerned, any claim I had to being an ethical writer was completely spurious. If I say so myself, I was at my scrappy best, but I had little stomach for the fight. "What, are you a member, too?" I hurled at the writer when he stated that simply by submitting my work to *New England Monthly* I was showing my lack of integrity.

But I knew what he was talking about. Just after the Raid, Barbara Grizzuti Harrison had written an article for *New England Monthly* entitled "The Children and the Cult." Even some local critics of the church felt that Harrison's treatment was a bit much. Apparently the sect had succeeded in "getting to her"—she wrote of checking into the emergency room of the local hospital with unaccountable chest pains after one of her interviews—and when she sat down to write her story, she had little sympathy for the subject. What she saw had reminded her "of a scene from *Village of the Damned*." The children were "preternaturally grave." Her reaction extended to Island Pond itself. She wrote: "It would not be a gross exaggeration to say that the entire town of Island Pond has gone haywire. Paranoia, anger, hopelessness, apathy, hysteria, bitterness, and fear are everywhere in evidence. And yet *haywire* seems almost too thin a word to describe what I truly believe (and in this belief I am not alone) to be the contagion of evil."

I had responded with a letter to the editors, which they had printed, criticizing Harrison's treatment of the town. I accused her of possessing a mentality not unlike that of the church people. "A cultist grows to the ripe old age of twenty-five and concludes on the basis of a few unfulfilled ideals that the entire world is damned; Ms. Harrison spends several weeks in a town for which she obviously can feel no affinity and concludes that 'paranoia, apathy, hopelessness . . . are everywhere.' " I mentioned my letter to the two men in Common Sense. For them it was just further proof that I should have known better. The sect member added that he hoped I would "repent."

I seldom know when to cut my losses. I probably would have remained there talking for another hour had I not needed to visit one of my parishioners in the hospital. It was already late. I drove to the hospital feeling somewhat shaken, praying—as much for my own sake as for hers—that I would arrive in Newport before Alma had gone to sleep.

When I got there the ninety-year-old Alma was not only wide awake but prepared to do battle with all comers. Earlier that day she had announced what amounted to a hunger strike, which she had every intention of continuing until her demands were met. "I was feeling a little sick before I came here, that's true, but I feel okay now. My family thinks I am senile [accent on second syllable]. Well I am NOT senile, and they are going to send me to home! I can make my own decisions and that's what I've decided and that's all there is to it!" We said a prayer together. Alma may never know how much her tenacious refusal to let anyone define her own mind strengthened me that night. I knew then, as much as ever before, what it means to "belong to a church."

Nevertheless, I also knew that my conscience was not at peace about the words I had written. They may have been the right words, but I had written them too carelessly. I prayed that I would look for the truth, find and recognize the truth, and faithfully record the truth.

I wrote to the sect member who had written to me. I told him of my plans to write this book and this chapter. I told him that though I might have some misgivings about my past choice of words, any gesture of "repentance," aside from choosing truer words in the future, was out of the question. Either of us could manipulate an apology, or feel betrayed by it later on. But I did indeed want to learn more about his church. I told him that my first point of entry would be a Sabbath celebration. I went so far as to suggest that he might want to warn the faithful of my intentions. I wanted everything aboveboard.

When, after some weeks, I did show up at a celebration, there were no recriminations or warnings. The man to whom I had written greeted me as warmly as if I'd been Nicodemus himself. My relief was checked slightly when he pointed to one of the musicians and asked, "Do you recognize your friend?"

It was the writer who had dressed me down in the Common Sense. "Do you remember when you asked him 'Are you one of them?' Well, it turned out to be prophetic. He's decided to join our community. We are so happy. I guess his book will be on hold for a while now. And Garret, you wouldn't believe the change that's taken place in him. All of that bitterness is gone." I should have felt quite satisfied at having been right, and to some extent I was satisfied. But I couldn't gloat. The experience was like that of finding the head of a former acquaintance hanging in a trophy room.

I went to other celebrations. Unfortunately, my contact was called out of town for an indefinite period of time, but I soon found myself with a replacement in the person of the supercilious elder who had asked me about "the gay question." During my first— and, as it turned out, my only—interview with him I asked for a meeting with church elders and other members who could speak authoritatively on the group's beliefs. I offered to submit a list of questions ahead of time. The elder seemed pleased, even enthusiastic, as he read over my list, which covered a range of subjects from circumcision to liberation theology. Several weeks passed without a word. Then a letter, hand-delivered to my church, informed me that the elder and his brothers had decided that they could not cooperate with me. The reason was that I had not shown myself sufficiently repentant for my clock-winder article.

So this was "the answer," wasn't it? I had been mailed a formal invitation to "fully understand," as the first letter had said, and now my attempts at full understanding had been thwarted. Well, wasn't this the way "a cult" always behaved? Did someone have to hit me over the head with a brick?

Still, something in me said that I was settling too easily on a conclusion. After all, I *had* offended them. They had no good reason to trust me. I resolved to attend yet another celebration that Friday. I would stay until the end. And when someone invited me to his house for supper afterward, as someone always did, I would accept.

I arrived about an hour after the celebration had started. Many of the people looked flushed and tired. It was a hot evening in August. A number of the community were away at the annual Bread and Puppet Domestic Resurrection Circus in Glover, Vermont, where they would provide their own unofficial sideshow of folk dances, and talk to some of the same people they might meet at a Grateful Dead concert. I only heard one man testify. He read the passage from the Gospel of St. John about the Good Shepherd and applied it at some length to the experience of coming to celebration with his children and those of some housemates who had gone to Bread and Puppet. "All those little lambs," he said, looking at the children seated at his feet, and then at the assembly. There was a simpering quality to his southern twang that made me wonder if he talked like that all the time.

It was to his communal house that I was invited for supper. He did not invite me directly; another man who lived at a different house extended the invitation, then approached this man and whispered to him. I was promptly made welcome.

At the house I was led to a seat in the living room, where I was eventually joined by two women and three men. A fourth man seemed to have the responsibility of tending to the children who filled a long table in the dining room next door. Each of us had a glass of juice, then a plate of quiche, green salad, corn on the cob, and a glass of water. "I can take back my own glass," I said to the pretty woman who came around to do so, but she replied softly, "No, I want to serve you." Did this reply have even the slightest effect on my male ego? Not a bit. I'm completely evolved.

Before I had my plate in my lap, my host had placed his chair face-to-face with mine and begun his "story." What interested me about his particular version, aside from the fact that he had been one of Spriggs's original converts in Tennessee, was his willingness to acknowledge the good influences of people outside the group. Granted, he sketched for me the three domains of Final Judgment, and left little doubt about who was going where. But he spoke with disarming affection about the role his Baptist grandfather had played in his own spiritual growth. He even credited Spriggs's honored mission to the prayers of Spriggs's "daddy." There was something reasonable, tender, and just plain right in this. I felt a bit ashamed of how I'd tried to size the man up at the celebration.

I was also asked about my religion and my ministry. Did I wear special clothes when I preached, my host wanted to know? I answered yes, that I wore vestments. There were questions about those. My host wanted to know if I ever "wore them walking down the street." I sensed he might be baiting me a little—surely he'd never heard of a minister parading down Railroad Street in a cassock and alb. But I tried to answer the question in good humor. "No, I don't wear my robes down the street, but that's mainly because so far I haven't found anyone who'll rent me a donkey." No laughs.

A woman said, "So then it's just like a costume? It doesn't mean anything?" If she was trying to mock me, she wasn't very good at it. I could detect nothing but genuine interest in her voice. It seemed to me I had to make a decision. Was I going to hold back, play the observer, make my mental notes—or was I going to answer these people in some spirit of mutuality? The latter seemed both more charitable and more honest. I was starting to enjoy myself.

I explained that you could say the robes "didn't mean anything"; they were "just a tradition," special clothes that served to remind us that we were doing something special in church. As I understood it, their design was based on ancient garments in daily use when the church began to form its liturgy. There were many such customs in my church. The way we worshiped was very prescribed. We used a prayer book. We certainly lacked the spontaneity of, say, our Pentecostal brothers and sisters. Some would find our worship dull. That was the word my host had stressed in his indictment of the denominational churches. But unlike my host, who saw no hope for any church to enter the Holy City but his own, I did not see any church "having it all." Mine lacked some of the advantages of informality; it had advantages, too.

For me, the prescriptions of liturgy helped me keep my mind on God, and minimized the distractions of individual performances. The old words and gestures were given life by the condition I brought to them each week. Didn't the Bible also work that way? I asked. It was like a beach upon which the ocean of our experience was always washing up something new. I repeated, we Anglicans had our limitations. No bride possesses all graces. But I had chosen one spouse, one church, just as they had. And perhaps in loving my spouse faithfully, I could attain a knowledge of the love that every lover knows.

The reaction of my host to this was practically metamorphic. The evening became surreal from that point on. As every member of the household watched in virtually uninterrupted silence, he began to castigate me like a man possessed.

"Now wait," I said when he started translating my own words for me. "I listened patiently while you explained your beliefs for nearly an hour. Let me finish explaining mine."

"I will *not* let you finish!" he cried. "I will not let you finish! What I told you was the truth. What you're saying is not the truth. You're *preaching* is what *you're* doing." It was like having someone in a nudist colony suddenly scold you for not wearing any clothes.

He raged on. I was a minister and that was why I was "preaching." I was a shepherd, and I would be judged a second time over for every member of my flock. I was their shepherd—"I prefer to think of myself as the sheepdog," I interjected—and I would be judged as such before the throne of God. And I was a false shepherd with a false gospel. I worked for money—"Do you want to know how much?" I asked, but he didn't—and all I did for my parish was preach on Sunday. "How do you know what my ministry is?" I protested. "I know, I know," he said looking into my eyes as if I were the vilest thing he had ever seen. "I know you and I know what's inside of you." He said it over and over, gleefully. "I know. And you will be judged for it."

It's safe to say that this experience was unique in my life. I have had people angry at me enough to hit me—perhaps angry enough within the moment to kill me. But this man did not want to kill me; he seemed to want to consign me to a living death. I have never faced such unmitigated hatred.

I am sure that a sect member reading this account would say that it was my own bad conscience, not the solicitous warnings of my good host, that had touched me like a brush with hell. My host *did* know me, didn't he? No, he didn't know me. But he knew my doubts about my ministry. It did not take a prophet to know them. With some practice, I could probably do the same thing for another minister, another parent, another writer. "If you are truly the Son of God, come down from the cross." A drunk squatting by a gibbet can do it; even the Son of God can be hurt by it.

The assault came to a head when he shouted that I stood on a "fallen, rotten, slimy system" and I took a small notepad out of my pocket and asked, "May I write that down?" He jumped up and hovered over me with his hands on his hips. The thought crossed my mind that I was going to take a blow. "Go ahead!" he shouted. "That's why you're here, isn't it? You wrote an article about us, right?"

No, I told him, taking my note with as much composure as I could summon, I had not written an article about them. I told him what I had written, I told him what I was writing, and I told him what steps I had taken to make my purposes known in the community. The poor fellow—there he was, disturbing his digestion and ruining his Sabbath to defend his faith in the best way he knew how, and his so-called brothers hadn't even bothered to hand him a photocopy of my "offense." All he'd been handed was the official word and the burden of having me for supper. He may have been thinking the same thing, because he began to cool down.

There were some other exchanges—a few clarifications from me, a few sober admonitions from another man with some kind of European accent. It was past midnight, and I was utterly exhausted. I told everyone that I made no apologies for the content of what I had said, but if in saying it, or in my way of saying it, I had offended a custom of their house, I was sorry. In "the world," where I came from, the custom was to hear another's idea and then to offer one's own.

I was ready to stand up. I wanted to stand on more than my feet. "It will not surprise me," I said, "if I learn one day that I was nothing better than your little brother. Perhaps I am a poor excuse for a minister. But all of this is I, I, I, and Paul says 'not I, but *Christ*.'" I said the name loudly—a cry, a curse, a prayer. "There's a lot I don't know. But I will tell you this, what we said here tonight doesn't amount to a hill of beans, because outside these windows are a lot of good people, who want to serve God, and who weep because they worry they haven't." In my mind I saw the face of my parishioner Martha, weeping only hours before when she had told me how she longed for reconciliation with her sister, weeping years ago at the edge of her driveway because the police had come and "taken all the children away." "Jesus loves those people," I said to my hosts, "and he died for those people, and he loves me, and died for me, and he stood by my side tonight—that I know—because without him I might have crumbled. And I did *not* crumble." I was preaching now, all right, and I didn't care.

"You're good," my host said as I rose to leave. "You're good at giving your gospel." He refused to shake my hand. I thanked the adults and I thanked the children who were just then finishing up washing the dishes, and I walked back to my church.

On the way home I found myself wondering how some old flower child with a few gray hairs and a few burned brain cells would have held up under hours of such abuse. According to Isaiah, the Messiah would not "break a bruised reed, or quench a dimly burning wick," but I saw no chance for a dimly burning wick in that house. And I wondered, too, about "all those little lambs" that had dutifully followed my host to the celebration. "A little child shall lead them," Isaiah had also said, but I could not imagine any child of that house volunteering for the job.

I went to the library and found the article by Barbara Grizzuti Harrison. It had been years since I read it, but I recalled her episode with "chest pains," and I wanted to see if she had elaborated.

An elder I'd not met before stared at me, unblinking (how do they do this?) for half an hour and told me (many variations on a single theme) all about the Lake of Fire, in which, if I did not change my evil ways, I would soon find myself. I don't remember his words. They were silly words. I remember what I felt—virulent hatred focused on me, the kind of hatred that is like an invasion of the body: I felt my heart being attacked. Nobody—pity the children—can stand being the object of such intense hatred. The women, their voices sweet, chanted about the Lake of Fire. The children watched.

Three hours later I was admitted to the North Country Hospital for chest pains. . . .

It was my experience and my impression—with the exception of the chest pains and the women, who in my case had seemed almost sympathetic. At least that is what I thought of the woman who said, "I want to serve you." If that had really been her wish, she had fulfilled it, and not by waiting on me either.

So my old contact at the Common Sense had been right. I needed to repent for something I had written in *New England Monthly*. He, too, could be "prophetic" without intending to. But it was not my piece on winding the clock that called for repentance; it was my letter about Ms. Harrison. I had sinned against her—an unexceptionally common sin, as most sins are. I had allowed my disapproval of some of her conclusions to excuse me from sympathy for any of her pain. Now I had felt some of her pain for myself, and I was sorry.

If this sounds like an oblique way of writing off the sect, it is not. I have no wish to speak the damning word, or to hear it spoken by God. The damning word, when it comes, will not be spoken by the likes of me, by one of those children of twilight who always insist on giving the Devil his due. No, the word will come from a man like my host, when he undergoes a cultic version of a mid-life crisis. Then the sole possessors of the Holy Spirit will be proclaimed the chief minions of Satan himself. The apostate will not allow himself to remember the circle of beautiful children singing "Shema Y'Israel, God is Lord" at the celebration as if the angels themselves had descended on Island Pond; or the joy of driving nails side by side with his brothers as they fastened the beams of the new restaurant, not for money or to kill time, but for a purpose that held them as firmly as they held their hammers; or the smiling bride he took by the hand in the bosom of his community, recalling the words of Job, "when the morning stars sang together, and all the sons of God shouted for joy." Those memories will all belong to the "darkness" then. He will admit none of them into the clear light of his raving.

But it was my own psychology, not his, that concerned me when I prepared for my church service that Sunday. I braced myself for testing—not by God, but by my own manipulated mind. Every tatter, every mistake, every omission was going to accuse me. A floorboard rotting since the nineteenth century would doubtless give way beneath my feet, and I would fall to the slimy rocks below. I would need to be ready.

Nothing happened. Or rather, everything happened. The words of the liturgy ran to meet me like old friends. And the faces of my old friends themselves—I could have kissed every one. The Gospel for that Sunday, about Jesus pulling Peter from the waves when he had dared to walk on the water, was like a beloved old joke I would never tire of hearing. After the service my daughter and my godson played hide-and-seek among the furniture, ducking behind the pulpit, crawling under the pews, giggling in the sacristy. And when one of them searched too long without success, when one of them stood still, looking the least bit lost or embarrassed, the other called out his or her name.

"Of such is the Kingdom of God."

Of Bishops
and Bait Fishermen

Jesus said to the twelve, "Do you also wish to go away?"
Simon Peter answered him, "Lord, to whom shall we go? You
have the words of eternal life."
—JOHN 6:67–68

One of my favorite lines from one of my favorite books occurs when the fly-fishing Presbyterian minister in Norman Maclean's *A River Runs Through It* tells his sons, "Izaak Walton is not a respectable writer. He was an Episcopalian and a bait fisherman." A part of what endears the line to me is its association, in my mind, with the senior warden of Christ Church, as venerably stubborn an Episcopalian and bait fisherman as one could meet. Tommy Waterman is an anchor, not only for the parish but also for me. When disappointment or weakness of faith tempt me to leave my ministry, or even the church itself, he is one of my defenses. Like Simon Peter in the epigraph above, I cry out, "Where else can I go?" But along with the "words of eternal life," I am thinking of Tommy, of the way those words have lived in a wild, vital, mortal life like his.

In many ways, Tommy is the personification of Island Pond. Toughened by hard work and the woods, humorous and inscrutable, he, like the town, is a good deal older (seventy-eight) than he looks (fifty-five?). His life is a story of rivers and brooks, pack-horses, howitzers, and freight trains, and of the church in which he serves, along with his wife, Margaret, as chief caretaker. When our church roof began to leak, and our bishop suggested we apply for a loan from the diocese, I was delighted to learn that the application process required vicar and warden to travel south to Woodstock, Vermont, to meet with a finance committee. This meant I had the rare opportunity to take a little road trip with Tom, who views travel away from Island Pond with about as much enthusiasm as most dogs view getting a bath.

It also meant my having the perverse pleasure of taking the quintessential Island Ponder to a town about as far from Island Pond as one can find on anybody's soul map of Vermont. Vacation home for the Rockefellers, Woodstock is a village of picturesque brick and white New England houses, posh little shops, golf balls, and Republicans. When a candidate for bishop of Vermont was once asked how he, a New York City priest, could adjust to the needs of a rural diocese, he replied: "I know Vermont. In fact, I've spent my summers in Woodstock for years." Needless to say, he failed to win the mitre, but the joke he told without meaning to will be around for a long time.

Tom and I arranged to meet early in the morning in the parking lot at church. We would travel down in his car. As I expected, he was waiting for me when I arrived. He always is. Every Sunday he is standing by the church basement door when I drive into the parking lot. He pokes his head out and calls, "Do you want to come in this way?" Sometimes I've fancied that he will let me into heaven just like that. Tommy and Margaret can be counted on above all others to show up every Sunday, and on those rare oc-casions when neither is able to come, special arrangements have to be made for unlocking the church, for turning up the heat, and for preparing the altar—all of which they make. I remember once driving to church in the worst winter storm of my experience, when the roads were varnished with ice and it was treacherous to exceed fifteen miles per hour, arriving to find Tommy seated in the pew nearest the door, in his habitual brown suit and white shirt, and in case he was needed outside, his worn work jacket and striped railroad cap. "I don't think anybody else is coming," he said.

The only exception to this fidelity, in Tom's case, are two Sundays in November that fall within deer season. On those days Tom presides over and cooks for a campful of hunters. It is a matter of speculation among the remaining parishioners whether he actually hunts, but this is not a question anyone feels like asking. For me those two Sundays are a short church season almost as clearly defined as Lent or Epiphany. They are the Tommy-less Sundays. They raise the question of Christ Church's future when the last of Tommy's generation has died. They raise the question of my own ability to last the entire funeral service in the likely event that Tommy dies before me. Most of all, they raise the question of Tommy himself. Like the conventional seasons of the church year, the Tommy-less Sundays focus my attention on a mystery. In this case, why does Tommy come so faithfully to church?

One could answer "habit," but how did the habit begin? One could answer that Tommy's wife, who was an Episcopalian before he was, simply tows him along—but why has she been so successful here and found him so utterly untowable in other respects? The fact is, I haven't the slightest idea of what, in specific, personal, "existential" terms the church means to one of my most faithful parishioners. I have never heard him utter a single religious sentiment. Only once did he tell me something remotely of that kind: he was tempted to chew somebody out, or cut some corner, I forget how, and he said, "But I thought what you would say." Strangely, as much as I was flattered to think I had influenced a decision in favor of Christianity, his revelation wounded me somehow. The thought that I had played any part in his conscience was "too much"—I can't explain what I mean, perhaps for the same reason that I am as yet unable to ask him to tell me the story of his faith.

Stories of his life's doings, however, are another matter. I was prepared to hear as many of those as I could get on the ride to Woodstock and back. And perhaps in the stories lies a key to unlock at least a chamber or two of his great, mysterious soul.

The road itself was a prompter. At one sharp turn over a bridge, he recalled an accident he'd had when he and a buddy were returning from a trip to a New Hampshire department store to buy hard candy and phonograph records. "I told the salesgirl down there I'd buy every record she could sing. You wouldn't believe all the songs that girl knew!" They'd hit the bridge, and the steering wheel had come off in his hands as records and pellets of hard candy flew all over the interior of the car. And that wild ride recalled several others: the night before his wedding day when he'd stood on his head on the running board of a moving car, only to have the frame break, leaving him to limp alone in the pitch dark until his fellow riders noticed he was gone; the supposedly tame bear he'd tried to ride in a diner lot with the urging of several friends, who probably didn't need to urge him much. Had he heard the call of the Gospel as a kind of dare or bet? I wondered. Would he have gotten out of Zebedee's boat and gone off to be a fisher of men in the same spirit as he'd gone off as a boy to help tote logging supplies to the lumberjacks deep in the woods, or as his father, also while a boy, had worked the passage over from Wales to Canada—because something to do is better than nothing, because life is for those who "give it a try"?

His life had been one of hard work, and I was amazed at how nostalgic he seemed for much of it. When he was first married, he had held three jobs. During the day, he worked on the railroad, where he would be employed most of his life. At night he was projectionist at the movie theater, sometimes going by horse-drawn sleigh to show more movies in neighboring East Charleston. After the last film, he spent the remainder of the night and the rest of the early morning stoking the furnaces of an apartment building and napping when he could. Of course, the number of jobs was dictated by the Depression, not by desire. Yet he spoke of the work, especially the railroading and projectionist work, with as much delight as he recounted fabulous fishing trips along the Yellow Branch and Black Branch rivers northeast of Island Pond. On the railroad he'd repaired tracks, dynamited ice jams, operated the locomotive turntable, cut block ice from the pond in subzero weather, and later worked as a foreman for "bridge and building" construction. "I loved railroading," he told me.

Probably the rigor of his work contributed to Tommy's robust health—in the face of some unusual health habits. He has not seen a doctor since World War II, and claims not to have taken a glass of water in thirty years. His most recent ailment, a sty, was cured by pulling a wedding ring hard over his eyelid. Obviously, he has not come so faithfully to church because it is the conventional way to heal the soul.

In the stories of Tommy's working life I was surprised to hear how often he had worked for free. He once helped to haul a boxcarload of slate up the hill from the tracks to the Catholic Church, not because he was then a Catholic or there was a dollar to be made, but because the job simply needed to be done. I've wondered sometimes if his characteristic refusal to "keep score" on himself or on others is not also a source of his health. So many of us seem to make ourselves sick over an obsession with "bookkeeping." And I wonder, too, if this trait has something to do with the Gospel, if it was influenced by "the good news" of the Kingdom, or drew Tommy to that message.

I don't mean to suggest that Tommy is a meek, Franciscan soul with no sense of his own rights and prerogatives. I said he doesn't seem to keep score, not that he is above settling a few. He told me of being left in charge one night of a bootlegger's twenty-five-cent bottles of beer. Bootlegging, of course, was once a thriving business in the Northeast Kingdom; much of the alcohol came over the border from Canada. The bootlegger claimed he was going to pick up another fellow so all three could attend a dance, but it soon became clear that Tommy had been abandoned with a washtub full of commission sales. No doubt the load was worth something; twenty-five cents was at that time the hourly wage of a grown man in Island Pond. Tommy dutifully sold the first bottle for a quarter—then gave the rest away one by one. The next day when the bootlegger called him aside to "settle up," Tommy handed him a quarter. "You mean to tell me you sold that whole tub of beer for twenty-five cents!" the man fumed. "That's right," Tommy said, "and that'll teach you to never leave me stranded like that again."

It was a revenge story bound to appeal to anybody who's ever been "stood up," but what struck me was its juxtaposition in Tommy's "résumé" with hauling slate for the church roof, the way the sacred and the profane often seem to mingle in his life and in the tales he loves most. In Portland, Maine, while tearing down grain elevators on a railroad dock, he'd seen a Catholic priest pass by every day, walking his dog. "Good morning, Father," he finally called down.

"Good morning, my boy," the priest replied.

"Father, what kind of dog is that you have?"

"My boy, this dog is a son of a bitch."

He loves to tell that story, I think, because it surprised him, because it has an earthiness to it, and because on reflection the priest had simply told the truth.

For the same reasons, I often find Tommy on my mind when the lectionary provides me with a parable to preach on. So many of the stories he told me on our trip, and had told me before and has told me since, have a parabolic quality: they are about wonderful gains and drastic losses, about unusual venturings forth, about the strange joy glimpsed as it quivers beneath the surface of the lives our sins would render dull and dead. One day Tommy's father, who also worked for the railroad, went to the bar after work and then to the market, where he bought an enormous watermelon. To his great chagrin, he discovered he was in no condition to carry it home. So he hired a horse-drawn wagon, at double the cost of the melon, called to "Bucko" his son, then a boy in knickers, to "hop on," and together the father, the boy, and the watermelon rode home through the supper-hour town. Did King David himself ever ride through the streets of Jerusalem in such glory as these two rode home with their prize?

When Tom and I arrived in Woodstock, the scene we found there was a perfect image of what many people associate with the Episcopal Church. A group of well-educated white men in tweed jackets greeted us and each other with unobtrusive courtesy. I think a few were even smoking pipes. The room at the church in which we were to meet looked like a miniature dining hall from an English university. The stereotype persists, not least of all among

Episcopalians themselves, in spite of the fact that the worldwide Anglican communion is now less than half white, and the equally startling fact that in the United States we constitute a majority in only several communities, all of which happen to be Indian reservations. But there we were.

As I look back on the day, I remember Thomas Merton's ascerbic account of his boyhood encounter with the Church of England as recorded in *The Seven Storey Mountain:*

> His [the school chaplain's] greatest sermon was on the thirteenth chapter of First Corinthians—and a wonderful chapter indeed. But his exegesis was a bit strange. However, it was typical of him and, in a way, of his whole church. "Buggy's" interpretation of the word "charity" in this passage (and in the whole Bible) was that it simply stood for "all that we mean when we call a chap a 'gentleman.'" In other words, charity meant good sportsmanship, cricket, the decent thing, wearing the right kind of clothes, using the proper spoon, not being a cad or a bounder. . . .
>
> The boys listened tolerantly to these thoughts. But I think St. Peter and the other Apostles would have been rather surprised at the concept that Christ had been scourged and beaten by soldiers, cursed and crowned with thorns and subjected to unutterable contempt and finally nailed to the Cross and left to bleed to death in order that we might all become gentlemen.

There is much truth to what Merton had to say. And though Americans in the Episcopal Church have done a good job of substituting the banalities of the encounter group for those of the cricket green, the spiritual dwarfishness Merton attacked persists. I will never make the claim that Jesus, were he on earth today, would join my church.

Nevertheless, having granted Merton his point, I must go on to discuss a point of my own, one that I think Merton missed, and one that has something to do with that tweedy gathering of diocesan officers, with Tommy, and with this book. Behind the sermon Merton so despised is a belief that "ordinary human decency," if not the whole of the Gospel, is at least an essential part. What, after all, is the message of the Beatitudes, if not that true blessedness consists less of the grandiosity of "sainthood" than of the commonest forms of human emotion and kindness: mourning, meekness, forgiveness, peacemaking?

Attached to that first "article" of faith—in my very unofficial interpretation—is the belief that "ordinary human decency" can exist by nature and by grace in a good number of ordinary human beings. I think I see that belief implicit in the works of a number of writers who have been touched in one way or another by the Anglican tradition. You can find it in Dickens, Walton, Dorothy Sayers, Willa Cather, James Agee, George Orwell, and C. S. Lewis. You can find it, as traces of a sadly lost faith, in Swift. You'll not find even a trace of it in Nietzsche, of course, but he helps clarify my point with his contemptuous reference to "shopkeepers, Christians, cows, females, Englishmen, and other democrats." In any case, it may have been what Merton's chaplain, Buggy, was trying to get across.

Perhaps the best place to look for both "articles" of faith—the beatitude of ordinary decency, and the *possibility* of its existence— is in the life-and-death struggle with Puritanism from which the Anglican Church managed to emerge battered but still on its feet. In response to Calvin's teaching on the "innate depravity" of human beings, my church postulated a few kernels of "innate decency."

Now I am willing to grant Calvin his point, no less than I am Merton's. In fact, I think that in any argument over "innate depravity" the burden of proof falls on those who take exception to it. History is a persuasive debater for the Calvinist side. But if I were to assume my share of that burden of proof, then someone like Tommy would be my first supporting example. And if I were compelled to argue that Jesus just *might* have been "one of us," or at least could have stomached us, it is our reverence for the "ordinary" decency of a Tommy that I think would have attracted him. It is that quality, after all, that he went looking for on the shores of his own Island Pond: a fleshy, generous quality found in people who believe in hard work, and in fair play, and in casting one's lines into the deepest water to see what's there.

The first people who said "yes" to Christ were bait fishermen.
And they played, just as they fished, for keeps.

With Tommy like a bodyguard at my side, I sat down to make a
case for our loan. Actually, I had no good reason to be nervous.
The gentlemen on the committee did have a number of blunt
questions to ask—some on the viability of the parish itself—but
with Bishop Kerr to back us, the loan seemed assured.

If my bait-fishing warden can serve as the unofficial "representative man" of my church, then the bishop is the official one. Children in Episcopal confirmation and Sunday school classes are all
taught that "Episcopal" comes from the Greek word *episcopus* for
"bishop." Our denomination identifies itself as a worshiping community that has bishops. In my experience at least, this identifying
function seems to take priority over any hierarchical one. The
bishop is not so much "the boss" as the witness—or as I say above,
the "representative man." Now, finally, with the consecration of
the Right Reverend Barbara Harris, we also have a representative
woman. Like Roman Catholics and Orthodox, who do not as yet
have women bishops, Episcopalians believe in the doctrine of
apostolic succession: that bishops stand in an unbroken line of
continuity—one bishop literally laying his hands on the next, the
next on his next, and so on—from the Apostles to the present.
The bishop's main job, if he or she is doing it, is to shepherd the
people in that original apostolic faith, and to do so in times and
places the first Apostles never dreamed of. The bishop proclaims
the Resurrection, I was taught, as one who "has it from a reliable
source."

In regard to the characters in this story, if Bishop Robert Kerr
told me there was a Resurrection, and he did, I believe it. In many
ways he was one of the most reliable and attractive people I have
met in the church, or anywhere else. At the time he urged my
parish to apply for a loan, he was near the end of his time in office,
and also, though none of us (including him) realized it, near the
end of his life. As far as I could see, mortality seemed interested
in little more than his hearing and a bit of his hair. His main interest
then seemed in leaving his diocese in good order when he retired.

A part of that goal was a wish to do right by the more far-flung parishes of the northeast corner of the state. He was acutely conscious of the perception of his church as an institution governed by southern gentlemen, "southern" in this case meaning south of Montpelier. To some extent, he probably shared the perception. When the time came to choose his successor, he urged me to see to it that my parish assumed the full weight of representation to which it was entitled. "I fear," he said, "that in the last election the southern part of the state got its way too easily"—something to that effect. Several minutes passed before I registered that "the last election" was his own.

I wonder what Bishop Kerr would have said in response to what I've written above about my warden and about the religious tradition to which we belong. I know he was fond of Tommy. Tommy was equally fond of him; in fact, sensing the bishop's concern that we get our loan approved, Tommy took some pains to put him at ease. "Don't worry, Bishop," he told him, "if the diocese can't come up with the money, we can always raffle off a couple of pints of liquor." Yes, I think he would have agreed with me on Tommy. And whatever he had to say about my thoughts on ordinary decency and ordinary human beings, I know he would have instantly classified himself among the latter. When someone asked him how a meeting of all the country's bishops had gone, he gave the cryptic reply, "We are all very ordinary men."

On the surface at least, Bishop Kerr was an ordinary man. Homely in his rhetoric and unremarkable in his appearance, he gave one the superficial impression of unvarying ordinariness. The only outward exception was his voice. I am a collector of voices—and the bishop's voice will always be among the rarer objects in my collection. Even people presumably less fixated on voices than I agreed that Kerr was born to be a bishop by right of his voice. The best I can do is to say that his voice was that of a male lion with his great clawed paw resting as delicately as possible on the arm of a couch as he proposed marriage to a dubious lamb. I confess that sometimes when I am in the shower and grow bored with singing the name "Leah" and trying to make myself sound like Roy Orbison, I simply repeat my own name and try to sound like the late bishop. "Garret . . . Gah-ret"—somehow it restores a sense of purpose. "Garret, Father Castle has many talents, but record-keeping is not one of them. Will you please see that this service book is kept up to date from now on?" "Garret, that was as well-prepared a class of confirmation candidates as I have ever seen. Well done, Garret, well done." "Garret, your wife and daughter are tired, and it is late. Go home."

Of course I'm talking about more than a remarkable set of vocal cords. Voices, like the people who own them, have bodies *and* souls. And there was a definite soul within the bishop's voice. We sometimes talk about a writer's voice, E. B. White's voice or Eudora Welty's voice—we mean the integrity of a persona as mediated by his or her words. There is a religious counterpart to a writer's voice. Jesus spoke of it in his figure of the Good Shepherd. "When he has brought out all his own, he goes before them, and the sheep follow him, for they know his voice." I felt I knew the bishop's voice; somehow I had heard it before, and I responded to it. It did not always speak to me, or to me alone, of course. But even when he addressed his wife as "sweetie," which he always did, often to the surprise of a few bystanders, it seemed to speak to me of the sanctity of human tenderness. And when I asked him the vocational question I had once taken to a monastery, I finally heard, in his voice, the clear answer I had so wanted to hear then. "Garret, perhaps you shall seek Holy Orders. In many ways I hope you do. But my advice on the matter is this: Avoid it if you can. Seek to be ordained if you have the feeling that God has brought you to your knees, and left you no other choice." When people ask me, as they so often do, if I ever intend to "go all the way," I usually quote the bishop's advice, adding, "I guess I'm still on my feet."

Once a year the bishop visited our parish. People will remember him, if they remember him for anything, as a tireless traveler within the Diocese of Vermont. Unfortunately, he had no affection for road travel itself. He saw it as "wasted time." I sometimes imagine him resolutely folding himself into his nondescript midsize car, setting off on yet another hundred-mile trip, his vestments and crozier in the trunk, his stalwart "sweetie" at his side, but lacking the consolation of a four-speed shift or rock and roll. How often does sanctity manifest itself as this awful, prodigious plodding forward? In that regard, I also think of Samuel Issac Joseph Schereschewsky (yes, that's his name), a lesser known figure on the Episcopal calendar, also a bishop, who spent much of his life in almost total paralysis, typing his translations of the Bible into Chinese dialects with *one finger*. Perhaps true extraordinariness consists of the way one faces the horror of certain duties that are as absolutely ordinary as they are absolutely essential.

Though the driving may have been an ordeal for him, the bishop's visitation was always something special for us in Island Pond. For a parish with no liturgical frills, no smells or bells, often no music, not even a "real" minister, the sight of a fully vested bishop with mitre and crozier walking solemnly down the aisle retains its ancient excitement. And in a parish isolated both in a rural community and in the late twentieth century, the bishop's visitation retains its ancient necessity as well. Our little church is no less fragile than the first Christian footholds in Corinth or Ephesus. We need the reliable witness; we need the reminder that we are not alone. When the bishop called out "The Lord be with you," again in that amazing voice, I knew the Lord was.

His preaching was solid, sober, and to the point. It sometimes brought me to the verge of trembling, paradoxically because it was so direct and simple. Had he but once said, from the pulpit, that the church needed more priests, I might very well have found myself "brought to my knees" on the spot. What he did feel the church needed, and American society needed, was a good dose of liberalism. He said so, and in so many words. Bishop Kerr was a liberal in the classic sense of a principled, learned person ready to yield ground or resources to whatever appealed to those principles or that learning. I know it hurt him that "liberal" had become a dirty word both with some "progressive" activists and in the general mood during the Reagan Presidency. Still, he held fast to what he regarded as "the tradition." One of his favorites among the Church Fathers was Clement of Alexandria, who had tried to promote Christianity while assenting to the best of the pagan world. Clement was one of the first authors he commended to me in a wonderful tenure of book-lending that concluded with his taking me into his ceiling-high library just before he retired and saying, "Take whatever you want, Garret." Then it was my poor Ford Fiesta, filled to capacity with books, that was almost brought to its knees.

Of "liberal" issues, the two on which he preached most tirelessly were the new Book of Common Prayer and the ordination of women. Both had happened during his episcopacy; in fact, he had ordained the first woman priest in New England. He seemed to feel it had been his special historical task to stand behind both changes and then to spend whatever energy he had calming down the people upset by them. I'll only add that sometimes being a liberal is a damned thankless job. I wish he had lived to see the consecration of Barbara Harris as the Episcopal Church's first woman bishop. He would have applauded it—and her. But then, he might have been tempted to ask, in view of the rising defiance of episcopal authority by militant supporters and would-be saboteurs of women's ministries, whether the Church had at long last elevated a woman to the episcopal throne, or merely lowered the throne.

In any case, he fought a good fight—doggedly, and without getting, or seeking, much glory. In the end I think he was tired out by all of it, by the visiting, the bickering, perhaps even by the repeated reminders that he and his fellow bishops were "very ordinary men." But any weariness I detected in his voice only served to make it dearer to me. When the committeemen in Woodstock finished with me, they turned to him and asked, for the record, what he thought about the loan.

"Gentlemen," he began—and I wish Thomas Merton could have heard that despised word in my bishop's voice—"gentlemen, you know where I stand." We always did.

Another project in Island Pond to which the bishop also gave his nod was a lecture series on Christian mysticism. He liked the idea as soon as I proposed it, and probably my wish to please him helped me to overcome my tendency to procrastinate, and get it done.

My reasons for wanting a lecture series on Christian mysticism, aside from my own interest in the subject, were several. First, I was impelled by a little of the chutzpah that possesses most people who undertake "cultural" projects in depressed or rural areas: I was throwing down my gauntlet to those who would say, "Christian mysticism in Island Pond! It will never fly." Second, I was convinced it *would* fly, and needed to fly. Along with what might be perceived as the spiritual hunger of the general population, we in Island Pond are sitting in the midst of a counterculture population with spiritual interests all its own. Those interests often incline toward the esoteric. And therein lay my third reason: I wanted to show those disaffected with the "established church" the breadth of the tradition they were rejecting. Granted that Christians are not sole possessors of the truth, let us be clear about the truths they *do* possess.

And so with the bishop's blessing and suggestions I put out the call to men and women, ordained and lay, throughout the diocese who might be interested in doing a lecture for us. Many of those who responded, while having explored some of the less-traveled regions of spirituality, had never been to Island Pond. So here was yet another good reason for the series: we could put Island Pond on a few more personal maps. If I say so myself, we assembled an impressive series. There were lectures on Thomas Merton, the Desert Fathers, Evelyn Underhill, contemplative exercises, psychology and mysticism, Julian of Norwich, and icon painting.

In spite of his unwavering attendance at all church services, Tommy did not come to the lectures, not because he had a bone to pick with the mystics but because the lecture series belonged to the class of evening events, which includes concerts, town talent shows, and American Legion dances, and which Tommy generally keeps away from. Nevertheless, he did see that we had everything we needed at church, he did go in his railroad cap to hang up mysticism posters around town, and he was quite interested in hearing about the turnout when we launched the series with a lecture on Thomas Merton.

Even I was amazed at the number and variety of those who came, and of the revelations that came with some of them. There were two men from the Community Church. We had asked as a goodwill gesture if their print shop would take the job of doing up our posters and programs, but they had politely declined. Nevertheless, here were two of them. This was the first time, to my knowledge, that any of their number had set foot inside Christ Church. One of them told me later, rather superciliously, that he'd found the lecture "entertaining," and that interest in monasticism and in Merton was "on the decline." But apparently the interest, in his case at least, had not declined so far as to disappear.

There was also one of Island Pond's wealthiest and most prominent men. It turned out he had read every book by Merton in print. I had several times shaken his hand at well-attended funerals and civic functions, never guessing that this gregarious businessman and I shared such an interest. A young farmer from Quebec had also come to hear the talk. Later during the question-and-answer period he spoke of his wish to find parallels for the strange "awareness" he had sometimes experienced while riding his tractor. As with the businessman above, I wondered how many people had driven by that farmer's field in summer, never guessing that the man on his tractor was tedding hay in the midst of the Cloud of Unknowing. How little we see of our neighbors—and that, for me, is as "mystical" a realization as any. We are like tourists in Bethlehem, remarking that we might be better able to appreciate the spectacular star if it wasn't for some brat hollering in a stable.

As I had hoped, at least one person came down from what remains of Earth People's Park in Norton, just this side of the Canadian border. Probably the most notorious of the Kingdom's communes, it was reputed to be a "wild place" in the early seventies. Someone had even been murdered there. Our guest was harmless enough, however. A middle-aged man in shabby clothes with a slight resemblance to Allen Ginsberg, he told me after the lecture that he had taken "a lot of acid" at one time, and that he had also spent some months with the Community Church in town, but was "not ready" for their life. A year or so later he would become convinced of the need to defeat the Equal Rights Amendment in Vermont. To the naughty pleasure of those of us who supported it, he haunted the anti-E.R.A. booths of fundamentalist women at country fairs. At the time of the lecture, though, he seemed less sure of things. He was just another mystery, seeking some answers in the mystics.

Not everyone who came to the lectures was a seeker, of course. There are those who seek nothing but confirmation of their own biases. The visitors from the Community Church probably belonged to this category, though they said nothing during the talks. The "Sufi" from some distance away was more vocal. He had once met Merton, he said, and told him to his face that *The Seven Storey Mountain* was "the biggest phooey," adding for Merton's consolation that this was "okay" because Merton had "needed to write it." I wonder what the man would have said had he met God.

Perhaps the most interesting person I saw at the lectures had come with me in my car. The way we met was nearly as interesting as he was. I was hanging a mysticism poster one evening outside the West Burke General Store and Taxidermy. Though it stocked X-rated videos and seemed to do most of its business in milk, soda, and beer, it was at that time a stubborn holdout in the dismal transformation of general stores to brighter, more streamlined "convenience stores." There were benches by an old wood stove where people sat and talked in winter, and a bench for warm-weather talking outside on the porch. In addition, the store's second business meant that its walls and counters were decorated with examples of taxidermy, including some novelty pieces like the deer's behind, the joint-smoking weasel, and my favorite, the woolly trout ("The winters get so friggin' goddamned cold up here," etc.). When I went to hang my poster on the bulletin board outside, there were two men in feed caps sitting on the bench. One of them wore a long macramé belt hanging down his leg, which I took for one of those hippie touches, like Willie Nelson's braids, that often seem to be an inexplicable part of redneck chic. I recognized him as the new part-time clerk and felt I ought to ask permission before tacking up the poster. Frankly, in spite of the lecture series' missionary purpose, I was hoping that I wasn't going to be asked to explain Christian mysticism or *which* Island Pond church I came from to these two guys at nine-thirty at night. Taxidermy's a nice thing to look at, but I had no wish to join the display.

"Yeah, you can hang the poster," the clerk said. "I saw one of them the other day." Oh, boy, here it comes, I thought. "I was a little disappointed you didn't have anything on the Jesus Prayer. I was happy about the icons and patristics, though."

It is scenes like these that make me glad I write nonfiction. I could never come up with them on my own. The Jesus Prayer consists of the silent repetition of "Lord Jesus Christ, Son of God, have mercy on me, a sinner." Also called "the Prayer of the Heart," it has been practiced by monastics of the Orthodox tradition from at least the fourth century. The prayer was first given exhaustive treatment in the *Philokalia*, a Greek anthology of spiritual writings initially published in 1782, and was popularized in a nineteenth-century Russian devotional novel called *The Way of a Pilgrim;* in America, a century later, the prayer occurs in J. D. Salinger's *Franny and Zooey.* The store clerk knew of the prayer because as a teenager he had left West Burke, Vermont, and attached himself to an Orthodox monastery in Texas. He was back home to decide his next step, one that he felt would include sharing his Orthodox faith with others. The belt at his side was in fact a rosary, with which he counted off his repetitions of the Jesus Prayer, thousands each day, as he rang up live bait and salami grinders beneath the icon of the woolly trout.

He didn't have a car, so I offered to drive him to Island Pond for the lectures that especially interested him. He was a bubbling fountain of details and anecdotes about a religious tradition with which I have long been fascinated, and to which my own denom-ination owes a number of debts. At nineteen, he was amazingly conversant in theology—and orthodox with both a capital and a lower-case "O." A long white beard would not have made him any more Orthodox. He told me of St. Seraphim, and how the Russian Church had opened his tomb by the river to find it redolent with the fragrance of blooming roses. He told me of the dreadful Or-thodox Lents—no meat, no fowl, no dairy products, and scarcely any fish, oil, or wine for forty days—befitting a tradition that was suckled in the Levantine deserts, but also befitting its festive East-ers, and its magnificent weddings, where bride and groom are crowned as the king and queen of creation; here is an engine that must be powered by a terrible furnace. He told me without the slightest hint of skepticism about weeping icons, and about the golden domes of Russian Orthodox churches polishing themselves miraculously in defiance of weather and atheistic communism. He spoke so convincingly that I have wondered if someday the weathered copper shingles of Christ Church might shed their green tarnish and shine like God's new pennies in the sun. As it is now, they're blowing off—or vibrating off with the striking of the clock—and Tommy dutifully picks them up and stores them away for a time when we might have enough money to hire a steeplejack to nail them back on. But there is Providence, too, in the fall of a shingle.

When my new acquaintance wasn't working at the General Store or practicing the Prayer of the Heart, he was visiting with kids in town, trying to persuade them away from alcohol and drugs, or saying Orthodox liturgies in a local meeting house. The Unitarians, God bless them, were unorthodox enough to permit an Orthodox service or two to be held in their sanctuary. Since the time of our lecture series, he has moved on. He still sends me the newsletter he edits for an Orthodox society in Massachusetts. I rarely find time for more than a cursory skim of its articles, but I do think of him often. I think of him saying his rosary; and I imagine him working somewhere in one of those "convenience stores," which are in some ways the true churches of America. In answer to the questions "How does one redeem time?" and "How does one face the terror of existence?" they offer the answers of beer, grade-B videotapes, and a sign over the gas pumps proclaiming "self-service." And yet, if you have trouble serving yourself, there is a young man in a feed cap who will come out to the pumps to help. He wears a funny macramé belt at his side, and his lips move silently, unceasingly, on behalf of himself and the whole world. The Calvinist in my soul must never forget that he is a part of the picture, too.

It occurs to me as I look back over my catalogue of lecture participants that nearly all of them were men. Well, all of the oddest ones were. The most committed, on the other hand, were women. One woman, who probably could have matched St. Teresa for sheer determination, lugged her sleeping toddler and a cumbersome tape machine to almost every lecture. And of course the members of the Ladies' Auxiliary of Christ Church, who come to every church function bar none, were also there. Ranged in a row across a single pew, they were usually the first to arrive.

It is common knowledge that a number of churches, American and English, black and white, Episcopal and otherwise, are maintained and attended largely by women. And I fear we often betray our bias by asking why the men are missing rather than why the women are there. I have asked the conventional question, too. Sometimes I've felt that the absence of men is traceable to our categorization of religion as a strictly emotional phenomenon, and our definition of women as largely emotional (and thus inferior) creatures. I've even wondered if the masculinity of Jesus and the male bias of our liturgical language are not, ironically, reasons why heterosexual women "worship and adore" more readily than heterosexual men. In other words, I've wondered if a greater harmony between sexual orientation and spiritual orientation is offered to the majority of women than to the majority of men. Feminists are in the forefront of arguing for more feminine imagery and a more inclusive set of pronouns, but it may be that men need them more than women do. I only wish that both the feminists and the nonfeminist men would at least *ask* each other if that were so. It would be worth an oceanful of Maundy Thursday foot washings if they did.

In the case of Christ Church, the missing-men question is probably not so complex. Given the older ages of many parishioners, and the differing mortality rates for men and women of their generation, a lot of the "missing men" are simply dead. But what of the faithful-women question that is too seldom asked? Is that not a mystical subject deserving of our contemplation? I am hesitant to venture an "answer." If there is one, I think it should come from one of the faithful women themselves. I do not think the answer or answers can be given entirely in the reductive terms of feminism, or any other -ism, even mysticism, but I have come to recognize that we men who love our churches are doing them a disservice if we think feminism is only the concern of a radical fringe. I'll never forget a visit to one of the oldest women in my parish, as serene and devout a Christian as ever I've met—and one with an ever-searching soul. "Why," she asked me with an earnestness that would have brought tears to the eyes of an icon, "are all the saints and important people in the Bible men?" I was glad that she had the opportunity to hear a brilliant woman lecture on Julian of Norwich and her *Revelations of Divine Love,* one of which affirms "Verily, God is our Mother."

Anyway, thanks to the faithful attendance of women like her, and the interests of an odd assortment of others, the lecture series on Christian mysticism in Island Pond, Vermont, was deemed a "success." Of course, the real success of this or any other "church function" is hard to gauge. We do our work; only God knows what we accomplish, if anything at all. When I asked one of my parishioners what she thought of the lecture series she replied, in words that echoed Meister Eckhart's meditations on the Godhead, "I'm completely lost!" I've always regarded this woman as something of a saint. If she was "lost" in a lecture series on Christian mysticism, then I say she was lost the way an immigrant wandering down Broadway and asking directions to Manhattan is lost. By God's grace may I come to be as lost as she.

I fear that Tommy was feeling even more lost in Woodstock. I have tarried for a while, and I should not leave him stranded there. (I remember what happened to the bootlegger.) We got our loan. We said thank you and good-bye to the bishop and his men. We stopped briefly in the church before we left. Out on the sidewalk I was inspired with a bit of mischief.

"Tommy," I said with as straight a face as possible, "it's still early, and here we are in Woodstock with all these little stores. Would you like to do some shopping?"

He looked at me as though I'd just said, "Let's go over to Montpelier and moon the legislators when they go to lunch"—except that he probably would have regarded that as much less of an outrage than what I'd just suggested. "No," he said, "do *you?*"

"No, no, no, I just wanted to make sure you didn't."

"Well, no," he said, somewhat relieved. "I don't want to do any"—he forced himself to say it—"*shopping*. I will buy us a beer though."

So we pulled into a convenience store, then headed home, with a loan for our leaky church roof, a prayer for the parish, and two cold Genesees for our thirst. And that, I guess, is the story about Tommy and me and our trip to Woodstock.

But what is the story really about? Surely any reader who has borne with it all this way has a right to ask. Well, it is about bishops and bait fishermen, spirit and flesh, and the Word made flesh. It is about the voices of two good men, and the still-to-be-won struggle for the voices of women to be heard. It is about mysticism and orthodoxy, ordinariness and sanctity, unity and diversity, and about the intersection of all these things in a design that looks to me like a cross.

It is, above all, my descriptive "amen" to the sentiments of a man I met in a monastery some years ago, who told me that although his church was as corrupt as the Mafia, he would gladly die for that church. I would die for it, too, not because I am so brave or the church is so needy, but because without it I could no longer say what living meant.

My Friend Pete

*"Why is light given to him that is in misery, and life to the
bitter in soul . . ."*
—JOB 3:20

Peter Hughes was an old man I visited in a nursing home for three
years, and with whom I had almost nothing in common. The sixty-
year difference in our ages was but one example. He loved sports;
I had little interest in them. He was conservative; I was—not
conservative. He wondered how days could be so long; I wondered
how they could disappear so quickly. I was bound by strong ties
to my family, my work, and my church; he often felt himself utterly
alone. Eventually, none of this really mattered. The main lesson
of my association with Pete was how few of the reasons we give
for a friendship really matter. For in spite of all that could not be
spoken or shared between us, he was my friend. And though his
death relieved me of a sometimes burdensome duty, it also removed a mainstay from my life. I sometimes feel as though I shall
never recover the emotional stability I knew as a result of visiting
Peter Hughes.

I first heard of him not long after I had started my ministry,
when Father Castle announced to me one afternoon in the St.
Mark's kitchen, "We've got a problem in Island Pond." There was

an old man, an Episcopalian, living in a nursing home on the Canadian border. Father Castle had buried the man's wife, and visited him thereafter, but it had been awhile since he had seen someone from the church. His affiliation, such as it was, was to the Island Pond parish. Therefore, he was "mine."

Soon afterward I drove north to the home. My first impression of Peter was of a corpse. He lay back in his recliner, mouth agape, eyes open but unintelligible, skin pale, skull prominent. I was always very conscious of his skull—especially when we became close enough for me to kiss the top of his bald head. Years after our first meeting, when I brought my young daughter to meet him, we found him again cadaverously napping, and she sprang back from him in tears. I don't wish to be unkind in my description, but it will always remain in my mind that the first time I saw Pete he looked like a corpse, and the last time like a crucifix.

He wasn't especially friendly on that first visit. Perhaps he felt insulted that the church had sent him this young deputy instead of someone "real." Perhaps he wondered what exactly was the point of my coming if I was only going to reappear sporadically after that. At the time, I felt he resented my intrusion, and that may have been a part of his cold reception as well. Anyway, I tried to be as deferential as I could, and I resolved to let some time pass before I returned. A month or so later I was surprised to find him irritated at my taking so long to get back.

Very soon, my visits to Peter came once a week and assumed a pattern consisting of a little conversation, a few chores, and a prayer. At least once a month the prayer included Communion. The chores, such as changing his razor blades or reading his mail aloud, were mostly things the nursing home staff could and in the past did perform, but Peter came to prefer my doing them. It gave him greater independence, and it enabled him to request a few other favors, which according to the home's regulations were *his* duties. I seldom minded. The chores insured that our visits would not be empty or purposeless. They stimulated the conversation. They took care of my end-of-day restlessness. (I usually visited after work and before supper.) They enabled Pete to give the orders to the young man who came to give the blessing. In many ways they were the sacrament of our relationship.

One of the first chores Pete gave me, and one that was never finished for long, was to adjust his sitting arrangement. Pete spent most of his day seated in a well-worn recliner by the side of his bed. On the other side of the chair was a lamp, and behind the chair, an end table that held his cache of cookies, soda crackers, and Christmas candy. In front of him was a coffee table where he kept his nail clippers, pens, and most important pieces of mail.

The goal was to arrange all of the pieces so that Pete could get out of bed without falling over the chair, so he could recline in the chair without knocking over the cache, and so he could reach the coffee table with his feet and still have the items on it within reach of his hands. This was not always easy to do. There was also a walker he needed to have close to the chair yet "out of the way." And I have not mentioned another end table, on the same side of the bed, which was not in the way of the coffee table and the chair, but which limited the space for moving the table that held the cache. All of the furniture and the items upon it were necessary to some aspect of Pete's physical or psychological comfort—so there was no question of moving any piece to another part of the room. I knew; I'd asked.

To do the rearranging it was necessary for Pete to get out of his chair so I could move it, and then to sit back down to check my work. This made the process painfully slow. Usually we could succeed, or at least make the situation "a little better," but the furniture would soon be out of whack again. Comfort depends on a certain precision, on a certain alignment between one's buttocks and the seat of a chair, and when we must rely on someone else to seek that precision for us—someone who must act as the interpreter between our body, our wishes, and the rest of the material world—we experience a terrible isolation. At least that is what I imagine, sitting here at my desk, shifting without thinking in my chair.

Pete liked to listen to the Red Sox on the radio, and another of my chores was to find the station that broadcast their games. Here, again, were isolation and grief. His eyes were too feeble to see the dial. His ears were not the best; neither was the radio. And he lived amid the static of a rest home full of other people's electric appliances and other people's right not to have their sleep disturbed by a roaring home run. Somewhere out there Boston was playing New York in an impenetrable haze. What in hell was going on? And if Pete touched the dial after I had set it, he almost always lost the station.

Quite soon Pete entrusted me with the management of his checkbook, which was a great and hilarious honor, since my wife and I have hardly bothered to reconcile a bank statement in the fifteen years we've been married. Fortunately, my inexperience was compensated by Pete's almost phenomenal ability to do arithmetic in his head. He had once worked as a ticket-taker on the railroad, handling cash under pressure. So with me fumbling through old checks and muttering, "Let's see, I'm sure I remember . . . ," and Pete declaring things like "Fifteen seventy-six take away 337.94 equals 1238.06, doesn't it?" (it does), we got the statement checked. Then I'd write his checks for rent and for small pharmacy bills not covered by Medicare and his two health insurance policies. Though Pete never ran out of money, he was always relieved when his bills were paid and the bank had said—and I had confirmed—that he was solvent. This sense of security was periodically shaken by hospital statements that would arrive as often as a computer could manage to spit them out. Sometimes it seemed that twice a week there would be a statement containing line items equal to a year's salary of Peter's working life. Each one was printed with the ominous reassurance "This is not a bill." For someone in Pete's situation, this was like receiving weekly mailings picturing a coffin and the caption "You are not in this box."

One of the checks I always wrote was for "cash," and with it I bought small articles, Lifesavers, aftershave lotion, postage stamps, as Pete directed me. But the bananas, I had gotten him to agree, would be my treat. Pete's craving for bananas was legendary around his home and mine. In the case of at least one nurse at the home, "alarming" might be a better word. My own feeling was that given Pete's age and circumstances, I would have cheerfully delivered him a case of Canadian whiskey once a week had he requested it, though for that item he'd have had to chip in. I took some bananas almost every visit. I do think they became part of my signature at the nursing home: I was the young man who showed up once a week with a black prayer book and a bunch of bananas.

On one banana run I had an experience that I regard as one of the important parables of my life. I was standing with my Chiquitas on line at the supermarket behind one of those people who seem to think they're at a bank instead of a store. She must have had three checkbooks, and if I tell this story enough times she'll have a little metal changemaker on her belt, too. I shifted from one foot to the other, sighing, glancing at the clock. I wanted to catch Pete before supper. No doubt I was feeling the tiniest bit righteous because I was about the Lord's business on behalf of my old man, who needed his bananas and was looking forward to my company, and here was this loser buying an armful of trivial odds and ends and taking my precious time to screw around with her appallingly disorganized finances. When I finally got through the line, I watched her walk to her vehicle—feeling that same uncharitable impulse that makes us glance at the driver of a car we're passing just to "get a look at the jerk." She got into the driver's seat of a van marked with the name of a local nursing home and filled to capacity with elderly men and women who had no doubt handed her their wish lists and checkbooks as soon as she'd cut the ignition. Never in all my times of transporting bananas did I feel so much like a monkey.

I would eventually get to Peter's room, and kiss his head, and hand him the change from his purchases, and put new blades into his shavers, and ask the ritual question: "Would you like a footbath?" The answer would always be yes, but I would always ask. Jesus taught by example that we should always ask people before doing the favor we know they want us to do, so highly does God regard their dignity as persons. "What do you want me to do for you?" "Master, let me receive my sight." Well, what else would a blind man want? Nevertheless, Jesus first asked.

The footbath routine was our answer to Pete's unceasing worries and complaints about his sore and swollen feet. Pete felt that if he could have them in warm water on a regular basis—even more regular than bathing and the staff's indulgence allowed—he'd be in better shape. At my suggestion, he had written a check to a medical supply store for a rather deluxe electric footbath.

It was not until I knelt to take his feet from the water and dry them with a towel that the staggering associations, the giddy sense of privilege struck me. I tried not to think about what I was doing—but for a Christian, that was as easy as a biographer of George Washington trying to take a nonchalant boat ride across the Delaware. In the end I may have been saved from pride or anxiety by noting that the Lord had performed this task without the benefit of a two-speed vibration massage. As is often said, technology prevents us from making vital connections—sometimes for our own good.

With Pete's puffy feet in the water, I read the week's mail. Sometimes I couldn't make out the handwriting, but in the case of proper names he could usually guess the one intended, and so we got through. His daughter, a soon-to-be-retired computer analyst in Arizona, was his most faithful correspondent. She usually wrote him a brief note several times a week. She wrote about the weather, family news, events of her day, often writing "Ha!" to reinforce when she was joking. Pete would give a faint echo to her "Ha"—I never felt I read it with the right intonation—so it was a "Ha," then a "Humph," then on with the letter. Every one seemed to give him pleasure. Some he asked to hear twice. Reading these bits of her day, I wondered how many others in his family vowed to write him "a real letter" someday and never did it. In other words, I wondered how many were like me.

He also had a grandson, a medical student, who like his aunt sent a postcard or a brief letter faithfully. Mostly he told of the stage he was at in his studies and reminded his grandfather to keep up with his exercise bike. (Pete claimed he did, though I never once saw him on it.) I'm sure the grandson's own letters must have struck him at times as paltry, dull, even vain—yet he kept at it, like a routine on a bike, and as a result his grandfather had one more threadlike link to the larger world. It may be that few of the prescriptions he scribbles will effect as much healing as those postcards he disciplined himself to write in between lectures, labs, naps, and dates. I always felt a part of me saluting him; anyway, for his pains he often got a mention in the prayer Pete and I said together.

When chores were done, we talked. I soon had a stock list of questions with which to start the conversations: how were the feet, the appetite, the night's sleep, the Red Sox? For his part, Pete also had a list: the job, the wife, later the child. In such conversations, an elderly person is at a disadvantage because so much less appears to "happen" in his days. But if he is willing to touch on the past, then the advantage is his.

We did not talk often about Peter's past, however, because a good deal of it was painful. Like many of his generation, he had gone to work early; his first full-time job paid seven dollars a week, five of which he paid for a room. He then went to work for the railroad, quitting it in the hopes that he could get rich raising silver foxes. For a time it looked as though he had made the right choice. For at least one year in the 1920s he claimed to have made thirty-five thousand dollars. He met the Crash of '29 with an optimism I would have called uncharacteristic—meaning, of course, that I knew the man long after his hopes had been crushed. He bought while others sold, believing the bad times would soon pass. After five years of staying precariously afloat, he sank. Foxes worth $125 he sold for sixteen dollars. He lost his house and car. His wife, whose worsening health had required the hiring of a private nurse, died soon thereafter. Peter placed his children with relatives, moved, and eventually found work with Sears, Roebuck. He re-married, to a diabetic who would lose one of her legs, "so twice in my life I had to hire a woman to help out my wife."

He had three children by his first wife. The eldest, his namesake, "a big strong boy, all heart," had at one time been a candidate for a Montreal professional baseball team. An illness postponed his trying out, so he joined the military instead, where he was eventually killed in a jeep accident. Pete also had a daughter, whom I've mentioned, and a son who practiced medicine in New Hampshire. That son had four children, all of whom were doctors or about to become doctors, and three of whom had married doctors. In Pete's view, this preoccupation with medical school and medical practice had left too little time in his family's life for him. When I enrolled Pete in the Talking Books program of the Vermont Association for the Blind, he told me in a tone of profound disgust, "No books, please, about doctors or love."

A family with "eight doctors!" was a favorite example in any discussion of Peter's favorite theme: that the world had gone stark raving mad. "Crazy," he'd say, shaking his head. The salaries awarded to professional athletes? "Crazy." On one occasion he told me that much of the world's power was being seized by women, the French, and the Roman Catholic Church—a not-so-groundless theory in his immediate section of the global lunatic asylum, owned and operated by French-speaking nuns. When I announced to him that my wife and I were expecting our first child, he said with ingenuous melancholy, "Well, I hope it's a girl, but it will probably be a boy."

"Why do you say that?" I asked.

"Because a boy has nothing in this world."

With the election of Madeleine Kunin as the first woman governor of Vermont, the writing was indelibly on the wall.

"A woman for governor!" he gasped.

"Yes, Pete, but she may be a very good governor."

"Well, she may be a very good governor, that may be true, but a *woman!*"

I can't remember if I told him that I had voted for her. The question of "how much to say" is one that all people of conscience face, certainly one that many ministers face. If your concern is to speak with righteousness on every occasion, the problem is relatively simple. But if your concern is to help others find righteousness for themselves, if their progress is more important to you than your own "record," then the problem is harder. And I found it hardest of all when Pete turned from the crazy world to the seeming absurdity of his own existence.

On *that* score, he had two main questions. First: "What have I done to deserve this?" I felt competent to answer that one, only because Jesus had answered it first. "Who sinned, this man or his parents, that he was born blind?" I could tell Pete, with Scripture to back me up, that he had probably done nothing to deserve virtual blindness, great loneliness, and afflicted feet. The Lord himself had suffered—undeservedly.

It was the second question—in terms of frequency, Pete's first question—that I stumbled over: "Why does a person keep living? Why do you just go on and on? What is the point?" Of course there are ready-made answers to that, the catechism's or Camus's. But I knew, even as I told Pete about "God's unseen purposes" and about the value of each person's unique struggle in God's plan, that this was a question he had every right to ask and that no one but God could answer. I remembered Job's three friends, who had said all the "right" things about God and yet failed either to please God or to comfort Job because they had tried to contain the one's mystery and dismiss the other's anguish with words.

In the end, I realized that if I had an answer to Pete's question, the answer was I myself—not anything I knew or represented, but the part I played in our relationship. Why does a person go on living? Because he has a friend. Because in friendship there might be a reason—even a joy—in living. Nothing I could say was of much consequence. But that I was by his side to say something, and that I cared enough to say something, perhaps was. After all, God had given a similar "answer" to Job. His closing remarks about ostriches and sea monsters don't stack up to anything like a satisfactory answer to the question of human suffering. But his sudden, solicitous appearance—that is another matter. And perhaps that is a part of what Jesus meant when he said, "I am the way, the truth, and the life," that the "program" is a *person*. And perhaps each of us, to a much lesser degree, is a way and a truth as well as a life.

At any rate, as time went on, my response to Pete's big question became less theological. "I know God loves you," I'd tell him, "and I love you, too. You're my friend, and I'll never leave you alone." Then the question seemed to fade, to become less frequent, and less anguished when it arose.

Of course, the pain itself did not fade. And I was visiting but one old man in that old-age home on the border, so close to Canada and to eternity. I shall never forget an afternoon when I left Pete and was accosted by one of his neighbors on the second floor. She

was a classic French-Canadian grandma, *mémé*. There are Jewish
grandmas and Italian grandmas and German grandmas and African-
American grandmas and indisputably French-Canadian grandmas,
and they are all wonderful because they are grandmas, as opposed
to mere grandmothers, but they are all distinct, and sad, too, because a whole culture is dying with them—and this was a French-
Canadian grandma, dressed so like a "*bonne femme*," warm as cocoa
and nervous as a small bird. We had exchanged *bon jours* before.
She motioned for me to enter her room—I did not know why.
Perhaps she had a snapshot or a new piece of handcraft to show
me. Perhaps as a French Catholic female she felt an obligation to
warn me before the Big Takeover. I was startled when she seized
my hand tightly and squeezed it till the "How are you?" dissolved
in my mouth. She was crying. "I've lost my son," she said. "Life is
hard."

I don't know at what point Pete became more a friend than a
parishioner. I don't know when the reciprocal benefits of our time
together began to dawn on me. But I soon recognized that he was
every bit as much a special person in my life as I was in his. Never
mind that I had many more friends than he did, that I was simply
around people more than he was. That was the point, not beside
the point. How refreshing it was, after the day's long and intricate
dance around the unexpressed needs and subtle feelings of so many
partners, just to sit beside this affectionate old crank with sore feet
and talk about baseball games and bowel movements. There's a
Zen poem that goes:

> A sudden clash of thunder, the mind-doors
>   burst open
> And lo, there sitteth the old man in all his
>   homeliness.

I think it refers to the Zen goal of *satori,* or enlightenment; in my
Judeo-Christian mind-set I had taken it as a reference to God—
but in the time I knew Pete, the poem often came to mind as a
description of the experience of opening his room door at the end

of a working day, a day so often spent in a turmoil over trifles, and seeing him seated there like Ultimate Reality itself, lonely, dear, and enduring.

Here was yet another case in my ministry where the presence of God seemed very strong, where the sense of "two or three gathered in my name" came home to me. I began to place at least one petition on my own behalf in the prayers we always said at the end of a visit. In the crudest terms, I guess you could say that I felt the "magic was strong" here. Perhaps a worthier observation is that to put some of one's own cargo into a prayer said with and for someone else is to let it be known, both to that someone and to God, that we take the prayer most seriously. Throughout my wife's pregnancy I asked a blessing on her and the baby whenever I visited Pete. Sometimes I'd repeat the prayer silently downstairs in the little chapel, with the Blessed Virgin looking down, I almost thought with pity, on this poor Prot who wouldn't dare ask of her the favors she intended to give anyway. Once when we'd said the "Amen," Pete looked up and in a tone of voice close to annoyance he said, "You forgot to pray for Kathy." Back we went and finished the job.

Kathy and I would have liked to invite Pete over for supper, but our second-floor walkup apartment—Pete always took the elevator at the home—made a visit there out of the question. He also claimed to have no inclination whatsoever to go to a restaurant. One day I asked, "What about going just for a hot dog?" There were three foods Pete felt were lacking in sufficient quantity at the home: hot dogs, spaghetti, and, of course, bananas. We'd taken care of the third. How about one of the others? Pete said that might be nice.

I had forgotten since the time when my grandmother was alive that few older people will go out, even for a hot dog, without getting pretty dressed up. When I arrived for our first outing, I was impressed. Pete had chosen his best plaid pants and knitted pullover, both warm for the season but not for him, and with the help of the sisters had made himself quite dapper. He finished the look with a snap-brim canvas "motoring cap." Unfortunately, the motor car was less impressive than its elderly passenger.

At the time I was driving a VW Bug with an odometer on its way to the second turnover and a Darth Vader–looking flexible steel hose snaking up between the two front seats to defrost the windshield in place of the ducts that had long ago rusted out behind the rocker panels. As the holes in my muffler farted a desultory drum roll, and the bevy of French ladies who sat by the door nodded and smiled a look of "Ooo, *qu'il est beau,*" I maneuvered Pete and his walker to the car, folded him in, deposited the walker inside the lobby, and with Pete in his cap looking for all the world like Toad in *The Wind in the Willows,* we waved to the girls and headed for the open road.

Happily, my glove compartment lid had been designed to serve as a snack tray. Pete's coffee and french fries fitted there neatly while he held the hot dog in his hands or his lap. We tried a few places until we found the one whose wieners had "the right skin," and we went to that place until Pete grew too feeble even for such a modest adventure as this. Sadly, that was around the same time I began driving a slightly more comfortable used car.

As we grew closer, we became a small part of each other's holidays. I ran a piece of pie up to him at Thanksgiving. We exchanged Christmas presents. One year Kathy and I bought him a new bathrobe, which seemed to please him a great deal, and which he promptly had folded and put away, no doubt saving it for an occasion that required a superior bathrobe. Pete did all of his shopping by catalogue, usually from one of those gourmet cheese, cookie, and smoked meat varieties that come around the holidays, and I still recall the pleasure of being handed the catalogue and the checkbook and told, "Pick out what you want for Christmas and spend _____ dollars." I declined enough to be polite, but never so far as to be a fool—or to lose my shortbread and fruitcake. To tell an old man "You ought to save your money instead" is to suggest he can't please you and to pretend he won't die.

I noted with interest and some concern Pete's agitation over the Christmas holiday. His daughter came from Arizona and did up his Christmas cards months in advance. I mailed the cards at the beginning of December, and helped with the shopping. Until both were done, Pete knew no peace. I think it would be fascinating to see listed in order of increasing tenacity those attachments we abandon before death; I have a hunch that in many cases, long after vanity about our appearance, modesty, punctuality, even jealousy have departed, a man or woman will still worry about Christmas. I have little patience with those who would debunk Christmas for its pagan origins and trappings—it's a small step from trouncing paganism to denying that "the Word was made flesh and dwelt among us"—but there *is* something almost satanic in the way it grips us. The Old Boy has fastened his suckers on this feast like a lamprey—all the more proof to me of its true holiness. Anyway, for poor Peter it was like a bitter penance.

The annual Christmas party at the home was yet another looming preparation. Each resident was sponsored by someone who served as his or her guest and who provided the gift that Santa Claus would give to the resident at the party. I think that Pete always feared I would be unable to sponsor him, thus making it necessary for the sisters to supply some philanthropic stranger in my place. Status in a nursing home, as nearly as I can tell, is measured by the number of people you have in your life who visibly care whether or not you're still breathing. A bogus sponsor meant zero status. I told Pete I'd come.

I would love to know, and someday if I can I will ask the angels, who was feeling less festive on the way downstairs to those parties, Pete or I. But the truth is, we both warmed up to them once we were there. Pete began absently, or wryly. Once he turned to me and asked, "I wonder where the music man is."

"Music man?"

"Yes, there's a man here at the home, he comes to all these things and plays all kinds of instruments, piano, accordion—the music man."

"Well, Pete," I said, "maybe he's away."

"I sure hope so."

But with a little time and a cupcake in his stomach, Pete began to half sing, half groan a carol or two, and he always smiled when Santa handed him his gift—in part, I'm sure, because that meant he was free to go back to his room whenever he wanted—but also because at ninety years old he still liked getting a package from

Santa. For my part, the party provided plenty of stimulation—far more than many intentionally "stimulating" parties that inspire little more in me than a headache or the wish to be struck dumb. For one thing, there are few sights as charming and silly and "out of this world" as that of nuns having "such a good time." If they are not truly the brides of Christ, some of them are at least his kid sisters. I also liked the choir, which was made up of strong male and female voices who could sing in French and English. If anyone can tell me of a sight and sound in which spirituality and sensuality are as equally mixed and overpowering as that of mature men and women singing alleluias, I'd like to know what it is. Finally, I was a great fan of the Santa Claus, who shook his bell and ho-ho-hoed and swaggered about like something right out of a medieval feast of fools. With a few double-entendres and no tacky vulgarity, he was a thoroughly Saturnalian Nick.

I would leave the home hoping that the party had exhausted Peter enough for a good night's sleep. Along with his sore feet, sleepless nights were a major discomfort in his life. He dozed during the day. After supper he claimed he could barely keep his eyes open, so he was usually in bed by seven, sometimes earlier. At around one or two in the morning he woke up, and spent hours awake. It was "terrible." Exhausted by morning, he'd begin to doze—and so the cycle started again.

At first I suggested that since he didn't have a schedule to keep other than his mealtimes, perhaps he should just accept the sleeping pattern he'd fallen into. No, he couldn't accept it—he wanted to sleep through the night. Of course, that's not as stubborn as it may sound. Anyone who's worked a night shift will tell you that one hardly ever gets completely used to it; there remains that sense, biological as well as social, that night is for sleeping.

We decided to try a "cure." I would come to the home after supper and aggressively *visit* with Peter until late. By forcing him to stay awake until eleven or so, we'd force him to sleep until morning. Thus refreshed, he might take fewer daytime naps. Perhaps his whole routine could be bumped along to normalcy.

It was a long stretch. We talked, making each strand of conversation last as long as it could. We rearranged the furniture. I read to him. We listened to the radio. We broke banana together. I was sitting, as always, on the side of his bed, and I began feeling the urge to lean over on it—you know, just to change my position for a few minutes. Fortunately, Pete was getting the same idea, so he sent me home a little earlier than we'd planned. For a day or two, the cure seemed to have worked, but in a little while the old habits reasserted themselves.

Sometimes I think of Pete awake those nights, conscious against his will, while everyone around him slept. The border guards at their station down the hill had coffee and TV and the prospect of late-night drug runners to occupy them. Those few nights I kept watch with Pete at my home miles away were filled with some purpose—student grades to be tabulated, a nursery to paint—and they were barren enough. But to sit or lie bored and restless, and relatively healthy—I know where Pete's cry of "Why do you live?" came from. And he *wanted* to live; I realized that whenever a symptom hinted at death. He just wanted to be spared facing the darkness, the blankness that half of any civilization is erected to obscure. Perhaps God created the universe itself for the same reason. I always get a kick out of those who talk about abandoning the hope of heaven in favor of "embracing the eternity that lies within the now"—and the grin on their faces when they say so. (Salinger: "you know the way Orientalists laugh.") They seem to forget about nursing-home insomniacs and dry-cleaning drudges and gang-rape victims who know all too well about how eternity can exist within "the now." God save us from such nows!

I soon found out that nothing infuriated Pete like an attempt to comfort him in his ailments by comparison with those "worse off." In a sense, he asked for it by looking in dismay at those better off. His neighbor Vera, for example, was nearly as old as he, and she could see and hear and sleep at night and "jump all over the place." Well, I'd never seen, nor could I imagine Vera *jumping*. But she was in good shape, no question. "Yet look at the people twenty years younger than you, Pete, in wheelchairs, out of their heads, incontinent." Wrong approach. "Don't tell me about those worse!" he'd exclaim. "I feel bad for them. I wish they didn't have the problems they have. But that doesn't help *me*. That doesn't do a darn thing to make me feel better." Of course, to a large degree he was right. Admonitions about starving children in Africa have yet to make a helping of canned asparagus any more palatable. Pain knows no perspective but its own. Still, I felt a duty as Pete's friend even more than as his minister to steer him away from despair, to urge him to put resolution in the place of self-pity, to tell him, as Shakespeare's Malcolm says, "Dispute it like a man." Perhaps, though, I needed more often to remember Macduff's reply: "I shall do so. But I must also feel it as a man."

Once Pete turned on me in bitter anger. "You're with all the rest of them. You're working with them against me"—something like that. "Them" meant the sisters at the home, one in particular, who Pete felt never regarded him with enough compassion. Now it's possibly true that many nuns, with their belief in asceticism and the redemptive power of suffering, can sometimes be less than sympathetic in the face of another's pain. I've heard the complaint that they counsel patience more readily than they dispense aspirin. But I felt that Pete was often unfair in his complaints. I also felt that I was in some ways a cause of that occasional unfairness: I was the "better" alternative, the personal, the Protestant, the male caregiver. And it stung me to be accused in this way. I threatened to walk out. "Well, don't do that," Pete pleaded, and I immediately felt ashamed.

Looking back, I see that in some ways I was guilty as charged. No, I had never conspired against him. But I had sometimes talked about him with the nuns as if he were our troublesome charge, rather than my good friend. To be sure, I did so to further his interests, to catch some flies with honey, to give his helpers some of the recognition he was a bit stingy in giving. But there is an undeniable two-facedness to that kind of politics. One of the hardest things for a person to accept is that within a given set of circumstances he or she can be *both* "right" and still worthy of reproof. We can have done our best and still be short of the mark. Our problem is that we choose a relative good, but want it acknowledged as an absolute good. The hard words from Peter helped me to remember that the accessible commandment to "do justice, love mercy, and walk humbly with thy God" and the assertion "All have sinned and fallen short of the glory of God" are not in contradiction. To realize that is to be humbled—and to be free.

Things reached a point where Pete's feet and legs finally made good on their daily threat to fail him. He could barely move from one place in his room to another. One who knew his disposition might have been tempted to accuse him of mulish stubbornness. But that would have ignored all that Pete's mobility meant to him. In some ways his life depended on his feet. Like most homes for the elderly, Pete's was defined by its requisite level of care. To remain there, he needed to be able to manage his own hygiene with limited assistance, and to make it to the dining room under his own steam. Though there were canes and walkers aplenty at the home, no one I can recall was in a wheelchair. Thus Peter's feet, or rather his ability to stand on them, meant such things as a private room and bathroom as well as intangibles like status, familiarity, and independence.

Arrangements were soon made to move Pete to another home. I have since grown familiar with the place intended because of a parishioner who spent the last year or so of his life there. Almost none of the residents can walk. Hardly anyone seems to converse. One smiling woman wheels up and down the hall trying to exchange a few words in French with any willing passerby. Another groans incessantly, "Mother, mother, mother" in a voice that could be crying "My God, my God, why hast thou forsaken me?" You could stay away from that place for a month, a month that included ninety meals, sixty television programs, five movies, two novels, four church services, fifteen sexual acts, 125 pieces of mail, four paychecks, a haircut, an oil change, a game of basketball, and a twenty-four-hour virus, and return to hear the same "Mother, mother" as soon as you entered the door.

To the nuns' great credit, the arrangements were neither secret nor hasty. But within a week or so, Pete would move. At least I would still be able to visit him; in fact, the new home was even closer than the old. Our prayers together were a mixture of petitions that he be happy in his new home, accepting the move with courage, and a plea that even now he might be able to walk to dinner again. The former seemed like faithless defeatism, and the latter like a shameless instilling of false hope, but we said both every time we met.

One evening, before the supper tray arrived, and just as we had finished our prayer and our Communion, I asked Pete if he wanted to stand up. He did. And then—I forget exactly how we started or who suggested that we try—we left the room with Pete slowly, painfully trudging behind his walker. We finished the length of the hall. Then we entered the elevator. We descended, the doors opened—"Lazarus, come forth." We walked into the dining room and moved to Pete's place at the table, which had been ominously vacant for weeks. He sat down. I wish his senses had been better able to hear and see the stir he had caused: the pointing fingers, the nodding heads and smiles, the exclamations of "oh" and the murmurings of "miracle."

At this point, I think that Peter, who would have the use of his feet and an address at this home until the day he died, was mostly absorbed by how blasted long it was going to take some people to bring out his soup. But he grasped my hand tightly before I left and called me "my boy," which I guess by then is what I was.

We think of old age as living in the fear of imminent death, but I do sometimes think it is more a living in the fear of going to the hospital. I have taught young people for ten years now, and I have heard every kind of excuse for avoiding homework or staying home from school. But does any kid avoid an education as much as some elderly people avoid the hospital, or even a visit to the doctor if they suspect that will lead to the hospital? In their ears, the name of that place is like the roaring of white water: you enter and are pulled against your will to catastrophe. And I have to admit that I have seen few old people go into a hospital who did not seem to grow instantly much worse before they got better—if they got better at all.

Pete went to the hospital several times, for falls, stomach pains, disorientation, and he did come home after every visit but the last. The local hospital to which he was taken is the most humane I have ever seen, and if an ambulance ever picks me up, I pray to God it takes me there. But when I visited Pete in the hospital, I felt I came face-to-face with one more instance of humankind's propensity to create its own hell. By demanding perfect and eternal "health"—the Black Mass version of eternal life—by deifying physicians and then through our lawyers, crying "Crucify them!" whenever they prove to be less than gods, we have created an institution for healing from which we cannot be set free until every possibility is considered, every unknown probed, every method attempted. "Blessed are the merciful, for they shall obtain mercy"—and oh, what a curse it is to be at the mercy of our own merciless sense of entitlement.

Pete would go for one battery of tests after another. The tests did not always seem to be explained to him, or if explained, he could neither hear nor understand. One method of interrogative torture is to hood the victim, not only to conceal the identity of the torturer but also to increase the victim's terror. Nature had hooded Pete in almost complete blindness and partial deafness—not to mention an elderly layman's ignorance of his rights and his technological world—and in such a state Pete was taken upstairs, or downstairs, or wherever they took him to have his bowels explored, his skin pricked, his bony loins laid on the X-ray table, all with that kind and condescending reassurance that, I imagine, more than any pain, would drive me mad.

He pleaded with me to get him out. He was "playing on my sympathies," someone said. Of course he was, and what of it? When you are trapped and afraid, you play on whatever instrument will unlock the door. I called his doctor and expressed my concern. But not being a relative or clergyman, I needed as much time to answer "Who are you?" as to ask "What are you doing?" I called Pete's son, but he seemed to identify as much with the trials of the attending physicians as with the anguish of his father.

Even now, I find myself prone to ludicrous fantasies in which I enter the hospital with a shawl, a warm hat, and an automatic weapon, bundle Pete up, wheel him out in a spray of bullets, and head for the Canadian border—stopping just long enough to grab a hot dog on the way. I wonder, too, how many nurses and technicians and, yes, doctors might have had the same fantasy. We are all tangled in the same web. The wages of sin are death, and the fringe benefits are cynicism and a divided self: "Speaking professionally, as a doctor instead of a man . . ."

But as I said, Pete came back. As far as I know, little was ever resolved or repaired by the visits, but after a few days it was "okay to go home," and by that time one is so relieved that the question of why he left home in the first place fades in importance. Then came the list of expenses that was "not a bill."

In time I had my own brief stay in the hospital, as a labor coach, and it was a good deal happier than any of Pete's recent visits. In spite of his "grim" prediction, we had a girl. I drove to see him shortly after she was born, and it touched me how truly overjoyed he was by the news that mother and child were well. He was less enthusiastic about our move to a house a year later, in part because the price and the mortgage were "crazy"—and for once I agreed with him—and in part because we would now be twice as far away from him, more than thirty miles. But I assured him he would see me as much as before, and he did.

One thing the house meant was a ground floor, and so we could at last give Pete the third food he craved: spaghetti, with "a lot of meat in the sauce," and in this case prepared by an Italian cook to boot. Our memories rearrange chronology, and in mine this dinner comes almost immediately before his death—though in fact there were some months in between. He could see none of the things that we were still so proud to show our guests—the maple trees, the chunky beams, the old wide floorboards were lost on him—but he stepped up into the mudroom without too much trouble, and he ate his spaghetti with abandon. "Delicious!" he said with the same emphasis as "Crazy!" And so it was. After dessert he maneuvered to the couch, and I sat on the rocker opposite with the baby in my lap, who gawked at Pete, then grinned at me, fascinated as little children always are by the sight of an adult falling asleep. She soon followed, then I, and my wife came in to note with some amusement the soothing effects of her good pasta. Perhaps I distort the memory, but I think I rested then with that death-in-life sense that something important has been fulfilled, some sought-after plateau has been reached, where we know God's own sabbath—we see "it is good."

I always leave my name and phone number tacked to the bulletin board of any hospital room in which a parishioner stays, and on Pete's last visit to the hospital—he was simply "not feeling well at all"—I made a point to ask the nurses to call me if Pete was in trouble. I had always promised him that if he needed me I would come, and I needed the nurses' help to keep my word. I did not have to establish credentials with them; they knew from my visits and from the patient's own mouth that I was Pete's man, "my boy."

The call came when I was at work, about ten miles away. I drove as fast as I dared to the hospital. I came to find Pete in the middle of a fatal heart attack. His first words to me—and virtually his last—words I shall cherish until I die, were "Where the hell have you been?" He would not "go gentle into that good night." "I am right here," I said.

Pete was in considerable pain. I talked to him. I said prayers with him. When he fell into unconsciousness, knowing that the ear can often hear until the very end, I whispered the "Our Father," and my love, into his ear. By this time there were two of us in attendance, myself and a matronly nurse whose eyes were as moist as if she'd never seen a death or as if she'd known this one patient all her life. We each held one of his hands. I could not get over her tenderness for this perfect stranger who was only one small part of her messy job. I knew she would stay there until it was over; I may have needed her to do so more than Pete did.

I had never seen anyone die. He was at that point where the body inhales, pauses as if unable to decide or remember what to do next, then exhales utterly—"the last," you think—then after another pause, inhales again. "See how the body fights to go on living," the nurse told me. She spoke as if it were a beautiful and pitifully frightened animal resisting the hands that worked to free it from a trap.

With one terrible, final inhalation that raised Pete's neck and the hollow of his back from the bed, he opened his eyes as wide as I'd ever seen them and turned his head slightly on the pillow, as if scanning the heavens for some sign—and it was then, with the force of a thunderclap, that I knew as surely as I know anything in my life, as surely as I know that I shall die as he did, I knew *who* it was I had visited, and given Communion, and told with incredible irony and eternal comedy that Jesus also had suffered. And as soon as I knew, he gave up the ghost.

I did not drive back to my job with thoughts as sublime as that. In fact, a lot of what I felt was sadly trivial, even a bit wicked. I had seen my first death, and was as pleased with myself over that as if I'd witnessed a solar eclipse or met Woody Allen. How many of my friends could say as much? The long drives to the border, made longer by the demands of a new child at home, were over now. And in a very short while I had to compose myself enough to teach *The Scarlet Letter*. Would I tell my students where I had been? Would I look sincere? Certainly I'd preach an impressive funeral sermon; its words were already forming in my brain.

But in that dross was something else, a thought no less trivial or self-centered, really, but somehow not shameful either. It has stayed with me ever since. It is, I believe, a gift from God and from Peter, and apparently I needed it more than I could have known or would have admitted.

I had made a promise to a friend, and by God—by God, indeed—I had kept it.

An Island Pond Funeral

Son of man, can these bones live?
—EZEKIEL 37:3

Once at a meeting of parish leaders, the priest in charge asked us to "go around the circle" and tell what each of our parishes did best. "We bury people," I said when my turn came. I did not mean to be entirely facetious. There are often more people in Christ Church for a funeral than for an Easter. In a town that has been so conscious of its own decline, the liturgy and pastoring that attend a funeral may well be among the church's most important contributions to the healing of the community.

Island Pond funerals have that formulaic quality we expect of rites in a small town. There is often a vocalist, usually the same woman. The American Legion, the Masons, the Eastern Star come as a body to honor one of their own. The flowers are often distributed afterward among the sickest and oldest people in town— I hope without a meaning parallel to that of catching a bridal bouquet. The body is buried on a gently sloping hill overlooking the pond and its island. If the death occurs in winter, the committal will wait until spring. On a warm Saturday in April, coffins get planted almost as generously as onion sets and peas.

When I first attended these funerals, Father Castle was the officiant. I assisted. The "more or less" of that assistance was determined, as usual, by Castle's discomfiting mix of fraternity and impulse. When the time came to bury Mart, one of the parish's most venerable patriarchs, Castle urged me to do a homily side by side with his. I had grown very close to Mart and his wife, Bea, and I had been the last visitor to see Mart before he died. I spent most of a school day trying to shape my "eulogy" and woke very early on the day of the funeral to finish it. But as we vested for the service, Castle said that he had visited Bea, and her endurance seemed limited. We had better stick to his homily, he thought. On another occasion, again just as we were vesting, he said, "So you're preaching today, right?" "What?" I sputtered.

It was no disaster. Castle simply gave the funeral sermon as he did all the others, without notes, seemingly without effort, and with a loveliness that had the naughtier among us imagining ourselves dead in order to catch some snatches of what he'd preach over our corpses. He was talented, yes, and perhaps inspired by the Holy Spirit, but he also had an intimate knowledge of two important things: the person he buried, and death. He was a good shepherd, one who knew his sheep by name, and as I have mentioned elsewhere, he had buried his own teenage son and namesake. I never met anyone who had attended that service who did not speak of it with awe. It happened before I came north, but the other funerals I saw Castle do sufficed to give me some idea of what that great, sad service had been like. Infusing his warm recollections of the person who had died and his faith in the Resurrection was the experience of having faced death in its most dreaded aspect, and having stood firm.

In contrast to him, I said my first burial services almost without the experience of a death. I am still a relative neophyte. All of my closest family, I am thankful to report, are alive. This inexperience, even more than my lack of ordination, has often made me feel a helpless amateur when I stand facing the casket and the mourners.

But that condition is not without its own special grace. Perhaps that is true of many "disadvantages." I have often said to my parish in Sunday sermons, Look to what you do have; God is able to "perfect his strength in weakness." In the case of bereavement, though I cannot say "I know how you feel," I can say "I can't begin to imagine how you feel"—in either case one has done the mercy of treating grief with a sympathetic truth. And like Castle, I preach as a pastor now, as one who knows the sheep. Since a number of these "sheep" have become my friends, I am able to speak of death with at least the mourning of a friend in my experience.

Often, however, I find myself standing in my vestments beside the open grave of someone I never met. Frequently that someone is an Episcopalian who died in another state, perhaps Florida, and has now come home to be buried. Just as often, though, that someone is a local person with little or no affiliation to a church. The family approaches me to ask if I would "say the words" before the grave is filled. I never refuse. I can never know how those strangers stood with God in their lives, or at the moment of their dying. In cases where their religious faith seemed tenuous, I sometimes ask the survivors who knew them best to look over the committal service, and to tell me what prayers, if any, would be an insult to their loved one's convictions, or to the God who commands that we be sincere.

Perhaps nothing speaks to me as eloquently as these burials for strangers about the kind of society we have become, about the kinds of "community" we have made—or failed to make. I think of the last act of *Our Town*, where the dead sit in their congregation on the hillside, and wonder how that scene would be written in our time. *Could* it be written in our time? I think of the Beatles' "Eleanor Rigby," and wonder how many of us who grew up singing that song will die any less lonely than she. Even Father MacKenzie will not know most of us. Will our far-flying mourners feel anything so much as awkward, standing among people they scarcely know, hearing words they scarcely believe?

Sometimes, though, I am also struck at a stranger's grave by how the Gospel can speak intimately in the absence of the familiar. I was called not long ago to do the committal for a young soldier who had been shot in an incident elsewhere in the country. I knew neither him nor his family. All his mother had to tell me over the phone was that he had been "baptized Catholic" as an infant. But in the tremor of her voice I found "the text" I needed for the burial. "There was a son," I began, "who was killed, and a mother who wept for him. The mother's name was Mary and the son's name . . ." I was accompanied by the soundtrack from a nightmare. A loud plane flew overhead, and a gravedigger at a neighboring plot turned his raspy truck engine over and over before it would start. Yet when the plane had gone, and the truck had finally pulled out of the cemetery, we were left in the peace of the wind blowing softly over the pond. In the same way, I suggested, faith might come to us if we were able to wait out the noises of our lives' profane distractions.

If I sometimes do not know the person I bury, there are other things I also do not know, of which death can make me acutely aware. I am often struck by how little I really know about human emotions, about my own parishioners, about Island Pond. I once buried a poor local man to whom I had taken Communion, and later visited in a nursing home. Before he went to the home, that is, when he was still conscious, he would tell me how he had gone as a boy in a horse-drawn wagon to the Episcopal church. "I always went to the Episcopal church," he would pronounce as if daring someone, at the risk of physical blows, to refute him. Then, when I left, he would repeat in the same tone, "You are always welcome here," as I gently pulled my hand from his unloosening grasp.

At his wake, I felt as though I had entered Island Pond by a different door and had come into an unknown room, the oldest room in the house, perhaps, but one hitherto closed to me. I felt I was meeting some of the frontiersmen who had hunted and trapped and skirmished with the St. Francis Indians around Island Pond when it was still called Random, long before the railroad and the mills arrived. On a bench at the side of the coffin, a small cassette player filled the room with country-western music and some Elvis Presley. A son of the deceased explained to me, "A guitar is closer to what my father was than a, if you'll excuse the expression, damned organ!" With his own hands, he had cut out a wooden heart and attached a metal plaque engraved with his father's name and below it the words "father, husband, woodsman." This rested on the inside of the open casket lid. He had also given his "wedding suit" so that his father would have something appropriate to be buried in. Another brother added that he and his family used to go to church, but had stopped because of remarks about their clothes. "Was it our church?" I asked. "Is it I?" the disciples asked Jesus, when he said one of them would betray him. Each of us has the doubt. No, it wasn't my church. But I think he felt I was missing his larger point. "Church is supposed to be about you and the Lord, not some fashion show."

In his complaint I heard echoes of the great "justice" passage from Isaiah that is read for Ash Wednesday:

> *Is this not the fast that I choose:*
> * to loose the bonds of wickedness,*
> * to undo the thongs of the yoke,*
> *to let the oppressed go free,*
> * and to break every yoke?*
> *Is it not to share your bread with the hungry,*
> * and bring the homeless poor into your house;*
> *when you see the naked, to cover him,*
> * and not to hide yourself from your own flesh?*
> *Then shall your light break forth like the dawn*
> * and your healing shall spring up speedily . . .*
> *And your ancient ruins shall be rebuilt;*
> * you shall raise up the foundations of many generations;*
> *you shall be called the repairer of the breach,*
> * the restorer of streets to dwell in.*

The prophet was speaking as much to Island Pond and to its churches as to Israel. Haven't many of us middle-class Christians been hiding from our own flesh? I prayed that God would help us to do better. And I pray that God will help us to recognize that "the other America" of poverty and estrangement described in Michael Harrington's book is always a local phenomenon; it exists as the other Washington, the other Montpelier, the other Island Pond.

At its deepest level, I suppose, it exists as the other Garret Keizer—the impoverished "other part" of every human being that allows injustice and loneliness to exist for the sake of its own greed and complacency. The unknown "other part" of someone is yet one more truth that comes home to me at the grave. Whether we bury a stranger or bury our own son, how much, in the end, did we know about his darker side? Sometimes during a funeral sermon I can almost feel some of the mourners saying to themselves, "If only he knew what I know—if only he knew some of the pain this 'devoted mother' caused in my life." But I am not the only one in the church who "doesn't know," and darkness is not the only thing unknown. Do the mourners know—and sometimes I go so far as to ask, gently, if they know—the sanctity or the struggle for sanctity of the soul we "commend to God"? Do they know with what childlike trust a grandfather took his first Communion in more than forty years, not even remembering what he should do with the wafer—how humbled and seemingly relieved he was when his wife said, "You eat it, Ethan, you eat it"?

Or did they know how Emily, so frail and small at the end of her life, though scores of living souls traced themselves from her—how she sat in her chair giving tangible reality to the old cliché about "the patience of a saint"? She was kind to all comers, to the nurses, to the demented residents of the nursing home who meandered into her room muttering bizarre announcements. In perfect possession of her mind, she watched the birds at the feeder for hours, yet accepted without protest when the curtains were drawn in front of this single pleasure so that her neighbor could sleep. How many assembled in the church knew how she had joked that God must have momentarily misplaced her, to have her live so very long, and how on the day of her death she lay in a fetal position on her bed, almost the size of a child, sighing "Father . . . oh, Father."

How many would know, could know, how at the end of her funeral, when all had left the church, I walked into the sacristy and took hold of the bell rope and whispered, "This is for you, Emily," and pulled hard, ringing the bell once—immediately after which the long rope snapped high in the belfry, falling in a coil at my feet.

One of the funerary functions I have sometimes been asked to perform is that of chaplain at the Island Pond Memorial Day parade. I accept with a mixture of satisfaction, embarrassment, and awe.

Satisfaction, because the invitation means that I have been recognized outside my congregation as a parish leader. It is true that when I introduced myself as "lay vicar" of the Episcopal church to one prominent marcher, he replied, quite innocuously, "Those poor people over there—they *still* don't have a minister!" So I'll say *mild* satisfaction. Embarrassment, because a part of the "recognition" is riding in a parade car next to that prominent man and in front of the town's two surviving World War I veterans. I feel like the dog in the manger. And awe—need I explain the awe? It is a sad thing to hear people apologize for surges of patriotic feeling, as if they were confessing an enthusiasm for lady midget mud wrestling. I suppose it is a hopeful thing, too, in that such feelings can at least be "confessed." One of my favorite quotations from George Orwell goes: "It is exactly the people whose hearts have *never* leapt at the sight of a Union Jack who will flinch from revolution when the moment comes." What prophetic words they seem when we look at the flag-burning sixties and at all of the callow flinching that followed.

I'm flinching, too. Each Memorial Day parade reminds me that a few more years have passed of putting off "the project": a possibly idiotic idea I have of approaching the Island Pond American Legion, or VFW, or even the Masons or Lions, and asking if I might come to give a brief talk about "the other America," or the other titles of Mr. Harrington's books, about apartheid or U.S. policy in Central America. I have already addressed my parish on some of these issues. But I have so far hesitated to take the next step, a small, gingerly step back over the wreckage of bad faith and bad moves and bad taste that all but destroyed any hope of a progressive student-worker coalition in America. I wonder who would be more taken aback, the audience or the incestuous Vermont Left, if a few ministers went down to the local Legion Halls to make a case for the legitimacy of revolutionary struggle in the Third World, and of the necessity for a parallel struggle in ours. The nineteenth-century Anglican F. D. Maurice would not have shaken his head at such a move; neither would Simone Weil. I also wonder what effect it would have if one, just one, Legion Post passed a resolution condemning U.S. intervention in Central America or simply calling for a raise in the minimum wage. Finally, I wonder if I write all of this hoping that one of the marchers in the Memorial Day parade will read of my desire and offer me the opportunity I am apparently too timid to seek on my own.

We assemble for the parade in front of the Roman Catholic church on the hill containing all three of the oldest churches in town. The American Legion, the Legion Auxiliary, the VFW, young men and women now in military service, the regional high school band, Brownies, Cubs, and Scouts are all there; a pack of streamered bicycles waits to form the parade's tail farther down the street. It seems to me that the plan for the parade, the order of marchers and the method for linking them up as the parade begins to move, is never completely clear in anyone's mind. I've found myself wondering if the D-Day invasion was much the same. Did the generals have it all planned to the last detail, or was there a "pretty good plan" that eventually was carried forward and even overridden by the sheer momentum of so many troops on the move? In any case, I feel a great relief, as a public school teacher, that this is one assemblage I have no duty whatsoever to organize or police. Though I lack a clerical collar, I try to look as other-worldly as possible whenever someone approaches with that incipient "Do-you-know-what-the-heck-is-supposed-to-be-happening?" expression on his face. Don't be silly; I'm a man of God.

In the last parade for which I was chaplain, I noticed a fair amount of revolutionary emotion among the members of the Legion Auxiliary. It seems that for a number of years the women's place had been directly behind the leading cars, where they had breathed carbon monoxide for the duration of the parade. In a voice that meant "We've had just about all the garbage we're going to take," and which I interpret as prophetic for all "ladies' aid" groups from chorus lines to convents, one woman announced that this year the Auxiliary would *not* march directly behind the cars. This, too, made me feel patriotic, with all of the Orwellian implications—and also glad that I was safe in the car. Our middle-aged driver turned to me and said, "The World War II vets are probably the last of the male chauvinists."

I fear he has too high an opinion of men my age, but my thoughts at this point in the parade were with his generation. I should probably be in a more prayerful frame of mind, but before the parade begins I am caught up in imagining what some of the men and women looked like more than forty years ago. I envision one of them, his arms just as muscular, but his tattoo newer, his stomach flatter, his hair fuller, albeit cut the same way, strolling into a USO canteen with a whistle and a wink to ask, "*Où est les dames?*" Or the handsome woman in her smart blue cape and hat with the flag balanced on her hip and her mouth as red as blood—I see her writing her V-mail or boarding a WAC plane or stepping to her machine at the Island Pond shirt mill, an image of what I remember one film critic calling "those magnificent lacquered virgins of the forties." This is the generation of Russell Baker, Rita Hayworth, Charlie Parker, Joe Louis, Jack Kerouac, Marilyn Monroe, and the mothers and fathers of most of my friends. All in all they were a fascinating, sexy bunch, with their wicked cigarettes and black coupés and black-and-white romantic movies. Their adolescence was called Depression and their young adulthood was called War; their world demanded of them an aggressive sobriety, which may account for the faintly boozy quality of so many of their heroes and recreation rooms. They came home from Europe and the Pacific vowing to be prosperous and independent, and investing so much hope in their children that they sometimes drove themselves or their children mad. Maybe the men are the last of the male chauvinists, and maybe they are simply the last generation of men to grow old openly admitting what they are.

Finally, the parade moves. The sidewalks and lawns are full of spectators with cameras and little flags. We pass by some of the

Community Church people, who sit placidly on the grass watching us go by, perhaps as a small gesture of solidarity, though the less generous part of me imagines at least a few of them absorbed in an apocalyptic fantasy in which they stretch out on the green pastures of salvation while the rest of us march and drive with our drums and flags down into the Lake of Fire. Yet nothing or no one looks incongruous to me during a Memorial Day parade. The most erratic behaviors, the most apathetic postures, the wildest getups all seem to confirm, in spite of themselves, a value worth fighting for. The First World War veteran now snoring in the backseat behind me is more moving than a gun salute or the sounding of taps—what grander gesture, what higher honor could we confer on the oldest of our warriors than to give him a nap in a car chauffeured through the pomp and brashness of his home town? The barbecuers and the sun-worshipers, the early tourists and the hung-over denizens of the old hotel hanging over the porch railing—the "ugliest" Americans are beautiful to me today. I am glad that soon the parade will stop, and that we shall pray; I need that moment to prevent this rush of feelings from degenerating into sentimentality or cynicism.

The first stop is my favorite part of the whole parade. We pause by the bridge over the Clyde River, which empties out of Island Pond, and which after very heavy rains has been observed flowing in the opposite direction! But it is flowing west when we drop the wreath into the water for all who died at sea. The wreath is made of artificial flowers, unfading and sadly human in their manufacture. It floats under the bridge and out of sight. I suppose there's always a peculiar thrill in letting something go into the elements, a balloon into the sky, a sacrifice into a volcano. A mental image of a fierce storm at sea, or of a thundering sea battle, juxtaposes itself with the calmly flowing river, where some of those we honor may have fished as boys and girls. It is there at the bridge, after I've said the "official" prayer and tried not to flinch too noticeably when the guns salute, that I am able to wake out of my fancies and approach the spirit of heartfelt prayer. To the God I believe can hear me before the world began, I offer a silent prayer for the young sailors who died before I was born, that in their moment of mortal terror Jesus came walking to them over the sea.

I hope that one day I, too, will be buried in Island Pond. I want to be carried out of the church from which I have led so many coffins, and I want to come out into the light, facing the island and the pond, and be taken to the cemetery overlooking the water from its western shore. I am sure that any other place on earth is just as good for rising from the dead, but this one is my preference. From here I would like to rise up with Mart and Bea, and Pete, and Emily, and Ethan, with the smells of just-abandoned dinners at the Buck and Doe, and the astonished cooks in their chef's hats and aprons, and sail above the steeples and the train station amid a chorus of alleluias and an undertone of joyful greetings and incredulous "You too's?"—even tearful "Me too's?"

Though there may be some whimsy in that vision, I believe the hope it embodies with all of my heart. I believe "We shall not all sleep, but we shall all be changed, in a moment, in the twinkling of an eye." And I also believe there are resurrections that prefigure the final one. To put that more specifically, I believe there can be a resurrection in Christ Church, in Island Pond, and in America. Actually, the worldly resurrection of a community is one of the Bible's most potent and prevalent symbols of spiritual rejuvenation. One could argue that in the Old Testament it is not a symbol at all, but rather a cooperative reality. The passage from Isaiah that I quote above says that when we stop "hiding from our own flesh" our "ancient ruins shall be rebuilt."

When the prophet Ezekiel is taken to the Valley of Dry Bones and asked, "Son of man, can these bones live?" he is being led to an understanding of the rebuilding of Israel, beginning with the refortification of Jerusalem. The revival of a town stands more solidly for the resurrection than the blooming of a lily—and I am not referring to those blasphemous "revivals" of urban neighborhoods called "gentrification," which stand as Dracula fables in relation to the rising of Christ. Sometimes as I walk or drive through some of the lowlier back streets of Island Pond, or when I stand in the evenings on her corners, I hear the prophetic question as though it were addressed to me and anyone else within earshot: "Son of man, can these bones live?"

Ezekiel's answer is a very good one. "O Lord God, thou knowest." So God knows for sure if all the resurrections I hope for will occur. But I think I do know this: that if they occur, no one person, church, race, class, gender, or generation can bring them about. They will have to be accomplished by the grace of God working through the cooperation and mutual recognition of all the people marching in and watching the Memorial Day parade: the devotees of Yahshua and "the real Northeast Kingdom hairy bears," the aging veterans and the aging hippies, the members and the strangers, the women and the men—and in some mysterious way, the living and the dead. For the living will need to be eulogized as well as the dead, and the dead will need to be honored and consulted along with the living. I can see fragments of this hope in the efforts of the communards inside and around town, in the discipline of the military color guard, and in the solemn prayers of my own congregation.

Island Pond, I'm talking to you. I'm being just about as preachy as I dare. May God grant that as your pond mirrors the heavens, your little town can mirror that Kingdom to which so many of its varied, nutty, ultimately lovely inhabitants aspire.

Three Journeys

*And as he was getting into the boat, the man who had been
possessed with demons begged him that he might be with him.
But he refused, and said to him, "Go home to your friends,
and tell them how much the Lord has done for you, and how
he has had mercy on you."*

—MARK 5:18–19

We have come to the end of a story that began with a pilgrimage.
I went to a monastery to ask if I should be a priest, and if not,
what else I should be. It seems appropriate to close with some
other, more recent journeys, which, like the first one, did not
"settle" anything so much as they helped me to understand the
church and the God I was trying to serve.

So here is my ending. That is, here is the account of three
occasions where I chose to begin again.

HARTFORD

"I know a man in Christ," St. Paul wrote, meaning himself, "who
fourteen years ago was caught up to the third heaven—whether
in the body or out of the body I do not know, God knows." I have
never had an "out of body" experience like his, nor have I ever
met a person who claimed to have had one. But I did "know a
man in Christ," only a little younger than I, who had for most of

his life felt he was in the *wrong* body. Though a man, he was convinced that in every nonphysical way he was a woman. I could not even pretend to understand his conviction. Like Paul, I faced the mystery of soul and body by saying "God knows."

He was probably not the first transsexual I had met. I had once taught a student who had confided the same self-awareness to me, but he had wandered halfway across the country before I could learn more about him or his struggle. Nevertheless, in my attempt to help him find some "answers," I had made various contacts within my church. One of these was the priest of a small New Hampshire parish, who apologized for having no suggestions whatsoever. Yet he remembered me a few years later when a visitor to his church approached him with the same confidence my student had once shared with me.

That is how I came to meet "Gloria," and how we found ourselves driving south on the interstate, with all of his worldly belongings in the compartment behind us. Our destination was the Gender Identity Clinic in Hartford, Connecticut, and one of its founders, an Episcopal priest named Clinton Jones.

At dawn I had crossed the Connecticut River to pick up my passenger. He lived in one of those dreary northern valley towns one hopes never to see in the rain. It was strange to look west, in the direction of Island Pond, and to think of that familiar place as the last outpost of "civilization." My companion and I loaded the car from the rear exit of his apartment. We took a back way out of town. Our precautions notwithstanding, he probably would not have been recognizable to his neighbors. I had met with him several times before, but on that morning, my slender, swarthy, working-class acquaintance had been transformed into a voluptuous redhead dressed for a major event—dressed appropriately, I guess. In his company, I looked suspicious. At least I felt suspicious. I felt, and I believe my companion felt, that old monastery ambivalence: fall to your knees or exit screaming. And for him this journey was very much like the one I had taken to the monastery years ago. He had questions to ask about who he was and what he would become, and we knew of no one in the world as fit to answer them as Clinton Jones.

His full title was the Reverend Canon Clinton Jones. He was a priest at Christ Church Cathedral in Hartford, as well as coordinator of the Gender Identity Clinic. He had once served as a chaplain with the Maritime Commission. He was now near the end of a career as one of America's acknowledged pioneers in the area of sexual minorities. He was still active with the various gay and transsexual groups in Hartford and at the Clinic, which is one of the few places in the country that perform sex-change operations. He had invited us to come, and offered to help resettle my companion in the city.

Hartford's claim to fame among many Vermonters would seem to be its multilane intersection on Interstate 91. People who thought nothing of driving to Boston or Montreal told me of the passage through Hartford as though it lay dead center in the whirlpool of Kharybdis. The luckiest mistake was to shoot beyond the city. Less lucky was to take the wrong turn into it, where you would either be atomized by merging traffic or forced, by the impossibility of ever retracing your route, into permanent Connecticut residency. In spite of all the risks that lay ahead, especially for my companion, I think I feared our entrance into Hartford most of all.

But I did worry about him, too. He chattered and giggled the whole way down—of course, he must have been scared to death. We took turns tuning the radio. If the ancients had had radios, I am convinced, they would have used them for divination in place of entrails and the flight of birds. Every other song seemed to be about longing and departure. "Leaving on a Jet Plane." "Baby Don't Go, Pretty Baby, Please Don't Go."

As the signs for Hartford began to appear, I pulled into a tourist information center to see if I could improve my directions for finding the church. The woman at the counter seemed to have been waiting for me. Not only did she know the way to the cathedral; she went there every Sunday. An Episcopal lay minister from Vermont—wonderful. Clinton Jones was a wonderful man. I thanked her—I thanked God—and sped to the point of impact.

We navigated into the right chute and were in the alley beside the church almost as soon as we realized we were in Hartford. We got out of the car and stretched. The mood of my companion was now quite subdued. This may actually have been his first big city, I don't know. I had been to cities before, but I could still share some of his reaction. Entering a city for the first time or after some time away—the noise, the foul, heavy air, the staggering mass of concrete and steel, the packed masses of human bodies—it is like a medical procedure in which an orifice of your body is opened wider, packed fuller, or probed more deeply than you ever thought it could be opened, packed, or probed. You mutter some protest, but neither your body nor its invader pays any attention. A first-time rural visitor to a city must experience some of that same primal outrage as his or her senses are overwhelmed.

The interior of the church was an immediate relief, at least for me. In contrast with the world outside, it was cool, dark, ancient, and of course beautiful. I have yet to see an ugly Episcopal church. For someone who believes, as I do, that simply coming *to be* in a church is infinitely more important than any emotion one feels there or the details of any creed one professes there, it is good that the place itself be hospitable. Needless to say, some of my response was due to nothing more than familiarity. With no effort from me, the positions of altar, font, and pulpit, the pictures in the windows, the very colors of the windows and chancel cloths, all renewed old associations, repeated old promises, pointed to old and ever-new mysteries. I knelt down to pray as naturally as a dog who smells her bed lies down to sleep. The old words, the old relief. I prayed that whatever changes might come to the life of my companion, he would always have a place like this at the center of his life.

We went to the reception area of Canon Jones's office. The rich dark woodwork and brass lamps with lime-green shades, so suggestive of an Anglo-Saxon men's club, stood in sharp, prophetic contrast to the people who waited there—some of whom I could not distinguish as men or women. Very probably a few were in transition between the two. "There is neither Jew nor Greek, there is neither slave nor free, there is neither male nor female; for you are all one in Christ Jesus." It occurred to me that Canon Jones's work was as revolutionary as Paul's preaching to the Gentiles; that his insistence on the full personhood of those he served was as ground-breaking as the apostle's declaration that "Circumcision is nothing, and uncircumcision is nothing." Why are you nostalgic, O my soul, and why do you languish for the struggles of former decades and the witness of earlier centuries? "Behold, now is the acceptable time; now is the day of salvation."

We were invited into the office. Canon Jones shook our hands. In the nightclubs of my imagination, Lou Reed sings "Walk on the Wild Side" as the Reverend Canon Clinton Jones comes on stage in his gray pants, gray jacket, gray shirt, white clerical collar, and thinning gray hair. This, too, was a revelation for anyone able to receive it: viewed correctly, his work was not some eccentric hobby of the church, but its conventional, orthodox, everyday gray-and-white mission on God's earth. On shelves piled high around us were books of every kind on every dimension of human sexuality. Having introduced my companion, I offered to leave, but he whispered to me to stay a little longer. A din of traffic and curses came through the windows. Canon Jones tried to put my companion at ease. He sketched a strategy for his move to Hartford and a new way of life. He spoke with the authority of someone who is all the more authoritative for not claiming to have every answer. In the secular world this is called an "open mind." In the church it is properly known as "the fear of the Lord," which Scripture says "is the beginning of wisdom."

Soon I was able to leave the two of them alone. I used the toilet. I found myself hoping, amid much wiping of the seat, that I had been told the truth about the ways in which AIDS is *not* transmitted. I reentered the church and examined it more closely. When the meeting ended, my companion and I drove to the motel that was to serve as the launching pad for his first explorations of the city. It had been recommended to us for its inexpensive weekly rates.

The office at the motel was not designed to inspire confidence. First of all, you could not walk *into* the office. Its doors were locked and hung with a sign stating that it was absolutely out of the question for them to be unlocked at any time. The young black woman who registered us was sequestered in a glass guardhouse with a

metal drawer opening between her and the outside like the ones
at drive-up windows in savings banks. Every sign on the windows
was a warning of some kind; one had the impression of a great
tank of inflammable or toxic liquid. If you're here you'd better
watch it. And you'd better know that this is where you want to
stay. Reservations were paid for in full, in advance, and there were
no refunds. As the reader must know by now, we were at what is
commonly called a "welfare motel," and I wish all the people I've
met who imagine such places as an outrageous extravagance squan-
dered on the "undeserving" poor could stay in one for just a night.

Since it was late summer and none of the rooms was air-
conditioned, most of the doors were open, and people visited in
the parking lots throughout the evening. The tight security at the
office had unnerved me, and I took my walks to the phone booth
and the soda machine with a sweatshirt over my arm and a heavy
claw hammer gripped in my hand. This proved to be as unnecessary
as it was probably un-Christian. If there were any predators about,
they had all been cowed into corners by the groups of friendly,
mostly young, mostly black neighbors who returned my "good
evenings" and helped me find my way around.

Our dingy room was the scene of a sleepless night, the sighting
of at least one mouse, and the accidental knocking over of a lamp,
which left us in total darkness. It was also the scene of many tears.
My companion was not sure he was ready for all the risks and
changes that a move to Hartford would mean. I offered to drive
him back home, but he was determined to follow through with his
plan.

We drove back to the church in the morning so that he could
meet again with Canon Jones. I revisited the interior of the church,
then took a walk outside. Seated on the lowest church step, a man
in old, greasy clothes sat gripping a disintegrating paper bag. I said
hello, but did not want to gawk. I looked up at the church tower,
then crossed the street to a department store. When I came back
to the church, the step was empty—except for a lurid splash of
vomit.

There are sights one never forgets, often unspectacular things,
often things seen traveling, when one is alert and taking nothing

for granted. The little square "leper's squint" in the wall of George Herbert's church in Bemerton, where members of Wilton colony would come to receive Communion, because no faithful person, not even a leper, could be excluded from the Sacraments, stands out more than anything I saw in two weeks of driving from one end of England to the other. The sight of that vomit-fouled church step in Hartford is at least as memorable. When I tell people about it, they often shake their heads as if I've recounted a terrible sacrilege, but they miss the point. On that step a man had sat down, weary and sick, and emptied his stomach. Like others with "something wrong" inside of them, like my companion, who felt himself locked inside of something wrong, his own body, the man had found himself huddled at the feet of the Church. "How beautiful upon the mountains are the feet" that are in this world to be kissed, pierced, and puked on, to stand in accessibility to the poor, the brokenhearted, and the oppressed.

Looking at that step, and at the smiling faces of my companion and Canon Jones as they rejoined me on the sidewalk to say thanks and good-bye, I lost my sense of strangerhood in an unfamiliar city. I was in Hartford, Connecticut, and I was going back to Island Pond, Vermont, and I had been reminded of the work of healing and liberation that needs to be done whoever or wherever one is.

BAKERSFIELD

"They tried to teach him some things," said one of the cronies gathered for the afternoon card game at the counter of Lawyer's Store in Bakersfield, Vermont. They were talking about a family named Willey who had taken in an ex-convict named Kane.

"Yep," said another dryly, "taught him how to burn down schools."

I was in Bakersfield, notebook in one hand and seven inauspicious cards in the other, to do my first magazine article. The burning of the school was not even the "big story." *Yankee* had sent me to town mainly to investigate the alleged embezzlement of more than half a million dollars in town funds by the town clerk. The disappearance of funds had left the town nearly bankrupt. Then one Sunday the middle school on the green caught fire.

The man charged with setting it had been paroled after serving time for the stabbing death of another man in the notorious Earth People's Park commune. Somehow he'd come to Bakersfield to live with the Willeys. Lyle Willey, who worked as a creamery foreman over in Richford, was also a minister "or something" who visited the prison regularly. He probably got involved with the Kane fellow over there. Nobody really knew Kane was in town— that is, no one knew what he was—until he wrote a letter to the local paper in response to another letter calling for the return of capital punishment. Did people realize who was living right there in town? Kane's letter said. They did then. Still, nobody seemed too alarmed. "He can't be all that bad if he's out there with Lyle and Carol."

Then one day he showed up "in this very store" and bought some cigarettes. Mrs. Lawyer recalled very distinctly that Kane had requested "another book of matches." That same afternoon the school caught fire. On their way to Bakersfield, firefighters from another town noticed a man pointing at a small grass fire near the road. They reported him to the police, who later arrested John Kane, smelling of alcohol and fire smoke.

I had an appointment to visit the Willeys after the last card game. If the reader thinks that I was predisposed to like them, especially because Lyle was also a lay minister, the reader has guessed wrong. I had some hard questions to ask these people who had brought dynamite into their small town. And Lyle's lay ministry was the last reason I saw for excusing him. If anything, that fact added to the skepticism I was taking to his home. Flannery O'Connor has a short story in which a silly, pretentious, down-at-heels white woman buys a garish hat—she thinks it flattering—only to board a bus and sit across from a black woman wearing one just like it. They immediately detest each other. The "hats" we put on as avocations or part-time callings can have the same effect. "I'm inviting Jerry Anzio, he wants to be a painter, too—you're going to just *love* each other!" Don't bet on it. We would see what this one-man rehabilitation program had to say for himself.

The Willeys and their three children lived on a side street in town, in an old house that needed, and was slowly getting, "some work." Lyle was apparently handling that rehabilitation job by himself as well. He was not yet home from work when I arrived. His wife, Carol, invited me in and gave me something to drink. She was in her last month of pregnancy. Although she was good-humored and friendly, it was clear that she felt some uneasiness about my assignment. Some of the newspapers, she felt, had been unkind in their portrayal of her husband and of John Kane. Still, she had already taken in a convicted murderer; the average journalist is usually not any more vicious than that.

She asked that I hold off the interview until Lyle came home. I was at least able to learn that she considered Kane a friend of the family and had never felt a danger with him under her roof. Lyle soon arrived. He was an energetic man in his mid-thirties, unremarkable in appearance except for a pair of lively—I'd almost say laughing—eyes. If he felt any uneasiness about my being there, he did not show it. In fact I was immediately impressed by his sense of humor. It also became clear from the start that Carol's request that I wait for Lyle was not based on his holding any patriarchal reins in the family. Though he was the prison minister, and thus the main focus of my interview, they both spoke freely, both as individuals and as equal and affectionate partners. That appearance of partnership was not compromised when I was invited to stay for supper, and the family began to prepare the meal.

The story of the Willeys and their infamous house guest began when Lyle had gone to milk the cows of a seventy-year-old farm wife named Lois Putnam, who was a pioneering lay minister in the Vermont prisons. She inspired him. When he moved to his present home, he found himself within driving distance of the Franklin County Correctional Center, which had no regular chaplain. With the support of another woman, the minister of his Congregational church in Bakersfield, Lyle began holding prayer services for the inmates. He had no title, no certificate—as far as I know, no ceremony of institution. He was a lay minister with even fewer endorsements than I had.

In prison he met John. The picture *Yankee* took of him shows a man about Lyle's age, with a crude tattoo of what looks like a Confederate flag on his upper arm and a chiseled, Johnny Cash–type of face. Lyle was disappointed with the picture. It did not show what he described as the extreme gentleness of his friend, nor, of course, could the picture or my article tell the full story of Kane's life, of his incarceration as a teenager, of his addiction to alcohol, of the murder itself, which was committed after Kane had been drunk for something like six months. Not long after Lyle met him, Kane was paroled. He moved to Burlington, took a job, but was soon laid off. Then Lyle and Carol invited him to spend Christmas Day with their family.

For many of us, the threshold of our houses is where "Christian action" leaves off and relief from that pursuit begins. Even for those who would not draw as sharp a dividing line as I often do, there are certain times when the needs of the outside world are not permitted to intrude. Christmas morning is one of them. Whatever shortcomings the Willeys might have had, I was forced to give them that nod of recognition we accord to those who do good deeds that we ourselves wouldn't do.

For the Willeys, however, this was not a good deed. It was simply a good day. They were able to share in "the first real Christmas" of a full-grown man, who opened his presents with joy, and played games with their children under the tree. The lion lay down with the lamb. It was no easy thing to drive him back to the city. They missed him when he was gone. They felt a sad incompleteness in what they had offered him. "What kind of Christians are we," Lyle asked, "what kind of a church are we, to invite a man for Christmas dinner and then to send him back to the streets, knowing he'll have no family and no money and say, 'So long, hope you make it'?" The family had a meeting. It was quickly decided—they were going back to get him.

It was just after New Year's when they went to bring John Kane "home." Though he had only stayed one day out of January in his motel, the proprietor insisted on keeping one hundred dollars of that month's rent, which was most of the cash John had to his name. Not every crook is behind bars, of course.

"What would you answer those people," I asked Lyle, "who

would say that you and Carol were way over your heads, that however good-hearted you are, you simply lacked the training to help a man like Kane?"

"Amen!" he said, laughing. "We *were* over our heads. We *did* have a *lot* to learn. But who else was helping John? It's like being in a MASH unit and the doctor just got shot. You learn the best you can. You may be all the dying person has. You may make mistakes. You may kill him! But you're not going to lie back and do nothing just because you're not a doctor."

Obviously, this was not the creed of a man espousing the bogus "volunteerism" that has been the basis of social policy in the Reagan-Bush years. Rather, it was an expression of the desperation of a good man, a desperation mitigated by faith, but, sadly, not helped by any major commitment from the society at large. It was also a summary statement for all "lay ministers," for every dresser of sycamore trees who sees a need, and knows his or her own shortcomings to meet that need, but who knows just as well that help is not exactly "on the way." After Lyle's answer, only a small part of my attention was on getting what I needed of the Willeys' story for my article. Most of all, I was eager to grasp what I needed for myself.

Having John as a member of the household required some adjustments, but no more than would have been required "if *you* came to live here," said Lyle. It seems that after a while, the kindness of Kane's adoptive family began to overwhelm him. He began brooding over his inability to pay them back. And as he brooded, he began to drink. It was he who first pulled the fire alarm. Then he left the burning school and started down the road.

Since John's case was still pending, Lyle was very careful to say nothing incriminating. He never said, for instance, that Kane had set the fire. I did not press him. But I did probe to see what regrets he and Carol had over the experience. The only regret I heard was that John was not living with them still.

It may seem as though I came in a very short time to identify with Lyle as my fellow lay minister. That is so, but only to a very limited extent. I admired Lyle and Carol immensely. But the truth is, if I identified with anyone, it was with Kane. I felt that like him

I had been given asylum by the Willeys, a certain brief respite from my own dark places and from a cruel world of which they may not have been innocent, but for which they were surely too good. I walked out of their house and stood on the lawn, with the light of their kitchen at my back, and the stars shining overhead, and I understood how St. Peter felt when he drew his sword and cut off the ear of one of the guards who came to arrest Jesus. Faced with the goodness of people such as those I'd just met, my strongest emotion was the desire to protect them, even violently, from whatever person or thing might do them harm. And perhaps I understood even better than Lyle and Carol how Kane felt, too. What if I myself—the convict, the loner, and the murderer—stood as the chief symbol of the harm that could come to them? It might not take much more than a few swigs of whiskey to convince me that the best thing I could do to protect these people was to burn the bridge between them and me, even if the bridge was in the form of a school, and to head down the road lighting fires of warning as I went.

But the bridge was not burned. The Willeys stuck by their friend. I came back to interview them again after Kane had been sentenced for arson. Carol had accompanied him to court. In spite of some indications that the charges could be fought successfully, Kane had decided to take full responsibility for his actions. He was sentenced to serve four more years and the remainder of his previous sentence. He "got justice." For its part, the town got a sizable insurance settlement for an obsolete building that had been scheduled to close as a school within a year anyway. With characteristic generosity, Lyle saw this as an ironic reward for the town's kindness toward his friend. "Bakersfield, whether they liked it or not, reached out to John. The Lord has blessed the graciousness of this town in reaching out to that one person."

By this time, the Willeys' fourth child had been born. Carol nursed the baby while Lyle and the other children prepared supper. I checked out the bookshelves, a form of snooping I regard as perfectly acceptable. I found Dorothy Day, the cofounder of the Catholic Worker movement, keeping scandalous company with Billy Graham. Who were they, after all, but two distant and somewhat eccentric relatives of Lyle and Carol, whose Christianity I was finding it increasingly difficult to classify.

After supper I visited their bathroom, with careful instructions from Lyle on how to flush the house's miscreant toilet. Alas, I forgot to follow them; like Luther, I do a lot of my deeper thinking on the stool. I was repaid for my absentmindedness by the sight of a toilet almost brimful with fetid water. My last image of Lyle is that of him cheerfully guiding my feces down the drain with the help of a plunger and plenty of embarrassed apologies from me. There's a passage in Henry Miller's *Tropic of Cancer* where after a similar bathroom mishap he is led to wonder if the whole universe might "at the last moment" prove to be nothing more or less wonderful than "two enormous turds . . . in the *bidet*." (What are they saying these days about "diminishing expectations"?) For my part, I was led to wonder, and to hope, that all the waste and foulness of this world may ultimately be rinsed away with the same unshakable kindness as I saw in Lyle Willey.

I got a lot of mileage out of my visit to Bakersfield. I got my story for *Yankee,* and as one can see, I'm still finding other places in which to tell it. I also got the subject for that year's Christmas Eve sermon. I may have preached it in the same hour as the Willeys took John Kane's Christmas presents to the Franklin County prison. I told the congregation of Kane's first Christmas with the Willeys. I told them about the fire. I even told them about the strange surge of protectiveness I had felt leaving the Willeys' house. I closed as follows:

"What I have told you is a true story. There is another story I could have told you, about angels and a manger, but you know that story. I told you this story so you would remember that the other story is true. Indeed, if it were not true, the story I have just told you would not be true either.

"And I have told you this story so that you would remember the proclamation that is also true because Jesus Christ, who was born this night in Bethlehem, is true. When he had grown to manhood, Jesus rose in the synagogue and read from the book of Isaiah: 'The Spirit of the Lord is upon me, because he has anointed me to preach the good news to the poor. He has sent me to proclaim release to the captives and recovering of sight to the blind, to set at liberty those who are oppressed, to proclaim the acceptable year of the Lord.' The people in the synagogue looked at him the way I first looked at Lyle and Carol Willey. What are his credentials? they asked. Where is his training? Isn't this the carpenter?

"The Gospel always looks weak and underqualified. The Gospel always seems to need protection. The Gospel looks as fragile as a baby in a stable, as fragile as a scroll in a carpenter's rough hands, as fragile as a family with a convict under its roof. And yet there is no power on earth that can stand against it."

Amen.

HARLEM AND HOME

When I first saw Father Castle after stepping from the taxicab, he was watering the Garden of Eden outside St. Mary's Church on 126th Street in West Harlem. I stood there in silence until he noticed me. Slowly he trained the spray in my direction, a rascal's way of saying, "Be not afraid. It is I."

The Garden of Eden was planted only recently. When Castle came to St. Mary's there was little more than a patch of packed dirt beside the church and in front of the parish house. He had brought flowers, shrubs, and baby evergreen trees from Vermont. Through some arrangement with an Italian contractor, which I did not quite understand, a load of slate pieces had arrived at St. Mary's, and Castle had laid them as a small rectangular courtyard inside the rectangular garden. Not all of his plants were doing well. He showed me a few he had tried to save by transplanting. "We have a little replica of what is going on around us," he said. "Everything is dying. Crack, AIDS—it's horrendous. There's a lot of death here. A lot of little resurrections and a lot of big deaths."

We stepped out onto the sidewalk. A policeman from the precinct across the street backed out of the space into which he had just pulled his car. "We don't intimidate people, do we?" Castle said under his breath. For years prior to his coming to St. Mary's, the precinct had parked its cars, including some cars abandoned elsewhere in the city, up on the sidewalk in front of the church.

Castle had arrived to see mothers with baby carriages walking out into the busy street to get around the cars. So there had been demands, then protests until the sidewalk was opened for the first time in fifteen years. Occasionally it was still necessary to flour-and-water-paste the windows of a car with a sign reading "This Police Officer Disrespects Our Community."

"That is how I'll go down in the annals of history," Castle said. "St. Patrick got the snakes out of Ireland, and I got the cars off the sidewalk on 126th Street. Right now I'm working on the squirrels."

I took the latter statement as part of the joke until I saw him reach into a bucket of stones by the doorway to the rectory and fire two or three of them at a retreating gray varmint. From time to time throughout the morning, he stuck his head out the doorway like a child hoping for snow and muttered, "Any squirrels?"

Inside, the dining room table was covered with snapshots. There were pictures of baptisms and confirmations, pictures from the day the street had been painted with demands for a traffic light, pictures of Palm Sunday marches: vestments, crosses, palms, signs protesting drugs, racism, the need for housing—and a curious bodyguard of black cadets. Apparently one of the parishioners, a former marine, had started a cadet-training program, complete with dress uniforms, drill practice, and short clubs worn as sidearms. "We wrestled with it theologically, socially, and politically, and we decided we should have our own army," Castle told me. He had also told the boys to consider the possibility of being sent by the U.S. government to fight against their black brothers and sisters in South Africa. But in the meantime, St. Mary's sanctioned the program. "At demonstrations, they're our security."

There were also pictures showing the living conditions in surrounding tenements, broken toilets, garbage-filled alleys, all the features that have become clichés to those of us who do not have to see them outside of magazines. In a while, Father Castle would take me on a walking tour of the neighborhood, where I could see these conditions for myself, but for the time being I was free to look around the church.

St. Mary's is a beautiful brick church built in 1823, when Harlem was still a white neighborhood. There are still white people in the parish, and recently the church has begun holding a special service in Spanish, but Castle sees St. Mary's primarily as "an African-American church." That identity was reflected in such details as a Nigerian altar cloth, and a Haitian triptych at the rear of the church depicting scenes from the life of a black Jesus. The church was open during the day; a pair of volunteers sat near the door to greet those people who came for free coffee and donuts or to pick up their mail. Homeless people were invited to use the church's mailing address as their own. On a lectern at the rear of the nave were copies of a letter to the Presiding Bishop, asking that President George Bush be denied Communion for vetoing an increase in the minimum wage.

In the wings adjoining the church were other signs of its ministry and self-image. Pictures of black heroes lined the hallway—Martin Luther King, Paul Robeson, Marcus Garvey, the Honorable Elijah Muhammad, Bob Marley, the Virgin Mary at the center of a great company of nameless black women from every age and nation, and her black Son tending his sheep above Bible verses such as this from the vision of Christ in Revelations: "His hair was like wool." There was a great wooden coffin standing upright in a corner with a painted inscription: "DRUGS R.I.P." I saw the office of St. Mary's community organizer, a Muslim. Father Castle had actually been invited to address a gathering of the Nation of Islam on the subject of drugs in the inner city. He had been frisked several times on the way to the podium. When a speaker's words bring cheering from the assembly—and apparently Castle's were able to do so several times—the impeccably groomed and formidable Fruit of Islam men who guard the podium rise to their feet. Perhaps noticing that I was a little awed by his description of all this, Castle added with his best straight face that when the Fruit of Islam men rise, their bow ties spin around in circles. We laughed, but it was clear that his regard for the Nation's work in the black community, its strict moral code, and its militant nationalism was no joke.

Outside the church, behind the parish house and in coops fronting the Garden of Eden, were Castle's livestock. In Vermont he had always seemed a Jersey City boy, but in the city he could not be without his animals. He'd gone to the live poultry market several blocks from the church, one of the foulest-smelling places I've ever been, where cages of chickens, pigeons, and rabbits are piled as high as boxes in a warehouse, and bought twelve chicks. "We thought we'd get eggs, and sell them at church for fifty cents a dozen, or whatever—but they all grew up, and every one of them was a rooster." He also had a goose, gander, and a brand new gosling—which he saw as witness to the meaning of family. "That mother and father never leave that child alone. You go near that child and they let you know this is not to be messed with. And everywhere that little goose runs, the parents go nobly alongside."

We started out on our first walk. As we were leaving the church grounds, a girl of about nine or ten came out of the church and said hello.

"Father Castle, I was in the church, and I started reading the Bible out loud to the people in there, and they liked that so much."

"Well," he said, "that's nice, and that's a very special thing for you. Why aren't you in school today? School's not out yet."

"My mother let me stay home," said the girl, obviously a little disappointed that her Bible-reading did not impress Castle as she had hoped.

"And she let you stay home yesterday, too. She's got to see that you go to school. Otherwise, you won't be able to read the Bible."

As when he'd first turned his garden hose at me, there was that sign of recognition—this was the Father Castle I had known, seemingly reeling with frenetic energy and madcap humor, but perfectly clear in his vision and steady in his aim. He was just as familiar to me in our walk. Once at St. Mark's in Vermont, the Gospel for the service had read, "Beware of the scribes, who like to go about in long robes, and love salutations in the market places and the best seats in the synagogues and the places of honor at feasts." Afterwards, in the parish house kitchen, Castle had said, "I love all those things!" He still seemed to love them, as we walked down the street, through the playground he called "the country club"— "because people come here to drink"—and up the hill to the first street of tenements, and people called out "Hello, Father" every-where. But everywhere we went, he seemed to see what needed to be seen, and to say what needed to be said.

"God bless you, Father Castle. How are you?" a young woman called. "God bless you," Castle replied, but muttered to me, "I'm sure she's on crack. That's why she's so skinny." On the steps of each apartment building, after some banter with the people gath-ered outside or leaning from the windows—"Hey, Rosita, you want to go with me to the Dominican Republic?"—he focused the con-versation on rents, conditions, the need to stay organized and to support the tenant strikes.

There is probably no need to detail the conditions I saw. Behind every door was a story of woe. In one doorway Castle had held a service in memory of a young man killed there in drug-related violence. Several buildings we visited were run by a man known locally as "the Dracula landlord." Another no-less-despicable char-acter had harassed his tenants, many of whom had lived in his building for decades, by refusing to take their welfare checks and raising their rents until many were forced to leave. "They made people here in New York homeless, and then brought down home-less people from Westchester County and collected sixty-five to ninety-five dollars a day from the city for 'taking in the homeless.' "

We walked past a project whose tenants were engaged in a twenty-month-old rent strike, organized in large part by St. Mary's, over issues like inadequate security and services. Elevators were often broken; people were forced to walk up twenty flights of stairs to their rooms, or were stranded in elevators for hours. Of course, the neglect extended beyond landlords to the city itself. The "newly" installed basketball posts next to the building had been without hoops and nets for several years. The garbage brought to the curb might or might not be picked up that day.

"The thing is that nothing functions here, and it often doesn't function here because the people who are here are black and Latino and poor. And the only solution to changing this is for people to organize and have power." When Castle addressed me by name, I knew he was speaking from his deepest convictions. "There are two kinds of power, Garret, people and money . . . aside from the

Holy Spirit and all those other good things, but the Holy Spirit can be in people and in money. It just has to be organized people and organized money, and then people can change their condition."

It was a day for the recognition of obvious truths. Hundreds of Sundays I had seen bread and wine, money and people come to the altar, but now the statement of the ability of the Holy Spirit to dwell within an unworthy human being, or to sanctify a wrinkled dollar bill, struck me as though it were a brand new revelation. And there was one truth more. I think it struck home with the sight of black high school graduates walking proudly down the streets of their neighborhood, wearing their gowns home after graduation practice. The school colors, blue and white, were the same as those of the school where I teach. "This is great to see," Father Castle said. "But you wonder what they're graduating *for*."

Here was the second "obvious" revelation: not only that America's first order of business is the need to destroy racism, but also that a white person can choose only between believing that *is* the first order or being a racist himself. What excuse did I have for not grasping that all along? Like so many people of my color, I had somehow been lulled into thinking that the racial issue had pretty much been "solved," that white America had undergone a mass conversion, that in fact the word "racist" was applied a little recklessly in some cases. One shouldn't be branded a racist simply because he or she could not accept some faction's agenda for dealing with race-related problems.

But there in Harlem, and especially as I passed those black counterparts to my students back in Vermont—students who often had serious disadvantages of their own, but none so formidable as being black—there and then I finally got it through my thick white head that race is the "judgment seat" for my country and my church. Faced with this kind of misery and hopelessness, you must either believe in a do-or-die struggle to end it, or you must inwardly believe that somehow the misery stems from some implicit inferiority in those who suffer it. It is a clear choice, and it is becoming clearer with every month's headlines. It has been clear to many people for generations. It was first clear to this one soul on a day in June, on a walk with Father Castle.

When he said, "Let's go see the Italian shoemaker," I thought he was giving me one of his ironic introductions; probably we were off to the Jomo Kenyatta Shoe Shop, or to some Jamaican cobbler with two-and-half-foot dreadlocks and a ceiling full of Haile Selassie's face. But in fact there *was* an Italian shoemaker a block or two from the church, in a little shoe-piled shop just like those I'd known as a kid in New Jersey. There were cronies, too, except instead of elderly *paesani* with stogies, the steps outside were filled with old black men in neat sweater vests and dark baggy pants like old men everywhere, with caps, canes, and fedoras. Because of the heat, "the club," as Castle called it, was meeting outside, but in colder weather they would line the wall in a row of chairs parallel to the shoemaker's counter.

When we came in, he was sewing up an old suitcase. Not long ago he'd sewn a pair of the Father's shoes, doubtless worn out by innumerable walks through the parish. The shoemaker had been there for sixty years. "He's the true sole-saver of the neighborhood," Castle said, and as usual there was a meaning in the humor if you cared to look for it. Like the family of geese back at St. Mary's, this man was a witness and a symbol. He stood for the possibility of honoring one's own origins while remaining a neighbor to people of different origins. His accent, his name, his shop were as Italian as Garibaldi in a tomato garden, but his customers and the brides, grooms, babies, and graduates in his snapshots on the wall were mostly black. He had not fled when the neighborhood changed. He had remained—as a neighbor.

What a sight and what a thrill it was for me to walk down 127th Street, Martin Luther King Boulevard, one of the main thoroughfares of Harlem. The name "Harlem" is so often used as a synonym for the bitter depths of the black experience in America. Indeed, there are reasons, even increasing reasons, for that usage. In the last fifteen years, Castle told me, Harlem had lost five thousand of its hospital beds. Some blocks at its center were reminiscent of London after the Blitz. But there on the avenue I was nearly overwhelmed by the color, the vitality, the signs of pride and history all around me. I saw the famous Apollo Theater, which may have been host to more genius than any center for the per-

forming arts in America. I saw the Theresa Hotel, where Fidel
Castro had come on his visit to the U.N., and where Malcolm X
later had his headquarters after breaking with the Nation of Islam.
As far down as I could see, the avenue was being widened and
repaved. "Let's go see how many black guys are on the road crew,"
Castle said. As I recall, there was not even one.

On the sidewalk were a number of vendors; one had a cart almost
like a shrine in which he sold reproductions of his own artwork,
pointillistic paintings of biblical figures—all black. I bought an
eight-by-ten of the Good Shepherd, gently tending his white sheep
beside the still waters. I look up to him from time to time as I
write. It is an interesting thing for a white man to look into the
black face of the Savior who died so that he might be forgiven.
There are days when I am almost afraid to glance at that picture.
On the day I bought it, I wondered how many white neighborhoods
I could find with posters of Christ and the Blessed Virgin Mary
being sold on the streets as heroes and cult objects. Not too many,
I suspected. I remembered what Malcolm X had said, that black
men and women have been America's best—and least respected—
Christians. And I remembered the line that had almost prevented
George Herbert's poetry from making it past the royal censors:

> Religion stands on tip-toe in our land,
> Readie to passe to the American strand.

In the world at large, and perhaps in America, too, it is now passing
from white hands into brown and black. So perhaps the picture I
bought is a fragment, a point in some vaster pointillistic design by
which the Son of man will be revealed in all of his fullness.

We came back to St. Mary's. A young seminarian named Earl,
who served as Castle's assistant, was talking to a man laid out on
some police barricade planks piled on the sidewalk. "Too many
donuts, Earl," Castle shouted to him, adding in an aside to me, "I
think Earl wants to lie down there himself." But there was little
rest for Earl, Castle, or me that day. The church and parish house
were bustling with activities. St. Mary's was home or headquarters
for rent strikes, immigration classes, Boy Scouts, cadet corps, day-

care, and a Gospel chorus; the phone rang, the doorbell rang; one man came to "borrow" some money, and left quoting Christ's great promise to St. Peter: "You are Peter, and upon this rock I will build my church."

"And we believe that here," answered Castle, "and the gates of hell and the police department will not prevail against it."

We went out for several other walks. He took me through the campus of Columbia University, where he urged an old man with horribly swollen legs to raise up his feet; to Riverside Church, where he tried to hustle an Oriental carpet for St. Mary's (I do wonder if in a past life Castle was a Persian rug merchant); to the Cathedral of St. John the Divine, as breathtakingly ponderous, confusing, and unfinished as the Anglican communion itself, where services are as likely to be accompanied by African drums or acrobats as by a cosmic-barreled organ—then back to St. Mary's, where the phones and doorbells were still ringing.

"I'm tired," Castle said to me at one point. Really? I was about ready to ask for a tub of water for my aching feet—but he was talking about his life. What would become of him, I wondered. In two months he would turn sixty. Where would he be in another five years? Some of those who'd crossed his path in the early days, sometimes even joining in "the cause," were now bishops, high church officials, presidents of divinity schools. He was here, stirring things up. Would they eventually find him, as they had just found a controversial community organizer in the neighborhood, piece by piece, an arm, a leg, and a head? Just the week before I'd arrived, he had helped to break up a fight between some black and Hispanic teenagers. His relations with the precinct across the street were still not the best. Perhaps he'd be retired by a bullet. Perhaps he'd retire to Vermont. He was ruling out neither possibility.

But I am still too young and solipsistic to ponder anyone else's future for very long without turning to my own. A day with Father Castle was a day of spiritual carousing; my head was full of plans and resolutions for my parish and for myself. But it was a sobering day as well. Our paths were divided for good now. We were the most distant of companions. I have just found in an old journal a surprising entry from the time when Castle first left Vermont.

"Kathy said to me today that she knew I'd want to go to New York with Father Castle, and that if that were so, she was prepared to go with me."

It hadn't turned out that way, though. And it would never turn out that way, if for no other reason than that I could come to New York only to have Castle move elsewhere. But of course there were other reasons—and these, too, were sobering.

As I spoke with him, and the sun began to set in the window behind his chair, I realized that I would never have many of his most enviable gifts. I would never have his energy. I would never have his capacity for sacrifice. I would never be able to go among the outcasts without worrying about the toilet seat, or walk through the Valley of the Shadow of Death without carrying a weapon, or meet another minister without sizing the man or woman up. I would never, in all likelihood, become a priest.

But maybe I was not meant to be one. Maybe all these deficiencies will one day define my crowning strength. And maybe, along with the call to "go forth," is the less glorious but no less important call to stay put.

Anyway, I could not stay put in New York. Nor, in spite of my parents' invitation, could I stay any longer as a guest at their home across the river. Sunday, the best of my days, was drawing near, and I had a service to do in Island Pond.

Postscript
"Here Am I"

In the year that King Uzziah died I saw the Lord
sitting upon a throne, high and lifted up; and his train
filled the temple. Above him stood the seraphim;
each had six wings: with two he covered his face,
and with two he covered his feet, and with two he flew.
And one called to another and said:

"Holy, holy, holy is the Lord of hosts;
the whole earth is full of his glory."

And the foundations of the thresholds shook at the voice
of him who called, and the house was filled with smoke.
And I said: "Woe is me! For I am lost; for I am a man
of unclean lips, and I dwell in the midst of a people
of unclean lips; for my eyes have seen the King,
the Lord of hosts!"

Then flew one of the seraphim to me, having in his
hand a burning coal which he had taken with tongs from
the altar. And he touched my mouth, and said: "Behold,
this has touched your lips; your guilt is taken away,
and your sin is forgiven." And I heard the voice of the
Lord saying, "Whom shall I send, and who will go for us?"
Then I said, "Here am I! Send me."

—ISAIAH 6:1–8

This passage is one of the Old Testament lessons appointed by the *Book of Common Prayer* to be read at the ordination of a priest. It was read for me in Island Pond on December 19, 1992, a little over a year after this book first appeared in print.

The special conditions for my ordination to the diaconate and the priesthood are spelled out in the canons of the Episcopal Church, which provide for the raising up of indigenous clergy "in communities which are small, isolated, remote, or distinct in respect of ethnic composition, language, or culture." These so-called "Canon 9 priests" are authorized to serve in their home parishes only, and are expected to work under mentors and to earn most or all of their living outside of the church. A careful reader of this book will recognize that such conditions suit my needs and desires quite well.

It is tempting to say more about this new role, to attempt to describe the experience of one's first celebration of Holy Communion, which occurred for me on Christmas Eve, or first solo Baptism, which was of a baby girl shortly thereafter, or of blessing my congregation, which has grown in number and diversity since I last described it. But these things belong in another book, not in the postscript to this one.

It is also tempting to bring the reader up-to-date on people and places (to note, for instance, that Ronnie Langford of the Buck and Doe has died, and that Father Castle is now the subject of a documentary film called *Cousin Bobby*), or to qualify some of my thinking. (I no longer believe that "moral obesity" is such a bad thing, if it leads us to rely on God.) But every change I note will be followed by changes I cannot note; I cannot prevent my book from growing old.

So I will simply acknowledge how funny it seems for a man who wrote "I would never, in all likelihood, become a priest," to then be seized by his church and by God and called to pursue Holy Orders just as those words were about to be published.

And I would add this observation: Sometimes we resolve to do without an evil or harmful thing, and Grace enables us to do without it. But sometimes we also resolve to do without a *good* thing—

something that "for our unworthiness we dare not, and for our blindness we cannot ask" (*Book of Common Prayer*)—and Grace gives it to us anyway.

The main good thing that I and many people frequently, and despairingly, resolve to do without is not an ordained ministry, or even a lay ministry, but redemption itself. The work of Christ on earth was to make that resolution a joke. The purpose of the Gospel is to help people laugh at that joke, ever more heartily and in ever greater numbers.

I hope the little laugh that is my book will have played some worthy part in God's Comedy.

G. K.
February 1993